THAI CAPITAL AFTER THE 1

THAI CAPITAL
AFTER THE 1997 CRISIS

EDITED BY

PASUK PHONGPAICHIT

AND

CHRIS BAKER

CONTRIBUTORS

Chaiyon Praditsil
Nophanun Wannathepsakun
Olarn Thinbangtieo
Porphant Ouyyanont
Sakkarin Niyomsilpa
Ukrist Pathmanand
Viengrat Nethipo

Natenapha Wailerdsak
Nualnoi Treerat
Pavida Pananond
Rattaphong Sonsuphap
Thanee Chaiwat
Veerayooth Kanchoochat
Wattana Sugunnasil

SILKWORM BOOKS

This research for this project was supported by
the Thailand Research Fund

ISBN 978-974-9511-36-7

First published in 2008 by
Silkworm Books
6 Sukkasem Road, T. Suthep,
Chiang Mai 50200, Thailand
www.silkwormbooks.com
info@silkwormbooks.com

Set in Garamond Premier Pro 11 pt. by Silk Type

Printed and bound in Thailand by O. S. Printing House, Bangkok

5 4 3 2

CONTENTS

LIST OF FIGURES

LIST OF TABLES

ABBREVIATIONS

AFTA	ASEAN Free Trade Area
AICO	Asian Industrial Cooperation Scheme
AIS	Advanced Info Services
ASEAN	Association of Southeast Asian Nations
BBC	brand-to-brand complementarity
BOI	Board of Investment
CAT	Communications Authority of Thailand
CBU	completely built up
CEO	chief executive officer
CKD	completely knocked down
CP	Charoen Pokphand
CPB	Crown Property Bureau
DBS	Development Bank of Singapore
EGAT	Electricity Generating Authority of Thailand
FDI	foreign direct investment
FEER	*Far Eastern Economic Review*
FIDF	Financial Institutions Development Fund
FRA	Financial Restructuring Authority
FTA	free trade agreement
GDP	gross domestic product
GM	General Motors
IFCT	Industrial Finance Corporation of Thailand
IMF	International Monetary Fund
INN	International News Network (www.innnews.co.th)
IPO	initial public offering
JETRO	Japan External Trade Organization
MNC	multinational company
MP	member of Parliament
NESDB	National Economic and Social Development Board
OTOP	One Tambon One Product
PAO	Provincial Administrative Organization (*obojo*)
PPB	Privy Purse Bureau
R&D	research and development

FOREWORD

The 1997 crisis caused the decapitation of Thailand's capitalist class. Certainly the crisis caused great suffering among the poor. But it devastated the rich, too. In retrospect, the crisis seems to have left a mark on Thai entrepreneurship that threatens to become permanent.

Nobody deserves to be blamed for causing the crisis except the entrepreneurs themselves. They rushed off together like a pack of lemmings to borrow too much overseas. Their combined action put the whole financial system at risk. The Bank of Thailand's only mistake was its misguided attempt to defend the indefensible.

Our entrepreneurs have learned the lesson of the crisis, but perhaps they have learned it too well. Before the crisis they took too many risks. Now they seem to take too few risks, or none at all. The appetite for risk-taking has almost disappeared.

The banks, in particular, spent the years after the crisis learning how to manage risk and installing new systems for evaluating the risks of each loan. The amount of credit they now make available to the productive sector of the economy is half what it was in real terms prior to the crisis. The banks are swamped by excess liquidity. Perhaps they are now being too careful.

Our rate of savings has dropped since before the crisis, and our rate of investment has dropped even more. If you look at our industrial sector today, it is hard to detect signs of domestic entrepreneurship. There are a handful of old companies still surviving. There are a few pockets of domestic capital such as food industries. But it is hard to find examples of new industrial projects launched by domestic capital. Thai industrialists are no longer trying to obtain the best know-how from around the world, as they once did. We are all for multinational companies. Do not mistake this for nationalist sentiment. It's just a description of reality.

Look at the younger generation of our prominent old business families. They seem to prefer ventures in entertainment, media, or other service sectors like fashion and restaurants. They do not seem interested in the industrial backbone of the economy. In the last few years, Thai capital has been flooding back into real estate development, totally forgetful of the bubble and bust in 1997. I suspect that our entrepreneurs prefer these service and property ventures because they believe such projects have lower risk.

Throughout Asia we were traumatized by 1997. A greater emphasis on risk management is fine, but perhaps we have swung from one extreme to another. Entrepreneurship requires some element of risk. For the economy to grow, we have to invest, and since investment is risky, we have to manage risk and not wish it away. It's time we rethink the institutional framework to allow more risk-taking so that the economy can grow.

Ammar Siamwalla
Bangkok, September 2007

PREFACE

THIS book comes out of a project to understand the impact of the 1997 crisis on Thailand's domestic capitalism. The project was supported under the TRF Senior Research Scholar scheme (*methi wichai awuso*) of the Thailand Research Fund from 2003 to 2006. In all, fourteen researchers contributed. The idea was not to impose a single approach or single framework on the project, but to let the researchers examine the question from many different angles. The final papers were (titles translated from the Thai):

Chaiyon Praditsil and Olarn Thinbangtieo, "The roles of local bosses in the throes of globalization: A study of a province in the eastern region."

Natenapha Wailerdsak, "Capital groups and family businesses before and after the 1997 crisis."

Nophanun Wannathepsakun, "Case study of construction business groups."

Nualnoi Treerat, "Capital accumulation in Thailand: The case of the liquor industry."

Pavida Pananond, "The changing dynamics of Thai multinational corporations."

Porphant Ouyyanont, "The Crown Property Bureau and its investment roles."

Sakkarin Niyomsilpa, "Overall picture of the Thai automotive industry after the crisis."

Thanee Chaiwat, "Rent-seeking in Thailand."

Ukrist Pathmanand, "The telecommunications industry after the crisis."

Ukrist Pathmanand and Rattapong Sonsuphap, "Thai commercial banks after the 1997 crisis."

Veerayooth Kanchoochat, "The roles of institutions and the dynamics of transnational retailers in Thailand: A comparative institutional analysis."

Viengrat Nethipho, "Structure and dynamics of local business groups before and after the economic crisis: A case study of Chiang Mai." Wattana Sugunnasil, "Development and adjustment of agro-businesses in the south after the economic crisis."

The output was published in two volumes in Thai in late 2006 by Matichon Press under the title, *The Struggle of Thai Capital, Volume I: Adjustment and Dynamics;* and *Volume II: Politics, Culture and Survival.*

Natenapha's full paper has been published as *Klum thun—thurakit khropkhrua thai kon lae lang wikrit 2540* [Business Groups and Family Business Before and After the 1997 Crisis], Bangkok: BrandAge Books, 2006. Part of Pavida's research was published as "Thai Multinationals Before and After the 1997 Crisis," *ASEAN Economic Bulletin* 21, 1, April 2004; "The Changing Dynamics of the Thailand CP Group's International Expansion," in *Southeast Asia's Chinese Businesses in an Era of Globalisation: Coping with the Rise of China*, edited by Leo Suryadinata, Singapore: Institute of Southeast Asian Studies, 2006; "The Changing Dynamics of Thai Multinationals after the Asian Economic Crisis," *Journal of International Management* 13, 3, 2007; and "Explaining the Emergence of Thai Multinationals," in *Handbook of Research on Asian Business*, edited by Henry Yeung, London: Edward Elgar, 2007. An earlier version of Ukrist's research appeared as a chapter on "Thaksin and the Politics of Telecommunications" in *The Thaksinization of Thailand*, edited by Duncan McCargo and Ukrist Pathmanand, Copenhagen: NIAS, 2005. Porphant's chapter also appears in *Journal of Contemporary Asia* 38, 1, 2008. A summary of Veerayooth's research appeared in *Warasan Sethasat Thammasat* [Thammasat Economic Journal], 2007.

In this book, the papers have been condensed and updated. Key material from some of the omitted chapters has been worked into others.

For Thai personal names, we prefer to use the English spelling used by the person or family, and have been guided by the spellings used by the Brooker Group. Otherwise we romanize using the Royal Institute system.

For their financial support, cooperation, and encouragement, we are very indebted to the Thailand Research Fund, and especially to its director, Professor Dr. Piyawat Boon-long, and to Professor Dr. Vichai Boonsaeng, director of the Academic Research Division.

We are especially grateful to Professor Akira Suehiro of the Institute of Social Science, University of Tokyo. He gave us access to his extraordinary database, provided encouragement in many ways, and served as an inspiration through his own pioneering work on Thai capital accumulation.

We would like to thank many distinguished scholars, researchers, business executives, and professionals who read manuscripts or commented on papers at several project seminars. Our gratitude is due to Ammar Siamwalla, Apichat Sathitniramai, Banluesak Pussarangsi, Chirayu Isarangkun Na Ayuthaya, Deunden Nikomborirak, Jirapar Tosomboon, Kanoksak Kaewthep, Kevin Hewison, Krirkiat Phiphatseritham, Malcom Falkus, Nakarin Mektrairat, Narong Petprasert, Niphon Poapongsakon, Pairoj Vongvipanond, Pakorn Vichayanond, Phumsan Lertrotchanya, Pokpong Junvith, Preecha Piamphongsan, Ratchanida Nitiphatthanaphirak, Samart Chiasakul, Somboon Siriprachai, Somchanok Coompanthu, Somkiat Tangkitwanit, Witayakorn Chiangkul, Voravidh Charoenloet, Wirat Saengthongkham, and Yongyut Chopthamdi.

Thanks are due to Pairin Plaikaeo, Chanthra Thanawatthanawong, and Panya Loetsukprasert for excellent co-ordination and research assistance; and to Natchayakorn Kittrakun, Supaporn Trongkitvirot, and Khomsan Ninpairot for clerical help.

We are very grateful to Professor Takashi Shiraishi and the Center for Southeast Asian Studies at Kyoto University, and to Professor Akira Suehiro and the Institute of Social Science at the University of Tokyo for inviting Pasuk to Japan in 2004 and 2006 respectively, when work on this project was carried out.

A special thanks to Trasvin and everyone at Silkworm Books for their professionalism, dedication, and friendship.

Most of all we are grateful to the researchers who interpreted the theme of this project in different and fascinating ways.

Pasuk Phongpaichit
Chris Baker

INTRODUCTION

WHAT is the future for domestic capital in the economies of what we used to call "developing countries"?

The idea of development in the era after the Second World War imagined that any country could repeat the economic transition of the West by accumulating capital, reallocating labor, and developing industry. Development policy and planning was about nurturing entrepreneurial capitalists by creating the institutions that would help them flourish.

Over the last quarter-century, that model has been discarded. Most of the techniques for nurturing local capitalism in that development era are now outlawed under the rules of the world economy. The new orthodoxy is that capital should have the freedom to roam the world. In practice this means that big companies with the resources to develop technology and invest in marketing can generally out-compete their smaller, weaker, and more recent rivals. The production of all kinds of goods and services is under the control of large transnational companies, mostly based in the advanced economies but with some new additions from emerging giant economies of China and India.

For China and India, this issue is not so critical. They have huge internal markets that can incubate corporations of global scale. Their governments have the weight to bargain with the outside world while still protecting these markets in defiance of the new economic order. But for other developing countries, these special conditions do not apply.

What are the consequences of this trend for entrepreneurial capital in the old developing countries? What is the impact on politics (in the broad sense of the word)? What are the implications for state policy?

Major economic crises serve as a kind of reality check. In the short term, economies may be able to resist or disguise the implications of changes in the global environment. For many countries in Asia, the 1997 crisis brought home the realities of the new global economic order.

This book examines what happened to Thai businesses in and after the Asian crisis. The ten studies offer a variety of very different slices of this history. Three look at sectors or sub-sectors. Two focus on business groups. Two delve into provincial regions. Three take a topical approach. Most of these chapters set their analysis of the post-crisis period into a historical context stretching back over prior decades. As background, we present a general sketch of Thai corporate history from the Second World War through the 1997 crisis to the recovery.

THE POSTWAR ERA

At the close of the Second World War, Thailand was considered among the most backward economies and societies in Southeast Asia. It had a typical colonial-era economy, exporting primary produce of rice, teak, and tin and importing manufactures. Until 1932, this colonial-type economy had coexisted with an absolute monarchy, and the socioeconomic structure still reflected this history. Most of the indigenous population remained in a semi-subsistent agrarian economy. The urban economy was dominated by expatriate enterprise—either colonial trading houses, or sojourning Chinese migrant businessmen. There were only a handful of significant local firms, owned by former nobles or settler Chinese. Thailand lacked much of the basic infrastructure (physical, legal, institutional) needed for an urban economy, which colonial rulers had installed elsewhere in Asia. Fear of provoking a colonial takeover had resulted in very conservative economic policies. Bangkok was a modestly sized city of one million people, still in the old fort-and-port style. No other urban location had a population larger than fifty thousand. The economic surplus was captured by a small elite that included the old nobility, and a tiny new segment of businessmen, professionals, and officials.

After wartime distortions eased, the economy launched on a phase of rapid growth that lasted for half a century. Three main factors made this possible.

First, the US became Thailand's political and economic patron. The fear of colonial takeover evaporated. US advisers helped to install the legal and institutional infrastructure for a modern economy, and US funds helped to improve the physical infrastructure.

Second, a large Chinese mercantile population, stranded in Thailand by China's communist revolution, resolved to integrate into the local society and to apply their talents to building local businesses.

Third, as a result of prior neglect, Thailand had a prodigious stock of untapped resources, natural and human. The new physical infrastructure, especially a road network, put these resources within the reach of the migrant Chinese entrepreneurs. For the next thirty years, the economy grew largely by chopping down trees, putting more land under crops, damming rivers for hydropower, mining more minerals, exploiting the sea, and pulling people away from a semi-subsistent existence in the villages.

Banking and politics played special roles in shaping the corporate history of this era. Agrarian societies typically have high rates of saving. Beginning in the postwar era, a handful of banks found ways to collect the petty savings of farmers and shopkeepers, and amalgamate them as capital funds deployed in the growing urban economy. These largely family-owned banks grew at breakneck speed, expanding into merchant capital groups with many subsidiary companies, as well as serving as the hubs of networks of related business families.

The military government, which became the successor to the old royalist rule, provided no blanket protection for capital. Indeed, it withheld many rights from the migrant Chinese as a means to defend its own dominance. Business families thus had to negotiate their individual protection by placing themselves under the patronage of political leaders in return for a levy on their profits.

Access to the banks and access to the generals were both limited. The few families that had such access were in a position to dominate the business opportunities that became available. Besides the bankers themselves, there were two main clusters. The first included families that began by exporting primary produce, and then moved into agri-processing and expanded laterally into related businesses such as insurance, shipping, warehousing, and transport. The second included families that took over the import business vacated by colonial firms during the war, and gradually expanded into manufacturing under government policies of import substitution, often with foreign joint venture partners.

Profits were concentrated among a few tens of families. To strengthen their bargaining power, they networked together through marriage alliances, cross shareholdings, and cooperation in associations providing community welfare.

TRANSITION

This era came to an end in the mid-1970s and was followed by a decade of uneasy transition. After defeat in the Indochina war, the US patronage of Thailand declined. At the same time, the long phase of postwar growth and stability in the world economy under the Bretton-Woods institutions came to an end, announced by a series of oil shocks and financial crises. Thailand's military rule began to splinter under demands for a transition to parliamentary democracy. Thailand's earlier strategy of growth undermined itself by catastrophic depletion of the stock of natural resources.

At the same time, reserves of natural gas were discovered, offering new possibilities of energy and inputs for industrialization. Because of a decline in infant mortality in the postwar years, the workforce began to grow at 3 percent a year, providing a pool of young labor.

As the economy stumbled through this transition, the World Bank emerged as a new patron. The bank advised Thailand to liberalize its domestic markets in order to loosen the oligopolistic grip of the conglomerates, and liberalize its external markets in order to tap the increased mobility of goods, capital, skills, and technology in the world.

The Thai government accepted this advice, but with some major qualifications. Beginning in the early 1980s, external trade was gradually liberalized by reducing tariffs and abolishing other restrictions. In the mid-1980s, regulations and incentives for investment were reformed to promote export-oriented manufacturing. In the late 1980s and early 1990s, controls on cross-border financial movements were eased, permitting easier inflow of loans and portfolio capital.

But the business conglomerates were able to retain their political influence over the transition from military rule to parliamentary democracy. Liberalization of internal markets was much more limited. Most strikingly, the cartel of sixteen domestic banks defeated reforms that would allow any new bank to be formed, or any foreign bank to expand its business beyond a single branch. Investment rules forced most foreign firms, other than US firms, which were privileged as a result of earlier US patronage, to operate as a minority partner in a joint venture. Foreign firms were excluded from certain sectors, especially agriculture and agriculture-related industries, land ownership, and most service businesses.

In short, in the transition of the 1980s, many of the external barriers on trade, investment, and finance were removed, but many internal barriers were retained in an attempt to corral some space for domestic capital.

THE GREAT BOOM

Initially, this reorientation was a massive success. Thailand became attractive as a site for industrial production and for the expanding world industry of tourism. In 1987, Thailand entered on a decade-long boom based on rising investment in industry, and a transfer of up to a million people a year from agriculture to urban occupations. Over the decade, real per capita income doubled (see figure 1), and Thailand was dubbed a newly industrializing economy.

Many Japanese and other East Asian firms transferred manufacturing into Thailand (and other Southeast Asian neighbors pursuing similar strategies) to take advantage of lower costs. Domestic capital participated enthusiastically too, plowing back their own gains from the sudden lift-off, raising funds from the stock market, and tapping international loans under the newly liberalized financial system. The big established families took a leading part. They were attractive as joint venture partners for the incoming firms, and also launched many independent ventures, often acquiring technology by purchase or license.

FIGURE I Real GDP per head, 1951–2006

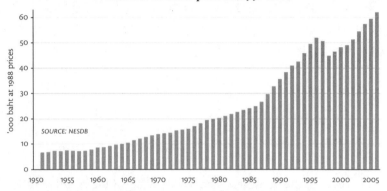

But the boom also threw up a new wave of entrepreneurs. Business success no longer depended on access to the banks and the generals. A new stock market and financial liberalization multiplied the sources of finance. Transition from military rule to parliamentary democracy multiplied the avenues of political influence, as well as providing a generally more secure environment for capital. Some of the new entrepreneurial groups were offshoots from the great families. Some rose from the middling ranks of the capital's business families. Several came from the provinces, and had accumulated their initial capital in the economy of resource exploitation—as loggers, crop traders, or land speculators. They moved into areas of new opportunity opened up by rising incomes and falling borders including telecoms, retailing, hotels, property development, and secondary financial institutions.

CRISIS AND RECOVERY

One consequence of the differential liberalization of the 1980s transition was the creation of a two-tier financial market. The cartel of domestic banks still lent at high rates, partially dictated by government monetary policies aimed at controlling the tear-away boom. But firms now also had access to dollar-denominated loans through offshore banks. Local banks borrowed from this source and lent onwards in baht, profiting from the interest differential. Local firms also borrowed directly from overseas sources. The offshore loans were so attractive that almost every significant business had used this facility to some extent. The private sector's foreign debt ballooned from 8 billion baht in 1988 to 74 billion in 1996.

FIGURE 2 Capital account flows, 1993–2006

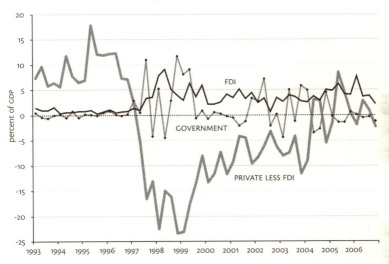

The baht was cut loose from the dollar on July 2, 1997, and sunk to half its former value over the next five months. The baht value of foreign loans doubled, destroying balance sheets. Foreign lenders hastened to collect their loans and withdraw. The drain of short-term capital swelled to the equivalent of almost a quarter of GDP in 1999, and declined only slowly over the next five years (see figure 2). Under the shock of the crisis, consumer spending shrank by a fifth in one year (see figure 3). The IMF intensified the shrinkage by applying a deflationary package designed for a crisis by excess government borrowing, and totally inappropriate in the case of a private debt overhang. Firms that had been gearing their planning to the pace of the boom decade now found they had enormous unused capacity for the foreseeable future. Many firms struggled to cut costs by reducing staff and stopped servicing their loans. In the past, default has been rare because it breached the rules of trust between bankers and clients, and placed any hope of future finance at risk. Now default became common practice, and bad loans rose to almost half the total credit advanced.

FIGURE 3 Per capita private consumption, 1993–2006

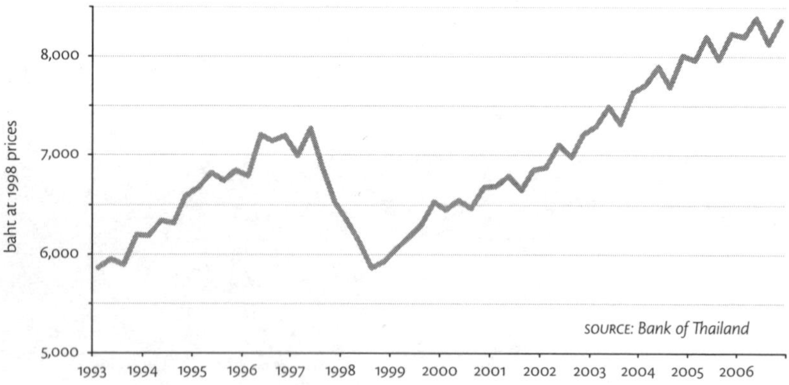

SOURCE: Bank of Thailand

The crisis was a massive shock. Over the prior four decades, growth had seemed as natural as the annual arrival of the rains. The only uncertainty was the relative scale. The shrinkage of 1997–1998 was not only unique but also massive in scale (see figure 4). While some kind of slump or crisis had seemed inevitable, few had predicted the severity, or the contagious effects on the region.

By mid-1998, the IMF admitted that its approach had been wrong. The deflationary policy was abandoned in favor of efforts to stimulate the economy through rising consumption. The government ran a budget deficit; the Japanese threw in some extra funds under the Miyazawa Plan; and the Thaksin government (2001–2006) extended the stimulus by expanding credit. With these measures, consumption regained its pre-crisis peak by 2003, and continued to grow strongly thereafter. This policy approach softened the social impact of the crisis and its potential political consequences. Employment climbed back to its former level.

FIGURE 4 Real GDP growth, 1955–2006

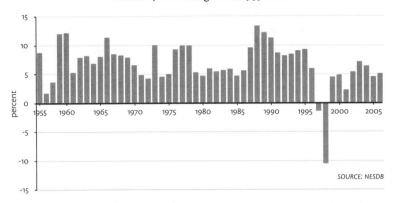

SOURCE: NESDB

The two million who slipped below the poverty line were hauled back above. But the consumer stimulus did not quickly translate into investment because of the existence of so much excess capacity and the collapse of the financial market. Banks refused new loans and shrunk the credit extended to business by one-third (see figure 5).

FIGURE 5 Distribution of commercial bank lending, 1990–2006

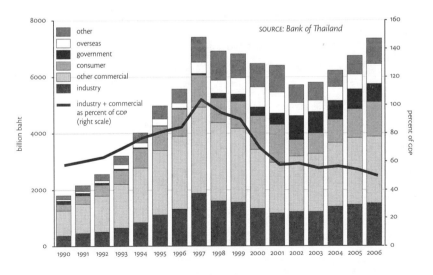

SOURCE: Bank of Thailand

But exports boomed because the depreciation of the baht cut the cost of labor and other local inputs. Between 1996 and 2006, exports multiplied 2.3 times in dollar terms and 3.5 in baht terms, dragging the economy out of the crisis. In the post-crisis years, almost all growth in GDP could be attributed to rising exports (Warr 2005: 37).

AFTERMATH

Over 2003–2004, the economy seemed to gain a new equilibrium (see figure 6). The leakage of short-term funds eased to a more moderate level (see figure 2). Most surviving firms had cleared their debts, straightened their balance sheets, and begun to show a profit. The stock market staged a dramatic revival over 2003, and then stabilized (see figure 7). After bad loans fell to reasonable levels, banks ceased shrinking their commercial loan portfolios and began to increase their lending to business (see figure 5). The overall level of investment in the economy edged upwards.

But some things had changed since the pre-crisis era, perhaps forever.

First, the overall level of domestic savings and investment, which had underwritten the high rate of capital accumulation in the pre-crisis era, had dropped down a step (see figures 1.8, 1.9). In particular, household

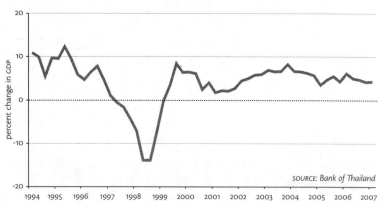

FIGURE 6 Quarterly GDP growth, 1994–2007

SOURCE: Bank of Thailand

FIGURE 7 Stock Exchange of Thailand index, 1997–2007

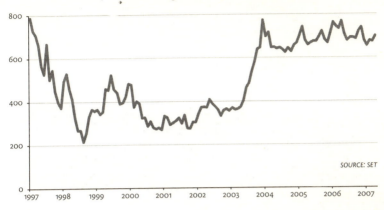

savings had fallen, and household debt had risen, as credit had become cheaper and more accessible. In addition, the banks no longer played such a prominent role in aggregating capital, and the stock market was only a partial replacement.

Second, the economy's integration with the outside world had risen a step. The simplest indicator was the ratio of foreign trade to GDP, which had risen from around 80 percent before the crisis to 150 percent in the

FIGURE 8 Gross national savings, 1994–2005

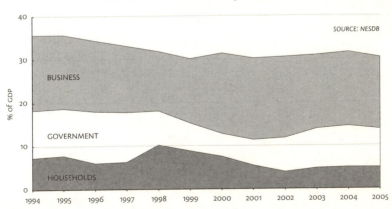

FIGURE 9 Gross domestic investment, 1994–2005

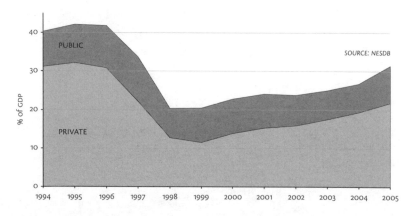

mid-2000s—a very high level for a country of Thailand's size by world standards (see figure 10). The involvement of foreign capital in the economy had also risen by a steep step (see chapter 1). The sectors that were driving the export growth underlying overall economic growth were technology-based manufactures, especially automotive, electrical, and electronic goods, which were almost all produced by transnational firms (see figure 11). The contribution of agriculture, resource-based

FIGURE 10 Trade as percent of GDP, 1995–2006

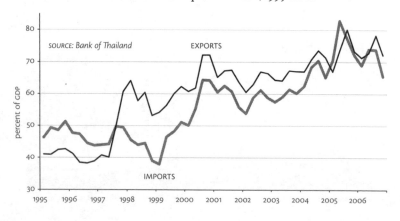

FIGURE 11 Export shares by sector, 1985–2006

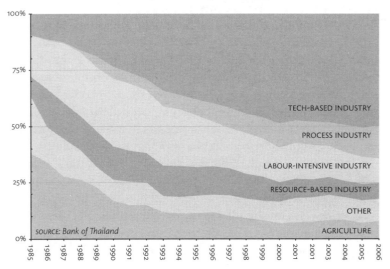

industries, and labor-intensive industries, where domestic capital still had a prominent role, had declined steeply.

Domestic capital had been at the center of Thailand's rapid growth in the postwar period. Government policy had provided stability rather than stimulus. Foreign capital had played only a subsidiary role. But over the crisis and aftermath, domestic capital had become of peripheral importance in the key activity driving growth in the national economy. Domestic capital had been moved from the center to the sidelines. How that happened, and what it may mean, is the subject of this book.

OUTLINE OF CHAPTERS

The first chapter examines what happened to Thailand's largely family-based firms in the crisis. It starts by calibrating the size of capital inflow in the post-crisis decade, and showing which sectors were chiefly affected. Next it sketches the nature of Thai family firms, and the dynamics of their growth. Finally it shows how their fate in the crisis depended on how far they had modernized their internal structure.

The next three chapters trace the fate of some key sectors of the economy. Liberalization of investment in the eye of the crisis opened up most manufacturing for full foreign ownership. Much of the capital inflow in the first post-crisis years was for acquisition of export-oriented manufacturing firms. A prime example was the automotive industry. After two decades of government policy nurturing a domestic automotive industry, the bulk of the sub-sector was transferred into foreign ownership. Automotive became one of the largest single industries in the Thai economy. Thailand became a minor hub in the transnational automotive industry. But only a handful of domestic firms remained as serious participants.

In theory, government still proposed to protect much of the service sector for domestic capital. In practice, it had neither the will nor the ability to enforce this protection. Big European retail chains entered promptly to take advantage of cheap land and limited regulation. Government, consumers, and local entrepreneurs generally facilitated their rapid expansion. The mobile phone market was carved up by concessions into a highly profitable oligopoly. Business groups invested heavily in politics to defend this arrangement against both local and transnational competition. The crisis probably worked in favor of the oligopoly. But after the crisis eased, this sub-sector came face to face with the logic of concentration on a global scale. The two major local firms sold out rather than taking the risky leap into global competition.

The next two chapters examine two business groups that not only survived the crisis but also prospered spectacularly. On first sight, the two cases could not seem more different. The first is Khun Charoen, the poorly educated son of a street vendor who emerged over the crisis as Thailand's richest entrepreneur. The second is the Crown Property Bureau, Thailand's oldest and most prestigious business group. Yet in fact, the reasons for their success over the crisis have a key similarity. Both had exceptionally deep pockets for reasons that were more about politics than business. Both were able to recover and restructure faster than their rivals, and hence reap the opportunities of the aftermath.

The next two chapters trace the interplay of business and politics in two upcountry regions. The first is a rural area where the local economy was in transition from an era of primitive accumulation on a resource frontier to a new era of urban growth on the fringes of the global economy. The second area is Chiang Mai where growth was founded on urban functions as a centre of administration, culture, education, and tourism. In both cases, the impact of the crisis was less severe than at the national level, yet it intensified local competition for business opportunities. In both cases, this intensification made local political influence even more important than before as an element of business strategy, especially following the expansion of elective local government in the late 1990s.

Two major themes run through all these case studies. First, the involvement of transnational capital in the economy has risen by a step, and in the long term the survival of domestic firms depends on their ability to compete in a global arena. Second, for the short term politics has *increased* in importance as a strategy for domestic capital's survival. The final two chapters address these two themes. The first looks at the readiness of Thai firms to venture overseas and compete in the global environment. The second analyzes the relations of business and politics within a framework of rent-seeking, focusing on Thaksin Shinawatra's failed attempt to create a new pattern of rent distribution.

The conclusion summarizes the key findings of these studies and attempts a partial answer to the question of what future there is for Thailand's domestic enterprise.

1

COMPANIES IN CRISIS

Natenapha Wailerdsak[1]

THE CRISIS of 1997 was the biggest shock to Thai domestic capital since it had started to accumulate on any significant scale from the Second World War onwards. How big was the damage? Which firms suffered and why?

This chapter starts by looking at the policymaking that framed how the crisis would affect domestic firms. Next it turns to look at the scale and nature of the inflow of foreign investment to acquire Thai firms' assets in the aftermath of the crisis. After sketching the background of the growth of Thai firms over the previous half-century, it examines the factors that sifted the winners from the losers.

CRISIS POLICY

When the Thai baht was floated free on August 2, 1997, and promptly sank like a stone, most major Thai corporations found their accounts were savaged. Over the past seven years since financial liberalization, they had borrowed funds overseas in foreign currency because the interest rates were far more attractive than those in the domestic market and because there seemed to be no exchange risk as the baht was tied to the dollar. They had borrowed a lot, too, as the booming rate of growth promised to separate those who stayed the pace from those who lingered behind. Even Siam Cement, widely admired as the country's most professionally managed company, had borrowed US$6 billion, mostly short-term and unhedged. When the value of the currency bottomed

---

1. The author thanks Professor Dr. Akira Suehiro for his kindness in providing data and his permission to use it for this study, and Chris Baker for his help in rewriting and editing.

in January 1998 at about 47 percent of its former value, the weight of these liabilities on the companies' balance sheets had doubled, rendering many of them technically bankrupt. Their income and cash flow went to hell, too. The economy slowed immediately from the shock of the crisis. Consumers stopped spending and investors stopped investing. The IMF imposed a severely deflationary package. Over the next year, consumer spending shrank by 20 percent, and overall GDP by 11 percent (see figures 1.3 and 1.4). Companies booked heavy losses and struggled to survive by cutting costs, adding to the downward spiral.

The IMF advised Thailand to keep interest rates high as one measure to prevent the currency spiraling downwards. This policy did not save the currency, but increased the hardship for indebted companies.[2] Several then stopped servicing debt to save costs. This was a dramatic move, as access to credit in the past had depended largely on personal relationships and trust. But as so many companies were in the same predicament, refusal to service debt became a common practice, known as strategic non-performing loans. As a result, virtually all financial institutions experienced the triple woes of technical bankruptcy, income losses, and illiquidity in extreme measure. Most of the finance companies had to be closed down. All the smaller and medium-sized banks effectively stopped operating. Burdened with mountains of bad loans, financial institutions virtually stopped lending, starving the rest of the economy of the funds needed to carry out business for several years.

As Peter Warr (2005) has shown, the various economies at the eye of the Asian crisis subsequently recovered at a roughly similar pace and timing. Since these countries pursued widely different recovery policies, this similarity suggests that these policies made only very marginal differences at the macro level. Economies recovered when the crisis bottomed out—when prices had fallen enough to lure back consumption, investment, and (most of all) exports.

---

2. The IMF admitted in January 1999 that the high-interest rate policy, recommended to Korea and Indonesia as well, was a mistake. Several World Bank studies found no correlation between the movements of interest rates and exchange rates.

But policy made a difference at the micro level, especially to the fates of companies.

Key US policymakers chose to attribute the crisis to weaknesses in the nature of Asian capitalism, rather than policy errors by governments, or the lack of any policing in the global financial market (Pasuk and Baker 2000: ch. 1). In particular they cited the prominence of closely held family firms (no clear separation between ownership and management), non-transparent accounting, the recourse to heavy borrowing from banks rather than fund raising from the stock and bond markets, and the cronyist reliance on relations with politicians and bureaucrats for favors and protection. These features were contrasted with the Anglo-American business model centered on the publicly listed company and a supposedly non-interventionist government.[3]

This view dominated discussion of the Asian crisis in international public space. It also provided a framework for the IMF's actions in managing the crisis, and was in broad measure accepted by the Thai politicians and technocrats who worked within this IMF framework over the four years following the crisis.

As a result, besides coping with the direct effects of the crisis, Thai companies had to face three further challenges.

First, government had no policy to protect and preserve Thai capital for some long-term benefit to the economy. In similar crises in other countries at other times, governments pursued policies to protect certain sectors for long-term benefit (Chang 1988). In the 1997 crisis, Malaysia's imposition of currency controls, and Korea's tough negotiation with the IMF, were based on such goals. In the dominant American view, this crisis was an example of the "creative destruction" at the heart of capitalism, and Thailand would ultimately benefit by allowing weak and flawed companies to go to the wall. The Thai government headed by the Democrat Party (1997–2001) was generally cold towards business lobbies that protested that government was abandoning its responsibility towards its own nationals, and inviting damage that would have long-term consequences.

---

3. See the review of this literature in Suehiro 2001: 1–5.

Second, among the IMF conditions were legal and regulatory changes designed to steer the Thai corporate sector towards the Anglo-American model or so-called international standard. Basel rules for banking practice aimed to make Thai banks more secure in the liberalized financial environment, but also threatened the close integration between banks and their major corporate customers, which had been a key characteristic of Thailand's brand of capitalism. New standards of corporate governance imposed on listed companies were again designed to make these companies more secure, but would reduce the prominent role of family ownership and management.

Third, owners of capital were exposed to a sudden increase in competition at a time when they were badly weakened and unable to respond. Since the 1960s, Thai governments had policies to nurture domestic capitalism, including providing some protection against foreign competition. Certain sectors were closed to foreign investment on grounds of national security or cultural protection. In other sectors, foreign firms were restricted to a minority shareholding (with the exception of US firms which were allowed full ownership as a result of the US's special relationship with Thailand over the cold war). As the economy had subsequently grown and become more integrated with the world, these policies were gradually and selectively relaxed. Especially after Thailand switched towards export-oriented manufacturing in the mid-1980s, non-US firms were allowed full ownership if they contributed to exports. For other firms, methods were found to circumvent the restriction on majority ownership through pyramid companies.[4] This practice appears to have begun in the 1970s, but have become significantly more widespread from around 1990 when more foreign firms wished to participate in the Thai boom.

---

4. In computing the percentage of Thai or foreign shareholding, the authorities scrutinized only the first level of shareholding. The common practice was to set up a holding company in which the majority of the registered capital was held in Thai names, but as preference shares with conditions that limited the owners of these shares to a much smaller share of the voting rights and the dividend payments. The law stated that it was illegal for a Thai to hold such shares as a nominee for foreign interests, but of course this was hard to determine. By allowing thousands of firms to adopt this work-around, the government relaxed the restriction on foreign investment *in practice*, while allowing it to remain in the law.

Still, sectors such as banking remained excluded from this practice, and many large non-US investors were content to conform to the pattern of minority ownership. Thai capital-owners had become used to entering joint ventures, especially in order to get access to technology and innovation.

In the dominant American view of the crisis, part of the "creative destruction" had to come about by easing ownership laws to allow foreign firms easier access and greater control. In the heat of the crisis, many Thai business-owners supported this move because they were desperate for an injection of capital to stave off corporate debt restructuring. The Thai government succumbed to this demand, partly in the belief that only injections of foreign funds could rescue many cash-strapped enterprises and hence preserve the productive potential of the economy. Several measures resulted.

Financial institutions were opened up to foreign investment but still subject to the minority rule. Companies under investment promotion, which were mostly in manufacturing, were allowed majority or full ownership. The Alien Business Law was reformed, shifting thirty-three industries into classifications that allowed foreign majority participation, and providing a few useful new loopholes.[5] Other reforms allowed foreigners to take fifty-year renewable leases on commercial land, to have 100 percent ownership in condominium units, and to own one rai for residence if they brought in at least 25 million baht. Foreign firms were encouraged to participate in auctions of the insolvent financial institutions' foreclosed assets which were seized by government at the onset of the crisis, and which were often sold at fire-sale rates.

---

5. The 1999 Act (following the earlier 1972 regulation) has three lists of sectors. Foreign firms (meaning a firm with majority foreign ownership) are prohibited from sectors in List 1, which include mostly agriculture and media. Foreign firms require permission from the Cabinet to enter the sectors in List 2, which are restricted for reasons of security, culture, or environment, and which include transportation, mining, and trade in antiques. Foreign firms require permission from a foreign business committee of the Ministry of Commerce to enter the sectors in List 3, which are restricted on grounds that Thai firms are not yet competitive, and which include law, accountancy, architecture, and engineering. Firms that are located in an industrial estate or have received promotion from the Board of Investment are exempt. This loophole effectively opened up most manufacturing.

FIGURE 1.1 Foreign direct investment, 1970–2006

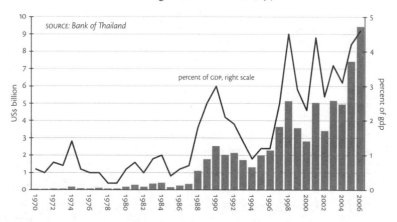

Besides, the financial crisis generated a lot of government business for foreign investment banks. Not only private firms but also the government needed advice on such complex matters as debt restructuring, privatization, bank recapitalization, and liquidation of the assets of failed companies. Thus, the names of foreign investment banks like Goldman Sachs, Merrill Lynch, Salomon Smith Barney, Lehman Brothers, and Morgan Stanley Dean Witter seemed to pop up everywhere.

CAPITAL INFLOW

Over the five years following the crisis, foreign investment flooded into Thailand. The recorded figures dwarfed the flows seen on the upswing of the boom, or ever before. Moreover, the official figures probably underestimate the true level. Several well-established foreign firms financed expansion locally by plowing back profits or borrowing in the local market.

Inflows of foreign direct investment (FDI) and foreign portfolio investment spurted from the second half of 1997 (see figure 1.1). In the ten years

FIGURE I.2 Shares of foreign direct investment by origin, 1970–2006

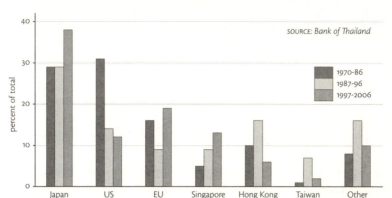

following the crisis, [6] the average annual inflow of FDI was almost three times higher than in the boom decade in dollar terms, almost five times higher in baht terms, and over double as a proportion of GDP.[7] Flows of foreign portfolio investment, while more erratic, were on average almost double in the post-crisis decade compared to the boom decade. As a proportion of the total stock of direct investment in Thailand since 1970, the foreign share increased from around 10 percent prior to the crisis, to over double that ten years later (Pavida 2006).

By far the single largest source of FDI was Japan, its share rising from 29 percent in the boom decade to 38 percent in the post-crisis era (see table 1.1 and figure 1.2). The US share dwindled slightly, while those of Taiwan and Hong Kong were reduced a lot. The share of FDI originating from Singapore increased from 9 percent in the boom decade to 13 percent in the post-crisis era. Singapore also dominated

6. In this calculation, 1997 is included in the post-crisis period because the FDI inflows in the second half of the year were double those in the first half.

7. The Bank of Thailand figures used for this calculation underestimate the contrast as they exclude investments in the banking sector, which increased after the crisis with the sell-off of controlling holdings in four banks.

TABLE 1.1 Foreign direct investment and portfolio investment, 1970–2006

	1970–1986	1987–1996	1997–2006
FDI YEARLY AVERAGE			
US$ billion	0.2	1.7	5.1
baht billion	3.5	43.7	202.3
% of GDP	0.0	1.6	3.6
SHARES BY COUNTRY			
Japan	29.5	28.9	37.6
US	30.9	14.3	12.1
EU	15.5	9.4	18.7
ASEAN	6.1	10.2	14.5
Hong Kong	10.3	15.5	6.2
Taiwan	0.6	6.9	2.5
SHARES BY SECTOR			
Industry	32.3	37.3	51.6
Trade	19.7	17.9	15.3
Services	7.3	3.8	7.3
Finance	5.2	6.6	4.7
Real Estate	2.8	23.0	5.6
Construction	15.2	8.3	0.8
Other	17.6	3.1	14.7
PORTFOLIO FOREIGN INVESTMENT, yearly average, US$ billion	0.0	0.9	1.5

the flows of foreign portfolio investment, accounting for over two-thirds of the total in the post-crisis decade. To some extent this reflected the fact that many international financial firms maintained a regional headquarters in Singapore. But Singapore corporations also plunged into Thailand in the post-crisis era, taking special interest in banks and property.

The major destination of FDI was industry, its share of the total rising from 37 percent in the boom decade to 52 percent after the crisis. Although the export-oriented boom is often attributed to foreign inflows, in fact the total foreign investment in industry in the post-crisis decade was over four times higher in dollar terms, and over six times higher in baht terms. Moreover, the foreign inflow into the electrical, machinery, and transport sectors (particularly sub-sectors such as automotive and hard-disk drives) increased from a 17 to 28 percent share of the total FDI inflow, and expanded by a factor of five in dollar terms.

Over the boom decade, almost a quarter of FDI had targeted the real estate sector, arriving late in the decade and swelling the speculative bubble that burst in 1997. This flow now dwindled but recovered strongly from 2005 and still accounted for 6 percent of the total. The destination of portfolio foreign flows are unknown but probably the upsurge in portfolio inflows in the mid-2000s also reflected a revival of foreign interest in the Thai property market.

FOREIGN-INVESTED SECTORS

Behind these figures, there were certain key areas of the economy where these post-crisis flows of foreign investment were concentrated.

Export industries

In many joint ventures, the Thai partner was rendered effectively bankrupt in the crisis, threatening the future of the joint enterprise. To help solve the illiquidity problems among local firms, government facilitated foreign investment in manufacturing. Foreign partners in projects promoted by the Board of Investment (BOI) were allowed to raise their stake to majority or full ownership. Many Japanese manufacturing firms had enjoyed their highest rates of return on capital from their Thai operation over the boom era, and judged that in the long term these operations were too valuable to abandon. Thus in many cases, the Thai partner was either bought out completely, or reduced to a small minority share.

In the automotive industry, for example, all the major Japanese assembly plants and most of their first-tier parts suppliers were converted to foreign-majority ownership (see chapter 2). Subsequently, further investment was required to reorient production towards export to compensate for the drop in Thai domestic demand. A similar buy-out, either by injecting new capital or accepting a debt-for-equity swap, took place among firms in the electrical and electronic sectors, and other areas.

Banks and finance

Commercial banks were saddled with a huge burden from non-performing loans, and faced the need to raise a large amount of new capital to repair their damaged balance sheets and to meet new standards of capital adequacy and loan-loss provisioning. Government offered to provide

TABLE 1.2 Changes in the banking system

	OWNERS, PRE-CRISIS	SHARE OF MAIN OWNER, 1985	RANK BY LOANS 1996
Krung Thai	Government		1
Bangkok	Sophonpanich	22.3	2
Thai Farmers	Lamsam	10.5	3
Siam Commercial	Crown Property Bureau	36	4
Ayudhya	Ratanarak	22.8	5
Thai Military	Armed forces		6
Bank of Asia	Euarchukiati, Phatraprasit		9
Thai Danu	Tuchinda, etc. (6 families)		10
Nakhon Thon	Wanglee		12
Laemthong	Chansrichawla, Nandhabiwat		13
Siam City	Sirivadhanabhakdi		7
Bangkok Metropolitan	Tejapaibul	24.9	8
Union Bank	Chonwichan		11
First Bangkok City			
Bangkok Bank of Commerce			-
Thanachart			

SOURCE: Data compiled by Akira Suehiro and Natenapha Wailerdsak

public funds to help in the recapitalization of banks but only under certain safeguards and conditions, including readiness to enter into corporate debt restructuring. Most major banks declined the government offer because they were wary of takeover. In view of the difficulty of finding the required capital in the local market, government lifted the ban on foreign investment in banks. Their fate varied according to size (see table 1.2).

The five largest commercial banks survived, in part through government assistance. In the three that were controlled by a dominant family, the family share was scythed down to below 5 percent, and

	NPL % 1999	RANK BY LOANS 1996	SHARE OF OLD OWNER, 2004	FOREIGN SHARE, 2004
	48.0	2	56.41*	12.42
	48.0	1	<5	48.32
renamed Kasikorn, 2003	40.2	3	<5	48.98
	34.3	4	24.04	38.14
	37.2	6	<5	31.25
	30.5	5	22.73	26.79
acquired by ABN Amro, later sold to UOB	38.5	10	0	97.0
acquired by DBS, later merged to Thai Military	48.7	-	1.77	51.72
acquired by Standard Chartered	39.9	11	0	75.01
acquired by UOB	69.3	12	<0.1	83.77
seized by government before crisis	56.4	7	47.46*	24.05
seized by government, merged to Siam City	70.1	-	-	-
seized by government, renamed Bank Thai	63.1	8	48.98*	5.75
seized by government, merged to Krung Thai	-	-	-	-
seized by government before crisis, closed down	-	-	-	-
received banking license, 2001		9		0.07

Government share.

foreign shareholders acquired major stakes, yet the family retained management control. In the case of the politically sensitive Siam Commercial Bank, the Crown Property Bureau was able to retain a more substantial share (see chapter 5). Thai Military Bank, in which the largest shareholders were the three branches of the military, was the subject of several merger schemes before eventually being merged with DBS Thai Danu Bank and IFCT.

Over 1998–1999, four medium-sized banks were sold to foreign owners—two Singaporean, one British, and one Dutch. DBS Thai Danu Bank was later merged into Thai Military Bank, while Bank of Asia/ABN Amro was resold to Singaporean UOB in 2004 and subsequently merged into UOB Radhanasin in 2005.

Five small and medium-sized banks were seized by government. Three were closed down and their assets merged with other institutions. The remaining two continued to operate with the Ministry of Finance's FIDF[8] as the major shareholder.

Of ninety-one finance companies operating before the crisis, fifty-six were closed down by government order in December 1997. Others lapsed over following months. Under the Financial Sector Master Plan adopted in early 2004, the remaining thirty-one were offered the options of elevating themselves into a universal (i.e., full) bank, or a retail bank (the main difference from a universal bank being a ceiling on loan size), or a specialized non-bank institution. Twenty firms or groups submitted applications. Three were granted licenses to become full banks, and another five to become retail banks.

All of the remaining banks understood that in the context of the Basel standards, increased foreign share ownership, and closer scrutiny, especially of credit practice, they could no longer primarily act as merchant banks providing loans to affiliated entrepreneurs, and taking capital stakes in outside ventures. All aimed to reorient towards

---

8. The Financial Institutions Development Fund (FIDF) was an institution under the control and supervision of the Bank of Thailand. It was established to function as a lender of last resort, assisting banks or finance companies to overcome serious liquidity problems. Since the currency crisis laid waste to the country's economy the FIDF has funneled 1.4 trillion baht (US$37 billion) into the banking system.

consumer banking, and consequently invested in new systems, internal reorientation, branch redesign, and corporate image. Siam Commercial Bank was the most aggressive, investing 7.5 billion baht in corporate restructuring, and claiming to make almost 60 percent of its profit from consumer banking by 2007 (*The Nation*, 8 May 2007).

The Financial Sector Master Plan of 1994 opened up opportunities for more non-bank financial institutions including credit card operators, factoring, mortgage, personal loans, leasing, and hire purchase. Several former finance companies took this route, while most of the commercial banks also opened subsidiaries. Under the Thaksin government (2001–2006) which was intent on boosting consumption through expanded credit, the credit card and personal loan sub-sectors expanded rapidly. By the end of 2004, the non-bank loan business in various forms was valued at 603 billion baht, or 9 percent of total loans (Chodechai et al. 2005: 170).

Prior to the crisis there were around fifty brokerage firms. Most of the major units were affiliates of the large banking groups. When the stock market slumped over 1997–1999, twenty-two of the brokerages closed down, and over the next few years, almost all those remaining were sold to international brokerage houses. When the stock market recovered in 2003, some of the brokerages were bought back. For example, the Kasikorn group's former executives bought back Phatra Securities from Merrill Lynch.

Property

Several foreign firms entered Thailand's property market in the later stages of the boom attracted by prices that were rising rapidly though still cheap in comparative international terms. These firms came especially from Hong Kong and Singapore, but also from China, Japan, and Europe. They concentrated on the high-end commercial and residential markets in the capital, and on major tourist resorts. Although some firms liquidated their interests and withdrew from the market after the crisis, several with deep pockets chose to stay on and take advantage of the slump in prices and the desperation of many owners to sell. A large volume of property, including land and unfinished development projects, fell into the hands of banks or the Financial Restructuring Agency (FRA), which acquired the assets of the collapsed financial firms. Foreign investors including developers and property funds, working through Thai nominees, were active in the auctions of these properties.

Real estate consultants such as CB Richard Ellis, Jones Lang LaSalle, First Pacific Davies, and Cushman & Walkfield worked as agents for foreign investors seeking prime properties at knock-down prices. Several prominent Thai business families lost control of their property companies when they were obliged to issue new shares as part of debt restructuring. For example, the Srivikorn family saw its 20.65 percent stake in Golden Land diluted to less than 8 percent. The Lamsam and Chutrakul families saw their stake in Sansiri diluted from 70 to 13 percent.

As the economy turned tentatively upwards in 2000–2001, several new property firms entered Thailand, either solo or as joint ventures. Singapore firms were again the most prominent. The Bangkok property market was also attractive for capital from China and the Middle East looking for offshore investment.

Construction-related industries

Another segment that was severely hit by the crisis were construction-related industries such as cement and steel. The long construction boom in the early and mid-1990s had tempted many companies to expand their businesses with the help of dollar-denominated loans, and hence these firms were crippled by the baht's depreciation. In addition, the property and construction markets collapsed, severely reducing the demand.

In the cement sub-sector, this resulted in three of the world's largest producers making acquisitions in Thailand. In August 1998, the Ratanarak family sold Siam City Cement, the second ranked Thai producer, to the Holcim group in order to raise capital to protect its banking interests. Subsequently Ciments Francais, the France-based international division of the Italcementi Group, bought controlling interests in both Asia Cement and Jalaprathan Cement, the fourth and fifth ranked producers, while Cemex of Mexico bought the small

Saraburi Cement from Italthai. Holcim and Cemex also hoped to gain control in the second-ranked TPI Polene, which was undergoing restructuring in an atmosphere of conflict between the owners and creditors, but ultimately failed (Yutthasak 2004).

Thailand has no upstream steel industry, but several firms shared the market to make sheet steel, construction steel, and pipe from imported materials. All of the five major firms were forced to enter debt restructuring. In 2000, the three makers of construction steel (NTS, STM, and SCG) merged to create a virtual monopoly under the name Millennium Steel. In 2005, Tata Steel of India bought a 65 percent stake in the merged company. The SSM company of the Leeswadtrakul family was acquired by its foreign creditors and renamed as G Steel. The main maker of sheet steel, Sahaviriya, had to allow two Japanese partners, NKK and Marubeni, to double their shareholding to 23 percent each, but the old management remained in control.

Big retail businesses

During the boom, three Thai conglomerates had launched into large-scale modern retailing such as hypermarket and discount stores through ventures with foreign partners. The Charoen Pokphand (CP) group had linked up with Dutch Makro. The Chirathivat family's Central group went in with Dutch Ahold and the French firms, Carrefour and Casino. The Mall linked up with Belgian Delhaize.

After the crisis, foreign firms bought out the cash-strapped local groups. Casino acquired a 68 percent stake in Big C, reducing the previously dominant Chirathivat family to a minority 13.4 percent. Ahold bought out the Chirathivats' 51 percent stake in the Tops supermarket chain to have full control. Tesco acquired 93.2 percent of Lotus hypermarkets, leaving the remainder with the CP group. Delhaize and its partners acquired full control of the Food Lion chain from the Mall group. Carrefour took full ownership of its Thai operation, buying out the Chirathivat family's 40 percent stake.

All five European firms launched programs of aggressive expansion (see chapter 3). They took advantage of the availability and low price of prime land, and of the lack of much regulation. Government had not yet created any special legal framework for this new kind of retailing and had many other distractions during the crisis period. Although local retailers protested against the rapid expansion of the foreign megastores, government was reluctant to impose controls that would halt this stream of investment, and that might appear as generally unfriendly towards foreign capital.

When the Thai economy revived in 2003, Central was able to buy back the Tops chain from Ahold which had found it impossible to manage its Asian operations profitably and was withdrawing also from Indonesia and Malaysia. Delhaize also withdrew, closing down eight outlets and selling the remaining twenty-six to Central.

Service businesses

A wide array of investments in service businesses appeared after a reform in the regulations on foreign ownership in 1999.

The new Alien Business Law of 1999 (see note 4) was designed to open up more of manufacturing to foreign-majority firms, but to retain restrictions on most service businesses. However, the law allowed firms in several sectors, including many professional services, to apply for special permission through the Ministry of Commerce.

Between 1999 and July 2006, 1,630 firms gained entry under this provision. In addition, 515 US firms were allowed under the Amity Act, and another 483 under promotion by the BOI. The largest proportion (38 percent) of these were regional offices. The next largest proportion consisted of firms offering an array of business services including consultancy, construction, engineering, repair and maintenance, and accountancy. Many others were firms providing specialized financial services including loans, leasing, mortgage, and hire purchase. Japan was the origin of 38 percent of the total, and Singapore of 12 percent (Deunden et al. 2007: ch. 3).

Many more foreign companies operated by evading the equity restrictions using pyramid shareholdings and nominees to control the decision-making in the firms. In 2007, when government threatened to close down this loophole, estimates of the numbers of companies involved ranged up to forty thousand (*Prachachat Thurakit*, 11 January 2007). This number included a vast number of restaurants and other petty businesses, but also some major ventures in property, telecommunications, retailing, and other services. Two foreign firms controlled 82 percent of the mobile phone market (see chapter 6). Three controlled 75 percent of large-scale retail (see chapter 3); five had a 44 percent of the market for express mail services (Deunden and Suneeporn 2006: iv).

A step change

In all these five areas—export-oriented manufacturing, finance, property, big retail, and services—the inflow of foreign capital in the aftermath of the crisis was a sudden and marked change from past practice. Overall, the involvement of foreign capital in the economy increased substantially. In 1988, 122 of the world's top 450 multinational companies had an operation in Thailand. By 2000, the number had doubled to 248 of the top 500, and the number of their subsidiaries had tripled from 214 to 630, of which 305 were in manufacturing (Suehiro 2003: tables C21, C22). The amount of tax paid by multinational companies had increased by 80 percent over four years (see table 1.3).

TABLE 1.3 Taxation levied on multinational companies, 2000–2004 (million baht)

	2000	2001	2002	2003	2004
Tax on juristic persons	145,554	149,663	170,430	208,896	261,928
Tax on profits	89,414	86,481	97,658	127,564	162,255
Service fee on profits remitted	23,313	25,144	25,976	26,819	35,337
Other	32,828	38,037	46,796	54,513	64,335
TOTAL	291,108	299,326	340,860	417,793	523,855

SOURCE: Deunden et al. 2007: ch. 3, p. 12, using data from the Fiscal Policy Office

Foreign investors have ranked Thailand among the most attractive investment destinations in the region because of investment privileges, relatively adequate infrastructure, and political stability. Various free trade agreements have attracted foreign investors to benefit from low tariff arrangements. After the crisis, the level of foreign investment in the economy took a step upwards and is poised to increase further in the future.

IMPACT ON DOMESTIC CAPITAL

Growth of family enterprise

The domestic firms that had come to dominate Thai business by the Asian crisis had some distinct characteristics. With only a small handful of exceptions, they were family firms founded by a Chinese immigrant over the past three generations.

Thailand's modern capitalism had had its tentative beginnings around the turn of the twentieth century in the era of high colonialism (Suehiro 1989). New businesses appeared in rice milling and exporting, timber milling and export, shipping, banking, and infrastructure. Participants included aristocratic families with capital accumulated from land, and immigrant Chinese with profits from trading and tax-farming. The major business of rice exporting was subject to vicious swings of glut and shortage in the Asian market, accentuated by instability among currencies, and competition from colonial firms with stronger capital backing. Fortunes were made and lost. The only investor that survived this endemic instability was the Crown because it had unique access to tax revenues and property to accumulate capital (see chapter 5). By the 1910s, the Privy Purse (which would late evolve into the Crown Property Bureau, CPB) had interests in banking, cement, and urban property development.

With this exception, all the other major business groups that emerged through the twentieth century were based around the families of immigrant Chinese, particularly those who first arrived in Siam between the 1880s and 1930s.

The engine of accumulation changed rapidly over time as Thailand's economy grew and integrated with the world economy. Between the two world wars, the rice trade remained the major business. By building integrated business, five families managed to acquire sufficient scale to survive the swings of the market, and pass on their accumulated capital to future generations. In the 1940s with war and the collapse of colonialism, new opportunities opened up in areas vacated by European capital, particularly banking and retail. Again a handful of families monopolized this opportunity and grew rapidly, largely by cultivating close and mutually profitable links with autocratic political leaders. In the 1960s, with the advent of development plans under US influence, the main opportunity was in agribusinesses to process and export the produce of a vastly expanded and variegated agricultural sector. The leading entrepreneurs included some of the old rice barons, but also a seed importer and several upcountry traders.

In the 1960s and 1970s, new opportunities arose to manufacture consumer goods and commodities under protectionist policies of import substitution industrialization. In both agribusiness and fledgling industries, entrepreneurs succeeded by cultivating close links with the banks, with political leaders, and with foreign partners that could provide technology. By the 1980s, the policy framework switched towards export-oriented industrialization. Firms initially focused on labor-intensive sectors such as textiles, but later the trend turned more towards joint ventures with multinational capital to participate in dispersed transnational systems of manufacture. In the later 1980s and 1990s, with accelerating urban prosperity, fortunes were made in providing the domestic market with consumer manufactures, media, telecommunications, entertainment, modern retailing, tourism, and electronic gadgetry.

Most of these immigrant Chinese businesses operated under the *kongsi* system, which roughly translates as "partnership." Under this system, all members and branches of the family are considered part of a single enterprise. The patriarch (or, more rarely, matriarch) has absolute control over both the direction of the enterprise and the distribution of the profits. All adult males, and many females too, are expected to work in the family concern. On the occasion of a son's marriage, the patriarch allocates the son a segment of the business for his family upkeep, though still within the patriarch's overall control. On the patriarch's death, control usually passes to the eldest son, but this may vary if another family member is clearly better qualified.

In such a system, the family demography matters. In the generation after the Second World War, many patriarchs of business families practiced polygamy to generate an expanding family workforce. Some also deftly deployed their daughters to recruit talented son-in-laws or to build strategic alliances with other families.

Some family firms grew into sprawling conglomerates over time. As the above sketch of a century of business history shows, the sectors and activities that offered the most profitable opportunities changed rapidly over time. A few families not only accumulated financial capital but also acquired intangible assets through their relations with banks, politicians, and foreign partners, which gave them advantages in exploiting new areas of profitable opportunity. Families often branched into new areas by indulging the ambitions of sons, especially those who had been educated overseas and had returned with new skills and a different view of the future. A few groups expanded by extending forwards and backwards from their original business. The Chirathivat family, for instance, built their initial business in department store retailing, and then extended forwards into various other retail forms (supermarkets, specialty stores, restaurants) and backwards into manufacture of some key areas of merchandise. Many more groups expanded sideways by lurching into new areas of opportunity. For instance, several of the families that dominated the agribusiness boom of the 1970s were among the key investors in urban property development, retailing, hotels, and telecommunications in the consumer boom of the 1990s.

Some of the biggest and most prominent conglomerates were based in finance. Prior to the rise of the stock market and financial liberalization, banks were the major mechanism for capital accumulation. As the economy grew, their deposits multiplied at a sustained rate of 20 percent a year over two decades (Suehiro 1989: 248). They distributed some of these funds in loans to affiliated business families, and invested some in their own subsidiaries. The biggest five banks became conglomerates in themselves, as well as serving as the hub of broader networks of business families. By using their financial power, they were able to protect a cartel of around fifteen banks from any new entry or from foreign competition. The prominence of these financial conglomerates was one of the distinctive features of Thai capitalism in the pre-crisis era.

Over the second half of the twentieth century, most of these family firms went through a transition from the first to second generation, and several also from the second to third. The transition from first-to-second was often a time of rapid expansion, especially for those families that had been demographically successful, and that had invested productively in education. According to common wisdom, the transition from the second to third generation was more difficult and risky because the migrant culture of hard work and self-exploitation had dissipated, while the chances of internal family dispute had increased.

Top firms, 1979 to 1997

The families that accumulated capital, human assets, and strategic relationships developed into sprawling conglomerates that dominated modern business. Krirkkiat (1982) identified the one hundred business groups of any significance in the Thai economy in the year 1979.[9] Altogether they owned 1,337 companies, and their combined revenues were equivalent to 30 percent of GDP. Even within this list, business concentration was marked.[10] The top thirty firms accounted for 81 percent of the total revenues, equivalent to over a quarter of GDP, and 90 percent of the total assets (see table 1.4). Among these top thirty firms, six had their core business in banking, seven in agribusiness, and thirteen in industry (Suehiro 2003: tables C2, C3).

Over the next two decades, the urban economy expanded, but the degree of concentration under a small number of family firms remained just as marked. Suehiro (2003) assembled data on the top 100 firms

9. His survey actually listed 112, but the bottom few are small and it is neater to round off the list at the 100 mark.

10. High concentration within a particular industry usually indicates significant barriers to entry including scale economies, product differentiation, and absolute capital requirements. High concentration on a national scale, such as this, probably indicates that such conditions are generally prevalent across sectors.

TABLE 1.4 Top thirty business groups, 1979 and 1997

		TOP 30 BUSINESS GROUPS IN 1979 (BY REVENUES)		
RANK	FAMILY	CORPORATE NAME	REVENUES (BAHT BN)	RANK 1997
1	Sophonpanich	Bangkok Bank	19.6	2
2	Crown Property Bureau	Siam Cement/SCB	16.4	1
3	Chawkwanyun	Thai Oil	9.9	56
4	Laohathai	Metro	8.3	20
5	Phornprapha	Siam Motors	7.3	19
6	Lamsam	Thai Farmers Bank	6.3	4
7	Boonsoong	Tri Petch Isuzu	6.1	62
8	Phothirattanankun	Sukree/TBI	5.0	132
9	Tejapaibul	BMB	4.9	22
10	Chearavanont	Charoen Pokphand	4.8	3
11	Darakananda	Saha-Union	4.0	26
12	Srifuengfung	Srifuengfung	4.0	30
13	Chokwatana	Saha/SPI	3.8	15
14	Ratanarak	Bank of Ayudhya	3.6	8
15	Bhirom Bhakdi	Boonrawd	3.5	10
16	Mahakhun	Mahaguna	2.7	-
17	Leophairatana	Hong Yiah Seng/TPI	2.7	11
18	Osathanugrah	Osotspa	2.6	23
19	Asadathorn	Thai Roong Ruang	2.3	65
20	Karnasuta	Italthai	2.3	17
21	Karnchanachari	Siew	2.1	44
22	Sukosol	Kamol Sukosol	2.1	79
23	Kanathanavanich	Laemthong	2.0	50
24	Lee-Issaranukul	MMC Sittipol	1.9	18
25	Bulsook	Serm Suk	1.7	41
26	Wisawaphonbun	G.S. Steel	1.7	-
27	Tharawanitchakun	Asia Trust	1.5	-
28	Sithi-amnuai	PSA	1.5	-
29	Chinthammit	Kwang Soon Lee	1.4	81
30	YipInTsoi	Yip In Tsoi	1.4	151

SOURCE: Suehiro (2003), using Krirkkiat (1982) and his own database

TOP 30 BUSINESS GROUPS IN 1997 (BY REVENUES)

RANK	FAMILY	CORPORATE NAME	REVENUES (BAHT BN)	RANK 2000
1	Crown Property Bureau	Siam Cement/SCB	238.2	1
2	Sophonpanich	Bangkok Bank	195.0	6
3	Chearavanont	Charoen Pokphand	161.0	3
4	Lamsam	Thai Farmers/Loxley	139.3	8
5	(public)	Krungthai Bank	127.3	7
6	Sirivadhanabhakdi	TCC	117.9	4
7	(public)	PTT	110.8	2
8	Ratanarak	Bank of Ayudhya	91.7	17
9	(public)	Thai Airways	88.3	5
10	Bhirom Bhakdi	Boonrawd	78.8	15
11	Leophairatana	TPI/Hong Yiah Seng	67.8	73
12	Army/Private	Thai Military Bank	52.2	27
13	Chirathivat	Central	48.7	11
14	Shinawatra, Damapong	Shin	48.6	9
15	Chokwatana	Saha Group	46.5	12
16	Bencharongkul	Ucom	41.8	16
17	Karnasuta	Italthai	40.8	22
18	Lee-Issaranukul	MMC Sittipol	38.6	10
19	Phornprapha	Siam	35.9	14
20	Laohathai,Tangtrongsakdi	Metro	35.3	25
21	Dumnernchanvanit	Soon Hua Seng	34.9	13
22	Tejapaibul	BMB	33.0	97
23	Osathanugrah	Osotspa /Premier	32.2	21
24	Phatraprasit	Phatraprasit	29.5	66
25	Chakkaphak	Finance One	27.9	-
26	Darakananda	Saha-Union	26.2	19
27	Wongkusolkit	Mitr Phol/Banpu	25.8	20
28	Limsong	Siam City/Ayutthaya	25.7	154
29	Chansiri, Niruttinanond	TUF	24.8	18
30	Srifuengfung	Srifuengfung	23.6	111

for 1997. Their total revenues were now equivalent to half of total GDP. Within this top 100, concentration had eased slightly but not by much. The top thirty still accounted for around three-quarters of the total revenues of the 100, and 85 percent of the assets.

But with the massive changes in the economy over these two decades, few family groups had been able to retain their rankings over the eighteen years between these two surveys. Of the top one hundred in 1979, only forty-five remained in the top one hundred in 1997, and of the top thirty in 1979, only sixteen retained that ranking, including four banking groups and the CPB, which was in part also based upon a bank. Not many of the 1979 top one hundred groups had totally disappeared. Most had simply slipped down the rankings, overtaken by firms that had successfully shifted into the new growth areas of the economy.

The background of the top thirty companies in 1997 was more varied than in 1979. The number in banking or finance was even higher at eleven, while those in agribusiness had dwindled to four. The new entrants in this business elite included firms in telecoms, retailing, construction, energy, and liquor. Moreover, most of these top firms now straddled two or more sub-sectors, reflecting the different generations of their growth. TPI had extended from agribusiness to petrochemicals, CP from agribusiness to telecoms, Phatraprasit from liquor to hotels and property, Wanglee from agribusiness to banking, and Sahaviriya from steel to property.

Family firms and the stock market

Using data from 1997, Suehiro (2003) compiled a list of 220 business groups that, like Krirkkiat's list eighteen years earlier, comprised all the significant groups in modern business (Suehiro and Natenapha 2004).[11] Their combined revenues were equivalent to 62 percent of GDP. Of these 220, as many as 212 were family-based groups with some Chinese origin.

They can be divided into three categories based on the degree of diversification. Some eighty-seven had specialized in one core business. Another

---

11. The details of how this list was compiled are given in Suehiro and Natenapha (2004).

106 were semi-conglomerates, meaning they had one core business plus one or two non-core businesses (particularly property or finance). Twenty-four were full-blown conglomerates, meaning their interests extended across four or more business segments. Only fifteen of the groups had made the difficult transition to the third generation, while the largest number, 102, were in the second generation, and eighty-nine in the first,[12] reflecting the large number of new enterprises that had appeared, especially over the great boom of 1987–1996.

Suehiro also showed that most of these groups had entered the Thai stock market. Until the mid-1980s, family business groups raised capital from their own resources, from their business allies, and from the banks. Under the 1978 act governing the stock market, listed firms had to distribute at least half of their shares to small shareholders, a provision that discouraged family firms from listing. In 1992, as part of a package of measures to boost stock-market growth, this provision was abandoned.

Many firms subsequently listed on the exchange. Private resources and bank capital still remained the major sources of capital for most groups, but stock listing provided an additional route to raise the large sums needed to grasp the opportunities created by the great boom. Family groups initially used the stock market rather haphazardly, often listing new ventures while retaining their major businesses under private family control. Subsequently many groups reorganized their internal structure in ways that enabled them to take fuller advantage of the stock market while still retaining the essential structure of the *kongsi*, especially the ability of the family and its patriarch to maintain full management control. This was done by forming one or more investment firms that were not listed on the exchange and that were wholly owned by the members of the *kongsi*. At the next level, these investment firms had a controlling stake in one or more holding companies listed on the market. These holding companies, in turn, had stakes in several listed and non-listed affiliates.

---

12. Suehiro is here counting the generations from the foundations of the enterprise, not from the family's arrival in Thailand.

Through this structure, the family was able to retain appointment over directors and key executives right down the ownership chain. The family or its allies generally retained control over a high proportion of the shares. A survey of 384 listed firms in 2004 found a very high concentration of share ownership (see table 1.5). In 105 of the firms, the top ten shareholders held over 80 percent of the shares, and only in four did they hold less than 20 percent.

TABLE 1.5 Percentage of shares held by top ten shareholders, 2006

	NUMBER OF FIRMS	PERCENT
More than 80	105	27.3
61–80	185	48.2
41–60	70	18.2
21–40	20	5.2
Less than 20	4	1.0
TOTAL	384	100.0

SOURCE: Natenapha 2006, from SET data

The family also maintained tight control over the appointment of directors. In all, 24 percent of directors were family members, 19 percent were other major shareholders, 24 percent were professionals recruited from other companies, and 15 percent were prominent political figures or officials. In short, company boards consisted of the owners and their family members along with a smattering of professionals for their expertise, and a handful of political figures for their contacts (Natenapha 2005: 68).

In 1996, almost half (48 percent) of listed firms were essentially family controlled. In most of these, a single individual or a family-owned investment company held over 20 percent of the total shares, while in the remainder several family members or family-owned investment companies held such a share. Meanwhile 36 percent were widely owned, with no single entity controlling 20 percent, 13 percent were foreign owned, and 3 percent were state controlled (see table 1.6).

Crisis impact

The immediate impact of the crisis on major Thai firms can be seen from the fate of the firms in Suehiro's list of the top 220 business groups in 1997. Three years later, the list had substantially changed (see table 1.4).

At the very top, the change was minimal. Four banking groups and the CPB still occupied the first five slots, though in slightly different order. A little lower down, six firms from the top thirty had slid down to the nether part of the list or disappeared altogether. Three of these were affected by the carnage in the financial sector. Three were broad conglomerates stretching across banking, industry, and finance, and headed by some of the most famous names in the Thai-Chinese business community: Tejapaibul, Phatraprasit, Limsong, Leophairatana, Chakkaphak, and Srifuengfung. Although these groups did not disappear completely, with the partial exception of the Phatraprasit and Leophairatana, these families disappeared from the forefront of the business elite.

Further down the top two hundred list, the disorder was greater. In all, fifty-one groups or almost a quarter of the total disappeared. The largest number of these fell into a few categories: finance-based groups; property developers; former partners in manufacturing joint ventures (e.g., with Isuzu, Toshiba); and some firms which had long been in decline through failure to shift with the changes in business opportunity (e.g., the Sukree textile empire, and Yip In Tsoi agribusiness-based conglomerate).

Between 1997 and 2004, one hundred firms disappeared from the stock exchange, almost a quarter of the total (compared to only eleven delistings over the prior decade). Of these hundred, fifty-three were mandatorily delisted, usually because of bankruptcy proceedings. Among the other forty-seven, many were Thai or joint-venture firms that had been bought out by a foreign parent company and removed from the exchange. Examples are Prudential Assurance and American Standard. Between 1996 and 2000, another thirty-three family-owned listed firms were transformed either into foreign-owned or widely held firms.

From 2003 onwards, several new firms were listed, and again these were largely family firms. Hence in 2006 firms with family-owned structures accounted for over half of total listed firms, even higher than before the crisis (see table 1.6).

TABLE 1.6 Listed companies by ownership (1996, 2000, 2006)

TYPE OF SHAREHOLDERS	1996	%	2000	%	2006	%
Family-owned	150	33.5	131	30.3	139	33.2
Semi-family-owned	66	14.7	52	12.0	72	17.2
Widely-held	160	35.7	145	33.5	127	30.3
Foreigners-owned	59	13.2	90	20.8	63	15.0
State or state enterprise	13	2.9	15	3.5	18	4.3
Total listed firms	448	100.0	433	100.0	419	100.0
Family-owned firms	216	48.2	183	42.3	211	50.4

SOURCE: For 1996 and 2000: Suehiro and Natenapha 2004; for 2006: Report of Major Shareholders of each listed companies, March 2006.

STRUCTURE AND SURVIVAL

Survival or disaster depended a great deal on which sector(s) the business group was in. It also depended on how the group was structured and managed. Prior to the crisis, four distinctive types of family firms had emerged, differentiated by three criteria: the extent to which they had diversified, the complexity of their management organization, and the degree to which they had brought in professional management (Suehiro and Natenapha 2004).

Authoritarian family conglomerate

The first type was the authoritarian family conglomerate. In this case, the family's business had become diversified on the conglomerate pattern, the management structure had remained simple, and few or no outside professionals had been brought into top management. In essence, this type was an unreformed *kongsi* in modern disguise. The patriarch was transformed into the chairman. Other members of the family filled other management positions, but under the patriarch's authoritarian control. The advantage of such firms was that a visionary patriarch or family group could drive the corporation forward along an ambitious and potentially highly profitable path. The disadvantage was that the capacity to achieve this vision was wholly dependent on the management resources within the family. Such firms were reluctant to hire outside professionals who would be difficult to integrate with the family structure. They also failed to attract the best middle management because there was no upward career path. This management constraint proved to be a major disadvantage in a crisis.

An example of this type is the Thai Petrochemical Industry (TPI) group. The family business had begun in rice milling, and had extended to gunnysacks, textiles, and insurance in the second generation. In 1979, the group consisted of nineteen firms still based mainly in agriculture-related sectors, and ranked 17th on Krirkkiat's list. The patriarch of this second generation, Porn Leophairatana, sent his sons to the US to study accounting, economics, and chemical engineering. Returning to Thailand in the era when the economy was shifting decisively towards industry using newly found supplies of natural gas, Prachai Leophairatana and his five siblings launched the firm into cement and petrochemicals. By the mid-1990s, the number of firms had expanded to forty-four, total revenues had multiplied twenty-five times, and the group's ranking had risen to eleventh. TPI had risen rapidly to second rank in the cement market, behind the venerable Siam Cement. It had also become a major player in the booming petrochemicals industry. TPI had financed this rapid expansion by listing its major companies on the stock market, but had also taken large loans from domestic banks and international banks.

Yet the management remained closely controlled by the family, and especially by Prachai, the eldest son and reigning patriarch, and two brothers. Across their twenty-five principal companies, the three siblings were directors in every one, Prachai was chairman of fourteen and CEO of five others, and two other relatives also appeared on the boards. In most cases, the members of the board and the executive committee overlapped. In the parent holding company, two independent directors were included to meet stock-market guidelines but had little weight against the family. TPI did not disclose detailed information on its debt.

When the crisis struck, it emerged that TPI owed US$3.2 billion in external debt to some four hundred creditors. In 1997, the group made exchange losses of Baht 14.5 billion. All expansion plans were put on hold, and TPI entered into acrimonious negotiations with its creditors. In an attempt to retain control, Prachai put both the holding company and the cement firm, TPI Polene, into the bankruptcy court in 2000. Over the next five years, Prachai used lawsuits, political connections, public advertising, and nationalist posturing in his attempt to retain control. However, in a bankruptcy court ruling in 2005, the state-owned petroleum corporation PTT became the major investor in TPI with a 30 percent stake and the family was reduced to a 15 percent minority. Subsequently Prachai and his siblings were ejected from the board, and the company paid its first dividend since the crisis (*The Nation*, 29 December 2005, 23 May 2006, 22 January 2007). By using similar tactics, the family retained fragile control of the cement company, but at the cost of it remaining mired in debt.

Several other firms that collapsed in the crisis had a similar structure under a powerful patriarch with little or no professional management. These included the Tejapaibul financial conglomerate, taken over by government in January 1998; and the Srifuengfung's Cathay Trust group. Others of similar nature ultimately survived but in much reduced form by shrinking their scope to a core business and bringing in some professional management.

Unreformed single business

Several family firms that had retained a basic *kongsi* structure but specialized in a single business rather then following the trend towards conglomeratization also faced difficulties over the crisis. Again these firms were governed by a patriarch, with other management positions filled by family members, especially the eldest son, and with few or no outside professionals in senior management positions. Typically they worked closely with one of the big banks, and cooperated with similar families by taking cross holdings in new business ventures. Several among such firms were forced into bankruptcy or closed down due to the heavy corporate debt they were carrying at the onset of the crisis. These included the Chansrichawla family's Siam Vidhya group in finance, Sukree Phothiratanakun's TBI group in textiles, Akorn Huntrakun's New Imperial Hotel group, and Charn Uswachoke's Alphatech Electronics group. Others entered bankruptcy proceedings, underwent restructuring, and ultimately survived but in much reduced form. Such firms include the Horrungruang family's NTS steel group, the SSP (Siam Steel Pipe) group led by the Leeswadtrakul family, and the Modernform furniture group led by the Usanachitt family.

A variant on this story is offered by the Boonrawd group, brewers of Singha beer. Since its foundation in 1933, the company has remained under the tight control of the Bhirom Bhakdi family. No companies in the group had been listed on the market, and family members dominated the management, though several professionals were also recruited. Due to conservative management, the group faced no major problem with debt over the crisis, but it proved vulnerable when beer production was liberalized, and its near-monopoly of the market was challenged (see chapter 4). The group failed to raise the money or the management and marketing skills to defend its position. Between 1997 and 2001, its sales revenues were cut to a third of their former level, and over 60 percent of the market was lost to the new competitor. Although its position improved as the beer market expanded in the 2000s, Boonrawd was reduced from a dominant monopolist to a secondary player.

Modernized single business

Groups classified as modernized single business have two main characteristics: they limited their expansion within a single industry, and they modernized their management structure and recruited many top professionals while still retaining ultimate family control. A prime example is the Chokwatana family's Sahapat group.

The founding father of the group began importing Japanese goods during the Second World War. Later he persuaded the Japanese Lion group to participate in a joint venture to manufacture consumer goods in Thailand. The second generation expanded through further joint ventures with Japanese firms to manufacture cosmetics, textiles, footwear, and processed foods, and by the 1980s the group had become the largest Thai-owned consumer goods manufacturer.

Throughout, the family retained close overall control. The head of the second generation, Thiam Chokwatana, behaved as a typical patriarch, closely directing all aspects of the business, and handing over the reins to two of his sons. At the same time, the group enthusiastically recruited outside professional talent, and allowed them to rise up to board level. It also floated its major companies on the stock market, including two family holding companies (SPI and SPF) listed in 1977 and 1978 (see figure 1.3). The family maintained close control by using both pyramid companies and cross-holdings. Through individual holdings and two non-listed family investment companies, the family has a strong controlling interest in these two holding companies (34 and 44 percent respectively). These holding companies have controlling interests in another six listed companies through a lattice of cross-holdings, and these six in turn control over a hundred non-listed firms.

These strategies provided the group with the capital resources and the talent to modernize all aspects of their business and remain competitive with the subsidiaries of global consumer goods conglomerates such as Unilever and P&G. The Sahapat group multiplied its revenues twelve times between 1979 and 1997, though slipping slightly from thirteenth to fifteenth in the ranking of corporate groups

Other firms with similar structure and practice include the Saha Union group (another branch of the same family), and the former Shin group of the Shinawatra family. These groups tended to weather the crisis with very little damage. Unlike most Thai firms, they took on less foreign debt. Shin had the prescience to hedge nearly 80 percent of its foreign-currency exposure before the baht was devalued in 1997. As a result, such business groups moved up the corporate rankings between 1997 and 2000.[13]

---

13. Shin from 14 to 9, Sahapat from 15 to 12, and the related Saha Union from 26 to 19.

FIGURE 1.3 Structure of the Sahapat Group, 2006

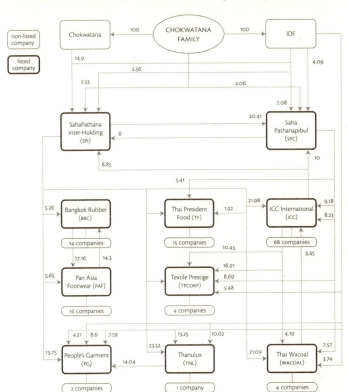

SOURCE: *Annual reports and 56-1 filings of each listed company, 2006*

Modernized family conglomerate

A handful of firms diversified into broad conglomerates, elaborated their management structures, and imported professional talent while still keeping central family control. During the crisis, they tended to restructure further by divesting non-core businesses, regrouping, and investing in new technology. The prime example is the Charoen Pokphand (CP) group.

The first generation began from importing seeds. The second, under Dhanin Chearavanont, developed an integrated agribusiness conglomerate based on poultry, extending backwards to feedmills and forward to retail. The group also became the most international of Thai companies by replicating this business pattern in other countries, mainly in Asia. By the 1990s, it had around a hundred companies spread across twenty countries with a workforce of more than 120,000. The group had also begun to expand its interests beyond its core area of agribusiness, especially into petrochemicals, and had become a major foreign investor in China with projects ranging from beer brewing to property development to motorcycle manufacture. In the early 1990s, in the classic pattern of diversifying to follow a new business vision of the next generation of the family, the group took a strategic decision to develop a second core area of business in telecommunications. Already by 1979, CP ranked tenth among Thai business groups, and notched up to third by 1997.

Alongside this rapid growth, the group constantly modernized its management structure and business practice. It employed professionals in finance and technology from the 1950s, introduced an American-style multi-division organizational system in 1985, listed affiliate companies from 1987 to raise funds, established a holding company and headquarters to centralize decision making in 1990, and launched an intensive human resource development program from 1995. While many family members were employed within the group, they were not exempt from the training and appraisal imposed on other executives, and could only hope to rise on merit.

Nevertheless, the group was severely rocked by the crisis. After commissioning a study from US consultants, it responded with a strategic decision to slim down to two core business areas in agribusiness and telecoms. It divested all its interests in petrochemicals, and many of its ventures in China (see chapter 9). In 1998 it revised the corporate structure to be more rational and more transparent. Each of the two core businesses was reorganized under its own holding company, and the structure of companies below them was streamlined. It invited more outsiders as board directors to promote transparency. The directors of the holding company for the agribusiness division, for example, included four family members and nine long-standing employees of the company. With these measures it was successful in

FIGURE 1.4 Structure of the CP Group, 2006

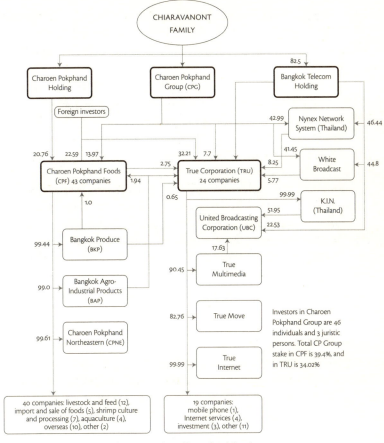

SOURCE: *Annual reports and 56-1 filings of each listed company, 2006*

attracting foreign capital. Institutional investors took up 22 percent of the agribusiness holding company, and 32 percent of the telecoms one. In 2000, CP retained its third ranking among Thai corporate groups, and has resumed its pace of expansion in the 2000s.

Yet at the core CP remains a family controlled company, though of a distinctly modern kind (see figure 1.4). Above the two divisional holding companies is an unlisted investment firm of which 89 percent is controlled by members of the family (Suehiro 2001). Below them is an elaborate pyramid of companies knit together by cross shareholdings. There is little doubt that the favored elder son, now running the telecoms division, will ultimately succeed to the chairmanship of the group.

A variant of this modernized conglomerate in which the core company is a bank is exemplified by the Kasikorn (formerly Thai Farmers Bank) group. As in the case of other banks which survived the crisis, it opened up to foreign shareholders rather than entering the government's rescue program. As a result, the Lamsam family saw a substantial cut in their shareholding and a significant rise in foreign ownership, yet the family retains management control. The family interest is structured similarly to that of CP, with a fully owned investment arm, Sombat Lamsam company, at the apex of a web of pyramidal and lateral shareholdings. The non-banking interests, which include importing and telecoms, are grouped under a separate company, Loxley, at the head of twenty-two affiliates. After the crisis, the flagship bank underwent an intensive program of modernization and reorientation towards consumer banking.

CONCLUSION

At the onset of the 1997 crisis, someone predicted it would be "the crisis of Yaowarat capital," referring to the firms of the immigrant Chinese families who had often started out in Bangkok's Chinatown around Yaowarat Road.

Until the crisis, the history of this era of "Yaowarat capital" had largely been heralded as a success. From very modest beginnings prior to the Second World War, Thailand's domestic capitalists had sustained a high rate of capital accumulation for over half a century without a crisis. A few families had begun to venture overseas.

The firms involved had some distinctive characteristics. They were founded by a Chinese immigrant. They were based on the *kongsi* pattern of family management. A few expanded into sprawling conglomerates, especially banks, which were the main mechanism of capital accumulation. Ownership and control were highly concentrated. According to one estimate (Brooker Group, 2001), there were only 150 families that mattered, and even within that small number assets were heavily concentrated at the top end.

In the years following the crisis, a significant fraction of the assets owned by domestic entrepreneurs was transferred to foreign owners. The inflow of foreign investment in these years was far higher than ever before. In the years immediately following the crisis, most of this inflow was used for acquisition, not new investment. Calculating what proportion of assets was transferred is impossible in any exact way. However, a rough figure is a quarter. That is roughly the proportion of all listed firms that were delisted, the proportion of the top 220 firms that disappeared from the rankings, and the proportion of the top 100 firms that slid far down the chart.

Life or death depended on several variables. First of all, it depended on government policy, or the lack of it. Government had no overall strategy to protect domestic capital. In order to sustain the export of manufactures, which had become the most dynamic factor in the economy, it decided to liberalize investment rules and encourage the multinationals to dominate. In finance, it provided some assistance to the major commercial banks, but allowed the remainder of the financial sector to be sold or rationalized. It continued to protect much of the service sector for domestic capital through the Alien Business Law and other regulations, but in practice allowed these rules to be overridden in the case of big modern retail sector and elsewhere.

The chances of survival also depended greatly on the management structure of the firm. The death rates tended to be highest among firms which had expanded into conglomerates while remaining organized under a *kongsi* system with a dominant patriarch, limited use of professional management from outside the family, and little transparency. Survivors tended to have modified this pattern by adapting the structure to take advantage of the stock market, recruiting more professional management, and becoming more transparent in their operation and corporate governance.

The domestic business community that emerged from the crisis was both changed and not changed. Many of the great surnames of the Yaowarat era had disappeared, especially those that had been involved heavily in manufacturing joint ventures or in the lower ranks of the finance industry, and especially those that failed to adapt their corporate structure. The commercial banks no longer played their old role as the mechanism of capital accumulation, the hubs of business networks, and the heads of some of the biggest conglomerates. Even those conglomerates that survived had generally slimmed down by shedding peripheral businesses. More of the leading family groups were now found clustered in service sectors where there was still some protection under the Alien Business Law, concession arrangements, or other regulations. Some of

FIGURE 1.5 Top 150 business groups by assets

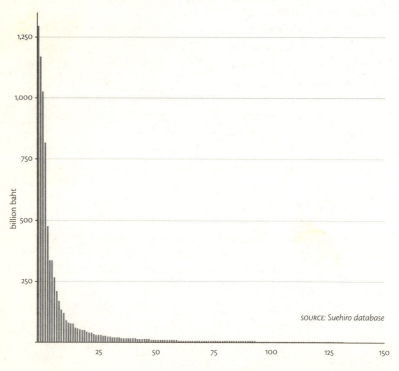

SOURCE: Suehiro database

the most successful business families on the exit from the crisis were involved in media, entertainment, telecoms, and property. More of the survivors raised funds from the capital markets.

Yet three-quarters of the business groups had survived. The family firm was still the dominant form. Even among listed firms that appeared to be "widely owned," there was a high concentration of ownership by a small proportion of shareholders. Despite all the changes in the banking industry, the old controlling family still hung onto control in four of the top five. The ranking of the top shareholding families on the stock exchange showed both change and continuity (see table 1.6). Families with interests in finance, steel, and manufacturing have declined down the rankings. Families in service sectors such as media, entertainment, and telecoms have risen or sustained their position.

In many sub-sectors, the crisis had killed off the weaker players and resulted in even more business concentration. The top five banks still controlled two-thirds of assets (as they had before the crisis). A handful of transnationals had an even firmer grip on the auto industry (see chapter 2). Three firms shared the mobile phone market (see chapter 4). Three transnational retailers had grabbed a major share of retailing from thousands of small stores (see chapter 3). Within Suehiro's list of the top 150 Thai business groups in 2000, assets were heavily concentrated among the leading twenty-five (indeed, among the top ten, see figure 1.5).

TABLE 1.7 Largest shareholders on Thai stock market by family name, 1995–2004

FAMILY	GROUP	CORE BUSINESS
Maleenont	BEC World	media
Shinawatra	Shin Corp	telecom
Damapong	Shin Corp	telecom
Chirathivat	Central	retail, hotel
Bencharongkul	Ucom	telecom
Damrongchaitham	Grammy	entertainment
Asavabhokhin	Land&House	property
Chansiri	Thai Union	agribiz
Leophairatana	TPI	petrochem
Photharamik	Jasmine	telecom
Karnasuta	Italthai	construction
Charanachitta	Italthai	construction
Vitayatanagorn	Thai Veg.	agribiz
Phaoenchoke	Thai Rung Union	auto
Sophonpanich	Bangkok Bank	finance
Winyarat	Theparos	agribiz
Niruttinanon	Thai Union	agribiz
Dumnernchanvanit	Soon Hua Seng	agribiz, paper
Wattanavekin	E.Sugar/Amarin	finance
Youngmeevidhya	Cfresh	agribiz
Ratanarak	Ayudhya Bank	finance
Piyaoui	Dusit Thani	hotel
Uachukiat	Bank of Asia	finance
Lamsam	Thai Farmers, Loxley	finance, telecom
Srifuengfung	Thasco	chemical, glass
Horrungruang	NTS	steel
Chokwatana	Sahapat	consumer
Karnchanapas	Bangkok Land	property
Tejapaibul	BMB	finance
Wanglee	Poon Phol	finance

SOURCE: Kan ngoen thanakan (*Finance and Banking*), December annual issue, 1997–2004.

RANKING

2004	2003	2002	2001	2000	1999	1998	1997	1996	1995
2	1	1	1	1	1	1	1	-	-
1	3	3	2	2	2	2	2	1	1
3	4	6	3	3	13	17	87	73	-
6	5	4	5	4	8	10	15	8	17
8	35	20	8	5	12	135	23	20	10
12	8	5	7	6	9	4	3	6	8
4	2	2	4	7	5	13	13	4	4
9	7	7	6	8	11	6	72	110	-
15	11	14	10	9	3	12	6	7	5
58	17	64	27	10	6	3	5	3	3
5	6	8	14	11	4	7	4	2	2
10	12	11	16	12	7	9	7	5	2
16	10	9	9	13	31	30	56	91	116
105	9	9	44	14	18	35	14	24	37
21	26	22	19	16	14	15	10	14	9
26	40	13	15	18	23	155	-	39	62
28	23	18	12	19	24	16	131	193	-
-	-	-	28	20	20	8	8	10	7
29	20	15	27	21	10	57	67	26	18
144	100	148	35	22	47	21	214	158	-
121	111	39	33	26	45	77	84	75	77
126	119	59	86	27	61	14	30	80	-
-	82	56	51	30	49	44	345	921	-
34	91	53	56	34	27	34	35	28	14
-	-	-	-	36	63	93	39	29	32
35	25	54	53	37	30	28	17	12	12
31	46	32	18	45	65	67	107	198	-
75	29	87	77	48	16	59	27	11	6
199	147	139	148	68	156	164	-	-	-
123	143	104	90	96	53	109	61	52	41

NOTE: The year 2000 is used as the benchmark year. Below number 22, the ranking is not sequential, but shows some selected major groups particularly in the financial sector.

SECTORS

2

INDUSTRY GLOBALIZED:
THE AUTOMOTIVE SECTOR

Sakkarin Niyomsilpa

IN the mid-2000s, the automotive industry was the single largest sector of Thailand's manufacturing by almost any method of measurement. It employed over one hundred thousand workers. It contributed a trillion baht to annual GDP. Alone among Thai industries, it could claim a place on international league tables. Thailand figured fifth in the world for production of commercial vehicles, and tenth among automobile exporters (1.8 percent of world total in 2005). One Japanese manufacturer had located a worldwide research facility in Thailand, and three of them had launched a new model for the first time in this market. The auto industry was also among the largest exporters, contributing 8 percent of the total, roughly the same as the total exports of the agrarian sector. The sector was also almost totally dominated by multinationals (MNCs). In 2005, 98 percent of the car market in Thailand was controlled by five multinationals, four Japanese and one American. Among the two hundred first-tier suppliers of parts to the assemblers, only around twenty were Thai firms. The policy framework for this industry was highly liberalized, and policymaking in the sector was largely the outcome of bargaining between multinationals, technocrats, and elected politicians.

Ten years earlier, on the eve of the 1997 crisis, the position had been very different. Thailand's automotive sector was already large, but not distinctly ahead of several other industries, and certainly not a factor in world rankings. It was still mainly oriented to the home market and only a minor contributor to exports. Several hundred domestic firms had a major role in the sector, both as partners of the multinational manufacturers, and producers of a wide range of parts and components. The industry was still hedged around by controls on importing, local content, and foreign investment. In policymaking, government bureaucrats and the domestic part-makers association were the most important players.

The transformation of Thailand's automotive industry over the crisis and its aftermath was very sudden. To a large extent it was inevitable. Over the prior two decades, the world's automotive industry had been at the forefront of globalization. A huge sprawl of nationally based firms had been condensed into seven world-spanning groups. Decisions within the industry were now made with a global perspective. Thailand had been protected from these trends by a policy regime based on the vision of a "national industry" which had become irrelevant. By transforming so rapidly in the crisis, Thailand took on a new role as a small but significant segment of transnational chains of production.

Yet this transformation still raises questions over the fate of domestic capital and domestic enterprise within this process of globalization. This chapter starts by sketching the growth of Thailand's automotive industry in the postwar era. It then looks at the rapid changes that took place during the crisis, and finally examines the way that policy is now being made in the sector.

AN INFANT INDUSTRY

Until the 1960s, all vehicles in Thailand were imported. From the 1940s onwards, some Western and Japanese manufacturers linked up with local business families, mostly Thai-Chinese, who acted as importers. From 1960, the government set out policies to develop a local automotive industry under the import substitution industrialization framework of the era. Import restrictions and high tariffs raised the prices of imported cars, while investment incentives and lower tariffs on parts encouraged foreign firms to establish assembly plants. Government laid down rules for the proportion of parts that had to be locally made, and gradually raised the figure to stimulate local investment and technology transfer. In the hope of cultivating local enterprise, foreign firms (other than US firms, privileged under the Amity Law) were limited to a 49 percent stake.

Under this policy, thirteen assembly plants were established. Western firms either judged the scale of the market as too small, or withdrew after the American defeat in the Indochina War. Japanese auto-makers targeted Southeast Asia, even though the small size and fragmentation of the markets made poor commercial sense, because they could hope to dominate this region. Most of the assembly plants were joint ventures between Japanese manufacturers and local business families, many of those who had earlier been their dealers, including Phornprapha, Sukosol, Yip In Tsoi, Boonsoong, Lee-Issaranukul, Lee-Nuttapong, Sitthi-Amnuai, and Sarasin.

Although the domestic partners had the majority share in these ventures, in practice the multinational partner had effective management control because of command over technology and expertise. Yet the protection offered by the import-substitution policy generated a large rent income for these families. Some of this income was used for lateral investment into other sectors, typical of the proto-conglomerates of this era. But a significant part was plowed back into the auto industry. Some families invested in increasing their share in the assembly venture. In the Bangchan assembly plant, local business raised their share from 40 percent in 1972 to 66 percent in 1983. Sitthiphon raised their share in the Mitsubishi venture from 40 to 60 percent in the same period. Even at the Toyota plant, the share of local capital rose from nothing to 35 percent. As for Isuzu and Mazda, local business partners raised their stake in this period also. The Nissan factory of Siam Motors, the plant of the Thonburi group, and YMC of Yontrakit were all wholly owned by local Thai business families in the 1970s.

Some of this rent income was invested to expand into motorcycle production, and to produce the increasing range of auto parts needed under the local-content policy. For more sophisticated parts, the local partners of the assemblers formed joint ventures with Japanese firms to import the technology However, simpler items were made by many independent small and medium enterprises (SMEs) using standard equipment, low technology, and funding raised locally through techniques like chit funds. All these firms formed a "club" within the Federation of Thai Industries to press their interests on the policymakers. In the late

1970s, they founded a separate Thai Auto Parts Manufacturers Association (TAPMA) in order to lobby for policies which were often against the interest of the assemblers, with some success. In 1978, they persuaded government to totally ban completely-built-up (CBU) imports to help ease the trade deficit. Subsequently, they persuaded government to limit the number of models each assembler could produce, in order to reduce the number of variants of each part, and pressed for a rise in the local content ratio from 25 percent in the late 1970s to 43 percent in 1983.[1] Under this policy, the number of Thai family firms involved in manufacture of auto parts rose to around a thousand. Japanese assemblers began to encourage their parts suppliers from Japan to move to Thailand to meet the rising local content requirements.

THE BOOM ERA

When the Thai economy boomed in the late 1980s, automotive sales grew even faster than GDP. In Bangkok, a rapidly expanding middle class moved out from the city center to new residential suburbs, and bought cars as commuter vehicles and symbols of new prosperity. Commercial vehicle sales boomed as the economy shifted towards industrialization. Wealth that trickled out to the provinces in the remittances of migrant workers was often invested in motorcycles and pickup trucks.

A similar trend was found across Southeast Asia. For the multinational auto producers, the region was no longer a sideshow, but one of the fastest growing markets in the world. American and European firms returned to Thailand after a thirty-year intermission. Korean firms arrived. Japanese firms geared up to defend their command of the market by designing cars specifically geared to the conditions and tastes of Southeast Asian buyers, rather than just selling models developed for Japan or the West. Under pressure from this broadened phalanx of multinationals, Thai government policy towards the sector changed.

---

1. True value-added was considerably less than the official local content figure because the system did not track the import content back up the production chain (Veloso et al. 1998: 17)

Industry relocated

The rapid rise in the value of the yen from 1985 prompted many Japanese firms to relocate overseas. The shift of auto parts producers into Southeast Asia, which had begun over the previous decade, now became a stampede. Japanese parts producers started fifty-one projects in Thailand over 1986–1990, and another sixty-one over 1991–1995.[2] Thailand was a favorite location for several reasons. Domestic demand was projected to grow to more than eight hundred thousand vehicles a year by 2000. The industry was less fragmented than in Indonesia and Philippines, which both had many small assemblers, but more varied than in Malaysia, where a government-backed national car project dominated.

Clusters of (mainly Japanese) auto-parts producers appeared on the outskirts of Bangkok, and in the Eastern Seaboard industrial zone. Government hurried to provide the supporting infrastructure, including an expanded road network and the Laem Chabang container port. Support industries appeared. Property developers built housing for the expanding work force, and for a new expatriate community of managers and technicians.

The increase in investment and in the size of the industry brought a rise in political bargaining power. Ever since the 1970s, Japanese auto makers had hoped that the idea of an ASEAN Free Trade Area (AFTA) would enable them to spread production networks across Asia, locating different functions in different countries in order to exploit local competitive advantages as well as keeping all the host countries happy. But progress towards AFTA was hindered by economic-nationalist concerns, and the simple fact that the various regional economies were often more competitive than complementary. But after the big shift in investment in the mid-1980s, the Japanese auto industry pressed harder. In the late 1980s Mitsubishi proposed to ASEAN a regional cooperation project under a brand-to-brand complementarity scheme (BBC), which reduced tariffs on auto parts produced and sold within the ASEAN countries by 50 percent. Mitsubishi executives lured the

2. In the same period, the total of projects in Indonesia, Malaysia and Philippines was ninety-five.

Thai government to support the scheme by promising in return to invest in the production of auto engines in Thailand. ASEAN approved the scheme. Later in the mid-1990s, Japanese car manufacturers proposed an Asian Industrial Cooperation Scheme (AICO) under which auto parts exchanged between countries would be subject to specially reduced tariffs in advance of the general AFTA tariff-reduction scheme scheduled for 2003. ASEAN agreed to the AICO scheme, which reduced tariffs on auto parts to a range of 0 to 5 percent.

Under these new trading conditions, auto producers began moving towards more specialized production spread across the region, with car bodies made in Thailand and Malaysia, batteries in Indonesia, brakes and axles in the Philippines, and electronics and transmission mechanisms still exported from Japan. Still more parts producers migrated out from Japan when the yen again inflated in 1994–1995. By 1997, Japanese auto parts producers had four hundred production sites scattered throughout the ASEAN countries. With the Americans preparing to reenter the market, the Japanese assemblers hoped that their well-established cross-country production networks would guarantee their competitive advantage and continued market domination for the long term.

Easing towards liberalization

The multinational auto firms also exerted more pressure on the Thai government to ease the regulatory regime. The Chatichai government (1988–1991) lifted a ban on CBU imports of cars under 2300cc, and removed restrictions on the number of models each assembler could make. The Anand governments (1991–1992) completely lifted the import ban, restructured tariffs to reduce the price differential between imported and locally made models, lowered the annual registration tax, and lifted controls on the number of taxis in Bangkok. These moves lowered car prices and further stimulated sales, leading to virtual gridlock in the capital, and hundred-kilometer queues on some provincial routes on national holidays.

A limit on new licenses for assembly plants was lifted in 1994. Government also encouraged assemblers and parts makers to orient more towards export, by providing promotional incentives, including permission for 100 percent foreign ownership in export-oriented ventures. Export regulations were also streamlined.

The liberalization of trade and production attracted Korean, American, and European firms. In 1995, Ford and GM decided to reenter the Thai market. GM first went into a venture with the Volvo assembler, Swedish Motors, to produce a sports utility vehicle, and then built a plant to produce Chevrolet pickups. Ford and its worldwide partner Mazda built a new assembly plant for pickups. BMW decided to locate its production for ASEAN markets in Thailand. Hyundai, Kia, and Ssangyong vehicles from Korea were imported by local agents. Several parts producers from the US and Europe established Thai subsidiaries to supply these ventures.

Through the 1990s, local auto-parts producers were still protected by the local-content policy and by some high tariffs on certain auto parts such as car bodies and engines. But assemblers became more skilled in evading the local content rules, and the Thai Auto Parts Manufacturers Association had less and less political clout with policymakers. The US firms Ford and GM pressed the Thai government to abandon the local-content policy, which the government agreed to do as part of its commitment to the WTO.[3] Domestically owned parts firms were also under greater pressure to compete against relocated Japanese firms, and against imports from within the region. A few were able to make strategic partnerships and joint venture agreements with the Japanese assemblers and their associated Japanese parts producers, and thus get the technology and connections to continue as first-tier suppliers.[4] Many more domestic firms slipped into the second and third tiers, producing sub-assemblies or replacement parts, and experiencing lower margins as competition in these sectors increased.

As cars had become more sophisticated over recent decades, closer coordination was required between assemblers and parts suppliers. As

---

3. The US auto firms had probably been behind the TRIMS (Trade Related Investment Measures) section of the WTO protocols under which Thailand agreed to abandon the local-content policy.

4. First-tier suppliers manufacture parts used directly in the assembly of new cars.

the market had become increasingly global, there had been an intense phase of consolidation among car makers, leaving only seven transnational groups. These car makers captured profit by concentrating on the downstream end of the production chain, and outsourcing more of the manufacture of parts and sub-assembly. This trend in turn put pressure on parts makers to have the required capability, and led to consolidation among parts makers, with a handful of mainly Japanese, American, and European firms spreading across the globe. In this process, local firms everywhere were increasingly downgraded to the second-tier—supplying the first-tier parts makers with inputs, materials, tooling, sub-assemblies—or further down the chain (Doner et al. 2005).

Crisis eve

On the eve of the crisis, Thailand's auto industry consisted of fifteen assembly plants, most of which were joint ventures between Japanese auto firms and domestic business groups, and some 1,200 parts producers which ranged from wholly Japanese-owned firms through joint ventures to domestic firms, and from sophisticated manufacturers to backyard workshops.

The industry was still very much focused on the domestic market. Mitsubishi had begun to think of Thailand not just as a market but as a production base for pickups exported back to Japan and other markets, but Mitsubishi was alone in such thinking. The strategies of the assemblers were based on projections that continued market growth. AFTA liberalization would bring greater scale and efficiency. Against the background of the Asian boom, the Japanese assemblers for the first time designed new passenger-car models specifically for the new urban middle-class Asian consumer. Honda launched its City model in 1996, and Toyota followed with the Soluna a year later. The US firms planned their market entries with similar models designed by Asian partners.

The industry was viewed as inefficient due to the limited scale of the market, and the overhang of protective policies from the import substitution era. The dream of cultivating a "Thai" auto industry through technology transfer was generally seen as a failure and a thing of the past. However, the accumulated investment in plant, skill development, cluster building, business networks, and relations with government was a significant foundation. As part of its promotion of agriculture, government had levied a lower excise duty on pickup trucks, with the result that sales of the 1-ton version had achieved a significant scale—as the second largest market for this model in the world after the US.

Government had begun to shift away from regulation and protection towards greater facilitation for exports within the AFTA framework. Export of vehicle parts, mostly within ASEAN, had grown from 3 billion baht a year in the late 1980s to 19 billion in 1996. But this volume was small, and half of it came from two Japanese electronics firms, Denso and Thai Arrow (Nipon and Wangdee 2000: 7).

CRISIS AND ADJUSTMENT

The transformation of Thailand's auto sector was the result of two decisions taken in the teeth of the crisis. The first decision was to liberalize ownership laws. The second was to abandon the vestiges of the old import-substitution framework, and to integrate Thailand as deeply as possible into the global production chains of the multinationals.

Liberalizing ownership

By late 1997, thousands of Thai firms were technically bankrupt because of the impact of the currency depreciation on their balance sheets, and starved of cash because of the sudden fall in consumption.

Among the auto assemblers, Sukosol Mazda closed its factory permanently (relocating the production to the Ford-Mazda joint venture, Auto-Alliance). Several other assemblers stopped production temporarily to lower stock and reduce labor costs. In some joint ventures, the foreign partner was able to arrange loans to keep the venture afloat, or to find opportunities for exporting to other subsidiaries within the group. Parts producers were affected in the same way, with many closing down, laying off workers, and searching desperately for new sources of capital.

In August 1997, the Thai parts producers asked the Board of Investment to allow foreign firms to inject more capital to keep firms afloat.

Government decided that one way to prevent firms from going out of business was to relax limitations on foreign ownership. In effect, the government decided to maintain the production base and thus limit the impact of the crisis by setting up a fire sale. The policy was applied to the export-oriented manufacturing sector as a whole. Some foreign partners were initially nervous about sinking more capital in a country where the extent of the economic wreckage was still unclear. But finally the Japanese assemblers and parts producers did not wish to see their Thai ventures crippled, and often welcomed the chance to gain the full ownership denied them in the past.

In December 1997, the Board of Investment (BOI) announced that foreign firms were now allowed to hold majority shares in ventures receiving investment privileges in zones 1 and 2. As these zones were the location for most of the assemblers and parts firms, and as most had BOI promotion, this announcement effectively liberalized investment for the automotive sector. In December 1998, BOI allowed 100 percent foreign ownership in new projects as long as they were approved for BOI promotion. Under this rule, foreign partners in existing joint ventures could apply to inject more capital, which would make them into full or majority owners. Over the following year, 180 firms applied to BOI under this provision, including most of the auto assemblers and major foreign firms in auto parts production. The total capital injected was around 20 billion baht.

Also in August 1999, government amended the Alien Business Law, allowing majority-owned foreign firms to operate in several service sectors with permission from the Ministry of Commerce. Although this did not directly affect the assemblers of parts producers, it indirectly enabled them to work with service companies (accountants, lawyers, finance, etc.) who were their global partners.

All the Japanese assemblers were converted to majority foreign ownership (see table 2.1). In the case of Mitsubishi, Mazda, and Honda, the remaining domestic share was insignificant. Only in Siam Motors (Nissan), did the Phornprapha family retain a modest stake of 25 percent.

TABLE 2.1 Structure of share ownership in auto assembly, 1972–2004

COMPANY	BRANDS	THAI SHARE OWNERSHIP				THAI PARTNERS
		1972	1983	1990	2004	
JAPANESE						
Toyota Thailand	Toyota	0	35	41	13.6	Bangkok Bank, Book Club Finance, Chiwamongkon
Siam Motors	Nissan	100	100	100	25	Phornprapha
Isuzu Motors	Isuzu	50	53	53	3.6	Sarasin, Chansue, Boonsoong
Sukosol Mazda	Mazda	30	35	36	7	Sukosol, Patchimsawat, Thienprasit
Thai Honda	Honda		51	n.a.	3	Sarasin, CPB
MMC Sitthiphon	Mitsubishi	40	60	n.a.	2	Lee-Issaranukul, Phenchat
Thai Hino	Hino	30	30	n.a.	20	Kowintha
EUROPEAN						
Yontrakit-YMC	BMW, Peugeot, Citroen, VW	100	100	100	n.a.	Lee-nutaphong
Bangchan	Opel, Daihatsu, Honda	40	66	66	n.a.	YiplnTsoi, Boonsoong, Sarasin, Chutakun, Tansakun
Thonburi	Mercedes	100	100	100	n.a.	Viriyabhan
Thai-Swedish	Volvo	40	40	30	n.a.	Sitthi-amnuai
AMERICAN						
Auto Alliance	Ford, Mazda				7	Phornprapha (2)/Swedish Motors (5)
GM	Chevrolet				0	

SOURCE: Doner (1992), JAMA (2004), and data from the Ministry of Industry

Among the minor assemblers specializing in European models, the arrangements were more mixed. The European parent firms had less commitment and stake in the Thai market. Generally, they injected

TABLE 2.2 Domestic automotive sales, 1996–2006

	4-WHEEL DRIVE VEHICLE	TRUCK, UNDER 1 TON	TRUCK, >4 TON	TRUCK, 2-4 TONS	TRUCK, 1.5 TON	PICK-UP, 1-TON	BUS/MINIBUS, <30 PERSONS	COMMERCIAL VEHICLE, TOTAL	PASSENGER CAR	TOTAL
1990	3,599	11,960	32,126	15,920		167,613	6,980	238,198	68,864	304,062
1991	2,338	10,200	15,895	10,312		155,366	7,670	201,781	66,779	268,560
1992	4,160	14,490	17,549	12,465		182,958	9,924	241,546	121,441	362,987
1993	3,687	14,207	15,573	12,717		224,388	11,727	282,299	174,169	456,468
1994	3,230	19,564	22,312	14,139		258,091	12,672	330,008	155,670	485,678
1995	7,420	16,402	31,766	16,383		323,813	12,425	408,209	163,371	571,580
1996	12,585	15,018	31,814	16,683		327,663	12,633	416,396	172,730	589,126
1997	8,481	5,642	11,275	9,021		188,324	8,353	231,096	132,060	363,156
1998	4,275	2,841	3,756	2,838		81,263	2,792	97,765	46,300	144,065
1999	7,199	3,018	3,434	3,750		129,904	4,167	151,472	66,858	218,330
2000	7,649	3,780	4,804	4,655		151,703	6,492	179,083	83,106	262,189
2001	6,371	2,686	4,398	3,807		168,639	6,582	192,483	104,502	296,985
2002	21,620	1,664	5,560	4,564		241,266	8,335	283,009	126,353	409,362
2003	16,492	1,478	11,216	7,366	16	309,144	8,489	354,171	179,005	533,176
2004	11,970	878	14,439	9,189	1,949	368,911	9,585	416,916	209,110	626,026
2005	5,406	580	14,406	9,616	2,638	469,657	12,891	509,644	193,617	703,261
2006	N.A.	608	13,023	10,375	N.A.	424,784	12,682	488,424	194,263	682,693

enough capital to help the venture survive, but not enough to acquire a majority. The Yontrakit company entered into agreements to produce Volkswagen, Peugeot, and Citroen, besides BMW. The Thonburi assembler continued to produce Mercedes on contract for Daimler-Chrysler. All agents of Korean cars stopped importing in 1997. Kia subsequently made an agreement with Yontrakit, and the first locally assembled Kia models appeared in 2003.[5]

Among parts makers, there was an estimated 1,200 firms operating before the crisis. Around 600 firms with some domestic stake were either closed down or sold to foreign owners (EEPC 2000). Estimates of the number of survivors differ. According to one study (Praphad 2002), there were 1,100 parts firms left in 2001. Of these, 709 were first-tier, capable of producing original parts. Among these, 287 were foreign-owned, 354 Thai-owned, and in 68 the foreign partner had a minority share. According to another study (Kriengkrai and Takahashi 2002), by 2002 there were only 700 firms still operating. Of these, some 200 produced original equipment and were mainly owned by Japanese, while the remaining 500 were domestically owned and mostly produced replacement parts. By and large, the Thai parts producers that did survive were relegated to production of replacement parts. Possibly less than twenty Thai-owned firms were now involved in producing original equipment. The assembly of automobiles, and most first-tier parts suppliers, were now virtually wholly under foreign ownership.

The Thai parts producers that managed to survive this shake-out used a mix of strategies. First, they sold off other businesses in order to maintain their stake in auto parts. The Somboon group sold their major stakes in nine companies to Japanese partners in order to remain a first-tier producer of axles and suspension. Sitthiphon and Siam Motors sold off their majority stakes in assembly plants in order to concentrate on parts.

Second, they tightened their relationships with the auto producers, often through shareholdings, in order to produce parts not only for the domestic market but for assembly elsewhere within the group. Thai

5. Hyundai began considering local assembly in 2007.

Rung, which had specialized in conversion jobs on pickups, went in with a multinational to produce ambulances and other specialty vehicles. Thai Summit strengthened its close relationship with Toyota, not only expanding its parts production in Thailand, but also laying plans to invest in India, Indonesia, and China to supply its patron.

Third, firms such as Summit and Sitthiphon invested in technology, management systems, and gaining certification (ISO 9000, QS9000 and ISO 14000) in order to qualify as first-tier producers. Fourth, they listed on the stock exchange to raise the capital for this upgrading. In the usual pattern, a family firm with several parts factories restructured as a group under a holding company listed on the exchange. The number of listed parts firms rose from ten before the crisis to eighteen.

Reorientation to export

Apart from liberalizing ownership during the crisis, government also abandoned the last vestiges of the import-substitution policy, and began to promote Thailand as a base for the international auto industry in Asia

The decision to abandon the local-content policy was taken in 1998 and implemented in 2000. In 2002, the auto industry was identified as one of the thirteen priority sectors in manufacturing. Government established a Thailand Automotive Institute as an independent foundation. The main roles of the institute were to coordinate standardization, quality control, R&D and training, and to propose policy changes to government. The institute produced a master plan for 2002–2006, and a vision for the state of the industry by 2011. Under these plans, Thailand would produce a million vehicles by 2006 (the target was passed a year early), and 2 million by 2010, by which time it would be the tenth largest producer in the world, employing 130,000 workers and contributing 9 percent of GDP. The industry would also be significantly reoriented to export at least 40 percent of the production, while retaining the proportion of local content at 60 percent.

Prior to the crisis, only Mitsubishi among the assemblers had seriously considered exporting as part of its strategic planning. In the eye of the crisis, almost all assemblers looked to exports for a short-term counterbalance to the decline in demand. Total automotive exports quadrupled from 18 billion to 75 billion baht between 1998 and 1999. With this momentum, and the changes in government policy, the principal assemblers all reconceived their operations in Thailand as part of regional or global networks, rather than principally as production facilities for the Thai market. Both the Japanese and the incoming American firms abandoned the idea of developing cars specifically for an Asian market, and instead took a global perspective. GM, for example, dropped the plan to pioneer its reentry into Thailand with a car targeted at Asian middle class consumers, and instead produced all-purpose models which could be exported anywhere in the world. Ford became the second firm after Mitsubishi to export vehicles from Thailand on any scale.

Among the auto firms, the most aggressive in this strategic reorientation was Toyota. It designated Thailand as a worldwide base for export of pickup trucks. Along with other pickup firms, it transferred more engineering processes from Japan to Thailand so that the local content of pickups rose from 60/70 to 90 percent. It invested 30 billion baht to build a new generation of pickups at an entirely new assembly plant in Chachoengsao. It also made Thailand a major base for its Camry and Altis passenger cars, supplying completely-knocked-down (CKD) kits to other Toyota plants in ASEAN. It redesigned its sourcing policy to maximize the benefit from AFTA. Finally, it located a technical center for the Asia-Pacific region in Thailand. By the mid-2000s, Toyota was not only the leader in the domestic auto market, but also the leading exporter.

Mitsubishi also invested 22 billion baht to develop new pickups and sports utility vehicles for export to all countries except the US. In 2005, it relocated pickup production from Japan to Thailand, increased the capacity, and increased the local content. Isuzu, which formerly had the largest share of the Thai pickup market, reacted more slowly but was obliged to follow suit. It designated Thailand as an international production center, reorganized its parts sourcing within ASEAN, and entered into a joint venture with GM for making additional pickup models.

For political reasons, Honda was against designating any specific country as a base, and maintained production sites around the ASEAN region. But in practice, production growth was most rapid in Thailand,

FIGURE 2.1 Automotive domestic sales and exports, 1995–2006

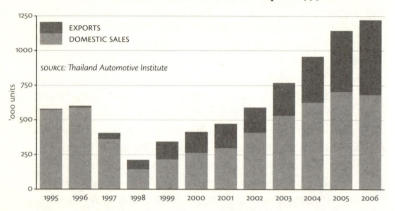

and exports increased. In 1997, the Thai plant exported small cars to Singapore and Brunei, and a year later sent middle-sized models to Australia and New Zealand. In 2005 Honda produced an entirely new model (in two forms, City and Jazz) in its Thai plant both for sale in the local market and for export to Japan and ASEAN. Subsequently, it designated Thailand as a regional center for the engineering research and design work on new models.

In 1996, less than 3 percent of vehicle production was exported. By 2006, the figure had grown to 44 percent (see figures 2.1, 2.2, and table 2.3). Over this decade, the value of exports multiplied twenty times, and grew from 1 to 8 percent of total Thai exports. By 2010, exports were estimated to surpass production for the domestic market.

The fall in the value of the baht in 1997–8 made it more expensive to import parts from Japan, and hence encouraged the assemblers to increase the local content. The rising usage of Thailand as a center of production for export increased the demand for parts of world standard. Both Japanese and American assemblers pressured their key suppliers to set up operations in Thailand. In the early 2000s there was another wave of investment by parts firms, sometimes buying up formerly Thai-owned companies, but more usually establishing anew. In 2002, for example, twenty leading parts suppliers from Europe and the

FIGURE 2.2 Automotive exports, 1988–2006

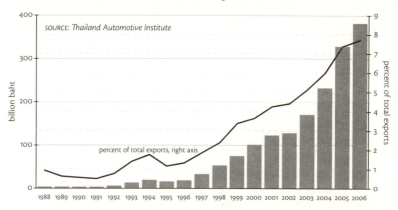

US invested in Thailand including Delphi Automotive system (a supplier of GM), Visteon and Hella Climate Control (Ford), and DANA
Spicer. Moreover, this wave penetrated down to the second tier and
beyond. The major US parts firm Delphi, for example, bought components locally from twenty suppliers that were all foreign-owned
or joint ventures. In response, several firms from Taiwan, Singapore,
Hong Kong, and Korea set up in Thailand to provide support services for the auto industry. Despite the ending of the local-content
policy, the level of local content increased, and imports of auto parts
and components declined after the crisis.

Policymaking

With the changes in the structure of the industry, the context of policymaking also shifted. Before the crisis, the major players in policymaking
had been domestic investors in assembly and parts, and bureaucrats, especially from the ministries of industry and finance. With deregulation, the
role of bureaucrats was substantially reduced (though not completely
effaced). With the transfers of ownership, the voice of domestic investors largely disappeared. The principal players became the multinational
firms that now owned much of the industry, as well as the politicians who

influenced decisions on excise taxes and government budgets to support the auto industry through infrastructure development and technical training. In the development of policy, both internal and external, Thai government ministers and industry leaders now fell captive to the multi-national assemblers. This was evident in the wrangling over the eco-car.

TABLE 2.3 Export of vehicles and parts, 1996–2006

YEAR	TOTAL VALUE	CBU		ENGINE (VALUE)	SPARE PARTS (VALUE)	CAST AND DIE		ORIGINAL EQUIPMENT	
		UNIT	VALUE			UNIT	VALUE	BODY (VALUE)	CKD (VALUE)
1996	6,296	14,020	4,253	802	215		44	374	602
1997	20,723	42,218	16,227	2,024	505	17	56	1,038	845
1998	34,110	67,857	28,126	1,537	723	6,013	64	1,347	2,288
1999	60,106	125,702	50,187	3,732	883	177	141	1,424	3,679
2000	83,245	152,835	63,349	7,106	1,246		120	1,556	9,531
2001	107,110	175,299	83,895	7,481	1,759	5	141	1,989	11,749
2002	107,730	181,471	82,475	6,087	1,796	18	145	2,880	14,196
2003	138,161	235,122	102,208	5,291	2,182	2	172	4,220	23,500
2004	202,080	332,053	149,233	4,316	2,909		797	5,385	36,489
2005	294,244	440,705	203,025	7,901	4,101		683	6,462	70,329
2006	342,980	539,206	240,919	8,448	5,026	135	690	6,647	80,489

NOTE: Values in million baht

Source: Thailand Automotive Institute (June, 2007)

In 2003, the Ministry of Industry's auto strategy committee proposed that government should support a project to make Thailand a base for production of small, economical, and eco-friendly cars suitable for Asian cities. Thailand was already a worldwide leader in pickup production, and this eco-car could become a second area of specialization. Government would lay out certain specifications, extend promotional privileges, and offer reduced excise tax rates (as with pickups) to ensure it would be commercially attractive.

The idea did not originate from the Thailand Automotive Institute, and was not part of the master plan. Rather, the idea came from Vachara Panchet, who had been appointed as vice minister of industry under the Thaksin government and deputed to propose ideas for developing the sector. The project generated intense debate. Mitsubishi and Honda supported the proposal since they already produced models elsewhere in the world that could be adapted for the Thailand project. Perhaps not coincidentally, Vachara belonged to the family that had long been Mitsubishi's partner in Thailand. The family had lost much of its stake in the assembler during the crisis but remained an important producer of parts. By contrast, Toyota perceived the project as a threat. Toyota had a leading share in Thailand's passenger car market, and no appropriate model available in its worldwide network, so it feared the project would result in either high investment or a fall in market share. The minister of industry at the time, Suriya Jungrungruangkit, belonged to the family of Thai Summit, a large auto parts group very closely associated with Toyota. The project wallowed between these conflicting pressures. In October 2002, Suriya was reshuffled from the industry portfolio to communications, and the prospects for the project increased. Government set up a committee to examine the project, and the NESDB came out in its favor. However, in 2005 Wachara ceased to be vice minister, and soon after Suriya returned to the industry portfolio. He announced that the project was not urgent, and that the use of excise tax to promote the idea would distort the market structure.

When Suriya then fell from power with Thaksin in 2006, the project revived. With Suriya no longer in a position to influence matters, the head of Toyota Thailand came out to oppose the project in person, using the prospect of future Toyota investments in the country as his bargaining chip. However, in June 2007, the Surayud Cabinet endorsed the eco-car project by agreeing to reduce the excise tax from 30 percent to 17 percent, and the BOI agreed to provide investment incentives. Honda promptly announced plans to build a new plant with a capacity of 120,000 eco-cars. Toyota (more reluctantly) said it would build an eco-car in Thailand by 2009.

In 2004, the government restructured excise taxes to promote energy saving, raising the rate on cars of 3000cc from 48 to 50 percent, and dropping that on cars under 2000cc from 35 to 30 percent. In addition it offered special rates to encourage innovations. Cars powered by electricity, fuel cells, or hybrids would pay only 10 percent, and those using at least 20 percent ethanol only 20 percent. Ford decided to bring in technology it had already developed in Brazil for ethanol cars, and to make Thailand a base for manufacturing an ethanol-using Ford Focus for Asia. Toyota looked to follow the same pattern. However, in 2005 the government postponed the scheme on grounds that local production of ethanol was insufficient. Ford showed its annoyance by muttering about future investment plans in Thailand.

Under AFTA, tariffs on cars within ASEAN countries dropped to a range of zero to 5 percent. Exports of vehicles from Thailand to the other ASEAN countries promptly increased sharply. Both government and the auto industry became supporters of concluding more free trade agreements (FTAs).

Thailand negotiated an FTA with Australia with the aim of increasing automotive and textile exports. In 2005, when the FTA came on stream, Thai automotive exports to Australia rose 15 percent. In the following year, total Thai exports to Australia increased 30 percent, led by commercial vehicles, automobiles, and components (*Bangkok Post*, 6 March 2007). In negotiation for an FTA with the US, the Thai side pressed for a reduction in the 25 percent tariff on pickups, but the US side refused to agree. The negotiation of the FTA was never concluded. Automotive issues were also a key factor in negotiations for an FTA with Japan, completed in 2006 and finally signed in 2007. Japan pushed strongly for reductions in Thai tariffs on auto parts and steel on grounds that these changes would improve the competitiveness of Thailand as an export producer of vehicles. The Japan Automobile Manufacturers Association met with the prime minister in April 2005 to lobby for these reductions, implying that failure to make these changes would tempt Japanese manufacturers to prefer locations in India and China.

The Federation of Thai Industries objected on grounds that the reduced tariffs on parts would place up to five hundred firms and three hundred thousand jobs at risk. Japanese parts makers already established in Thailand also opposed the reduction on parts tariffs. Meanwhile, Thai steel makers fought hard against reduction of the steel tariff on grounds that the steel industry still deserved protection. Eventually these two areas were compromised by allowing some phasing of the tariff reduction over a ten-year period, but essentially the auto makers got what they wanted with only a short delay. The FTA was finally signed in April 2007.

CONCLUSION

In 2006, Thailand had fourteen auto assembly plants, of which six were involved in exporting. These were supplied by some 386 parts firms, among which there were twenty-four major groups, with another thousand or so indirect suppliers of leather products, plastic, rubber, steel, electronics, glass, paints and petrochemicals; and numerous related industries including after-sales service, credit, leasing, logistics, financial services, insurance, education, R&D, and repair. Japanese firms held 80 percent of the market, with half of that in the hands of Toyota.[6]

The transformation of the auto industry over the crisis and aftermath exemplifies what happened to manufacturing industry in general over this period. Prior to the crisis, the industry was oriented to the home market, policy regulation still carried the legacy of the import substitution era, domestic capital still had a major stake within a joint venture

---

6. In addition there were four motorcycle manufacturers, three of which exported, and two major groups of motorcycle parts suppliers.

format, and policy was made by negotiation between domestic capital groups and government bureaucrats. Ten years later, all this had changed. The proportion of capacity devoted to exports had reached almost half and was still rising. The old protectionist format had been abandoned in favor of a bid to make Thailand an integral part of global production chains. Multinationals totally dominated, with domestic capital relegated to a minor role. Policy was made by negotiation between the Japanese firms and Thai elected politicians, with a subsidiary role for trade negotiators.

The auto industry had been promoted since the 1960s on an infant-industry development model in which protection nurtured local entrepreneurship, technology transfer, and skill accumulation. But over the subsequent four decades, the global context had totally changed. The auto industry was a leading example of a global industry within which ownership had become highly concentrated through mergers. Production chains snaked across the world, and key decisions were taken within a global perspective. Any prospect that the Thai auto industry would grow from an infant into an independent adult had long since passed.

The pressures to abandon the old policy framework had been building for some time. But this framework nurtured interests that wanted it sustained. Domestic capital enjoyed the rents. Bureaucrats enjoyed the power. Even the Japanese firms that had sunk their roots in the country were two-minded about liberalization that might reduce their advantages over global competitors. The key political decisions to liberalize the industry were all taken in unusual circumstances. The Anand government made the first tentative steps after the 1991 coup. The Chuan government completed the job in the aftermath of the 1997 crisis.

For all its faults, the protectionist era had created the foundations on which Thailand could bid for a place in the global industry. The Japanese assemblers had invested not only in plant, but in skill training, in understanding how to do business in Thailand, and in political connections. Several levels of support industry clustered around the assemblers. As a result of tax policies conceived as support for agriculture, production of the one-ton pickup had achieved sufficient scale for Thailand to become a global production center.

In 1997, when their domestic partners were crippled, some Japanese firms were initially reluctant to stump up the extra capital, particularly when the crisis had shattered optimistic projections of the domestic market's ability to continue growing at boom rates. Ultimately, though, they had little choice, and ultimately too they benefited from a relatively cheap acquisition. To make this investment pay, however, they had to convert their Thai operations from suppliers of the domestic market into more integral parts of their global networks. They did so by relocating production, changing sourcing, and becoming players in the politics of trade negotiation.

Among over a thousand Thai family firms that had lived off the auto industry in the 1980s and early 1990s, only a handful were able to keep up with the pace of this transition to a globalized industry. They did so by using the strategies outlined in chapter 1. They modernized their structure, took on more professional management, and invested in technology. They also worked closely with the multinationals and the politicians who now dictated the policy framework. It was no coincidence that the most successful Thai parts group in the post-crisis era, the Summit group, went into partnership with Toyota, and through Suriya into partnership with Thaksin.

BIBLIOGRAPHIC NOTE

On the boom era, see Doner 1991, 1992; Muramatsu 1997; Edith 2002, Nipon and Wangdee 2000; Veloso et al. 1998. *On crisis and adjustment,* see Doner and Ramsay 2003; Vallop 2002; Samart 2004; Higashi 2002; Iwasa 2000; Kriengkrai and Yoshi 2004; Masuyama 2000; Mori 2002; Minako 2002; Praphad 2000; Brooker Group 2002; Deunden et al. 2006. *On policymaking,* see Phatchari 1997; Thailand Automotive Institute 2002, 2006; Chaiyuth and Nipon 2003; Doner et al. 2005; JAMA 2004; Ninnart 2004.

3

SERVICES, SERVILITY, AND SURVIVAL:
THE ACCOMMODATION OF BIG RETAIL

Veerayooth Kanchoochat

ONE of the most striking changes in urban Thailand in the last decade has been the massive expansion of megastores. The trend began in the pre-crisis boom, when the pioneers were local business groups. The Central group expanded from its base in department stores into both supermarkets and then hypermarkets under the name Big C. The Charoen Pokphand (CP) conglomerate moved into big retail through hypermarkets under the name Lotus, and a joint venture with Makro. Central also helped Carrefour enter Thailand in 1996 by acting as a nominee partner. But by the eve of the crisis, there were only a total of eighteen big stores, mostly in the capital. Even in Bangkok, most consumers still made most of their everyday purchases at traditional outlets. Most goods passed through a traditional distribution chain from suppliers through wholesalers to retail outlets.

After the crisis struck, this pattern changed very rapidly. Both Central and CP sold their fledgling interests in hypermarkets to three large European multinational retail chains. These three chains seized the opportunity, created by the crisis, of low land prices and virtually no regulation, to expand very rapidly (Nipon et al. 2002; Yutthasak 2001). By 2006, the total number of branches reached 148. They were found throughout the capital, and in almost every provincial center of any size. The arrival of these new stores dramatically changed consumer behavior. People seemed to appreciate the low prices, the variety of goods, and the sheer experience of shopping in these palaces of consumption. The opening of a new store in a capital suburb or provincial town took on the celebratory atmosphere of a local festival. In the city, the siting of stores shifted traffic patterns and relocated traffic jams. In some provincial towns, the old central market areas very quickly began to decay from the new competition. Groups of retailers, wholesalers, and transport contractors began protesting to government against the new entrants, often appealing to nationalist sentiment against this new form of foreign invasion.

Debate over the arrival of the hypermarket multinationals tended to divide into two camps. On the one side, believers in the primacy of the market argued that the change was both good and inevitable. The multinationals had advantages through technology, scale, and financial might. Once the market was open, local retail and distribution systems were bound to lose against this powerful competition. The ultimate beneficiaries would be consumers, who enjoyed lower prices, and the economy as a whole, which benefited from greater efficiency. On the other side, people argued that government had a duty to protect domestic capital and the large number of livelihoods threatened by this new competition. Small-scale retailing had a special place in the history and mythology of Thailand's capital accumulation. Most entrepreneurial families were founded by a Chinese immigrant who earned his first capital from coolie labor, then multiplied that capital by investing in a small shop or similar business. The classic architectural form of urban Thailand is a shophouse—a one-story, one-room shop with a dwelling over the top. The arrival of mega-retail threatened not only livelihood but heritage, and a key piece of urban economics.

The proposition that large-scale retail will succeed and ought to succeed because it is technologically superior to traditional retail and offers benefits of economic efficiency to both consumers and nation is too naive. In real life, markets do not work by the pure laws of economics. Indeed, today's institutional economics asserts that markets are human creations that are shaped by a wide variety of factors including government policy, the business environment, and consumer behavior (Chang 2000, 2003; Hollingsworth 2000). Each country, each locality, each market has its own "rules of the game." This chapter examines the entry of big retail into Thailand from this perspective. For simplicity, the chapter concentrates on the hypermarkets (very large stores that sell a very wide variety of goods at low prices), as the expansion of this category of outlets was the single most dramatic part of the story. Transnational retailers (and some local chains) also entered with supermarkets, convenience store chains, and specialty stores.

To show that the success of transnational retail is not a simple function of technology, this chapter first sketches big retail's expansion into three other markets of Asia, showing that the results varied greatly. Then it dissects the factors in government policy, the business environment, and consumer behavior that shaped their success in Bangkok, and finally it highlights the varied welcome that the transnationals received in provincial Thailand.

BIG RETAIL INTO ASIA

Thailand is not the only country in Asia to have recently experienced the arrival and expansion of multinational retail chains. Several European chains have looked to Asia as a frontier of expansion beyond their home continent. In some countries, they have been very successful. In others, they have failed. The point is that the multinational chains are not guaranteed success because of their advantages of technology, scale, and financial resources. Here we will look briefly at three cases—Taiwan, Japan, and South Korea—in roughly the same time frame, as a prelude to examining what happened in Thailand.

Taiwan

In Taiwan, the multinational chains enjoyed great success. In terms of the number of outlets, Taiwan now ranks second in Asia behind China even though Taiwan's population is much less than several other Asian countries. Moreover, one company, Carrefour, has been exceptionally successful, able to take 35 percent of the hypermarket business despite a fiercely competitive market (Hitoshi 2003).

The Taiwanese government opened the door to the multinational chains in the late 1980s as part of a policy to encourage foreign investment in service sectors (PricewaterhouseCoopers 2005). Consumers quickly showed they had a liking for imported goods and shopping in large outlets (Chung 2001). Local producers, distributors, and retailers were small-scale and fragmented. They failed to combine on any strategy of resistance to the big stores (Chang and Sternquist 1993). Local business groups were happy to sell land to the multinationals, and to assist them in other ways. Carrefour went into a joint venture with Uni-President Enterprise (UPE), the largest food company in Taiwan, which conveyed several advantages over competitors including good political connections at national and local levels, and access to good retail locations (Wrigley et al. 2005; Hitoshi 2003).

In sum, the government was supportive, consumers were welcoming, some major local business (UPE) decided to cooperate, and others were too small and fragmented to resist, hence the multinational chains enjoyed rapid success.

Japan

Japan provides a contrasting example. The hypermarket chains were slow to enter the market, and ultimately not so successful. Again this can be explained as a function of government policy, consumer behavior, and the business environment.

From 1991, the Japanese government began to relax regulations blocking the entry of multinationals into the Japanese economy. But what government policy said and how it was implemented were rather different. The ruling LDP party considered that the thousands of small enterprises in Japan's highly fragmented retail sector were an important political constituency (Dawson and Larke 2004). Although multinationals could gain licenses from the central government, they also had to get permissions in the locality. For each store they had to undergo public hearings, which meant organizing forums to build local support, and investing in software to demonstrate that they would not have a bad impact on the local environment. Once through that hurdle, they had to negotiate the relationship networks and political connections of Japan's procurement and distribution systems, where making a partnership with a firm in one group might automatically exclude them from doing business with firms from rival groups (JETRO 2004). Finally, they confronted the consumer. Living in small accommodations with little storage, Japanese housewives were accustomed to making daily purchases in small amounts. They valued the convenience of a store close to home or work much more than price-ticket savings, greater variety, or the chance to buy in bulk.

No multinational hypermarket made a dent on the market dominance of the Japanese supermarket chains. Only Wal-Mart made some headway by going into a joint venture with the Japanese Seiyu chain, and spending time learning the market rather than going for rapid expansion (JETRO 2004).

In sum, government was highly equivocal, consumers were little tempted by the advantages of big retail, and the local business environment was unwelcoming.

South Korea

The South Korean story sits in between these two extremes. Multinational chains were able to succeed, but only in partnership with a strong local company, and only as minor players in a market dominated by local hypermarket chains.

The government carefully liberalized the market over a period of seven years, giving time for local business interests to learn, adjust, and compete. It placed limits on the number and size of outlets that the multinationals could operate, giving time for local rivals to expand in prime locations. Government spent US$21.3 million on balancing policies to support small retailers such as grants for upgrading stores, tax rebates for small retailers, and funding for purchase by cooperatives throughout the country (Sternquist and Jin 1998). In addition. Korean consumers approached shopping in ways that the multinationals found difficult to understand. The two major locally owned chains, E-Mart and Lotte-Mart, knew how to cater for the consumer, and led the market with shares of 32 and 12 percent respectively. After initially poor results, Tesco responded by entering into a partnership with the major local conglomerate, Samsung, and allowing the local partner full control over personnel policy, store design, and recruitment. This

Tesco-Samsung venture gained the third rank, while other multinationals such as Carrefour, Costco, and Wal-Mart, which had no local partners and which tended to apply their standard practices, languished at the bottom of the market (Coe and Yong-Sook 2006; Choi 2003).

Different rules of the game

These brief examples indicate that the technological advantages of the multinational hypermarket chains were not necessarily decisive. Government policy, factors in the business environment and consumer behavior could also influence the impact of their arrival in a new market. In Japan, the transnational chains could not compete with local firms. In South Korea, the transnationals had to cooperate with local firms and still gained only a minority share of the market. In Taiwan, the transnationals were very successful. In comparison to these cases, how should we understand the spectacular expansion of the multinational retail chains after the crisis in Thailand?

BIG RETAIL ARRIVES IN THAILAND

Retailing before the crisis

In the classic Thai pattern, manufacturers or importers of everyday goods supplied their products to "wholesalers" (*yi bua*), which were usually mid-sized retail stores with a secondary function of selling goods onwards to neighborhood retailers (*sa bua*). The whole distribution system was very fragmented, with very little aggregation by warehousing companies, transport agencies, or pure wholesalers. This pattern remained substantially unchanged until the great boom. Additions to this pattern were minor. Department stores led by the Central group of the Chirathivat family, added supermarkets to their store outlets. A handful of businesses founded to supply the large US presence during the Indochina War (especially Foodland and Villa) remained to cater for the resident Western expatriate community. From 1988, Jusco built a handful of supermarkets principally to supply the Japanese community. In 1989, the CP group, in a joint venture with Dutch Makro, began to establish cash-and-carry outlets that mostly sold to local retailers. By 1996, they had nine stores. These additions did not substantially alter the classic pattern of the retail trade. The supermarkets were limited to parts of Bangkok and a handful of other major towns. Their clientele consisted mostly of expatriates and a small, globalized elite. Makro functioned as an alternative to traditional wholesalers in a limited number of urban neighborhoods.

Change began in 1994, when Central established its first hypermarket under the name of Big C, and the CP group launched into hypermarkets under the name Lotus with the help of some know-how from Wal-Mart (Sombun 2002b). The French chain Carrefour entered Thailand in 1996 in a joint venture in which Central held 40 percent.

When the crisis struck in 1997, both the Central and CP groups embraced the opportunity to sell majority stakes to the multinationals in order to fund the rescue of their core businesses. For Central, the hypermarket business was a recent and relatively minor part of their business empire centered on department stores. For CP, the hypermarkets were one of many opportunistic expansions during the boom which had only a flimsy relationship to its core business of agri-processing. For Casino (French), Tesco (British), and Carrefour (French) this was an opportunity to take control and expand.

The Alien Business Law

Under the 1972 regulation that governed foreign business prior to the crisis, any foreign company (other than an American company) was limited to a 49 percent stake in any venture in retail. In 1999, government instituted a new Alien Business Act, for the first time allowing foreign firms to have majority ventures in the retail trade, on the condition that the investment was more than 100 million baht. In fact, however, no firm took advantage of this provision, because another clause of the law disallowed a foreign-majority venture from selling agricultural projects, food, and beverages. Instead, the multinational retailers circumvented the Alien Business Law by using nominee shareholders.

By convention, Thai law judged whether a firm was majority-owned by domestic or foreign capital by looking only at the first line of shareholders. If the majority owner was a "Thai" company, then the conditions were fulfilled. The law and regulatory agencies had no interest in investigating any deeper. It was therefore easy to disguise a foreign majority share by building a pyramid of holding companies, and by having Thai nationals as nominee shareholders. These nominees were credited with owning the majority of the capital, but then allocated a much smaller share of the dividend payments and voting rights (by using the conditionality of preference shares). When this technique was first used is now forgotten, but it expanded steadily as the economy liberalized. It became popular during the tentative early phase of liberalization by the Anand governments in 1991–1992, and then blossomed in the aftermath of the crisis. This technique allowed the Thai state the hypocrisy of pretending to protect domestic capital, while in fact welcoming foreign investment.

By 2000, Tesco, Casino, and Carrefour had taken advantage of this nominee technique to take control of their ventures in Thailand. CP sold 92 percent of Lotus to Tesco, and retained the remaining 8 percent. Casino took over 66 percent of Big C, leaving the Chirathivat with 13 percent and the remainder in the hands of small of small shareholders. The Chirathivat also sold all of their stake in Carrefour, which became virtually wholly owned under a nominee structure.[1]

All three chains promptly launched programs of rapid expansion to take advantage of the reduced price of land and the absence of any regulatory framework. Government was happy to see any signs of foreign investment and business expansion. While the three had a total of eighteen stores in 1996, the number spurted to fifty-eight, four years later.

---

1. Central had earlier held a 40 percent stake in Carrefour but had no say in management and was a pure nominee (see interview with Suthichat Chirathivat in Wirat et al. 2003: 126). SSCP, which held 20 percent from the beginning and added the 40 percent from Central, had Thai shareholders but was also a nominee. Carrefour annual reports show that SSCP's profits are fully consolidated into its worldwide accounts.

Central also sold a 50 percent stake in its Tops supermarket chain to Ahold of Belgium, but bought the stake back in 2004 when Ahold made a strategic decision to reduce its operations across Asia because of losses.

Local retailers protested. They argued that the government was favoring foreign over domestic capital. At the least, the local shops should be afforded some protection to give them time to adjust.

FIGURE 3.1 Number of hypermarket outlets, 1995–2006

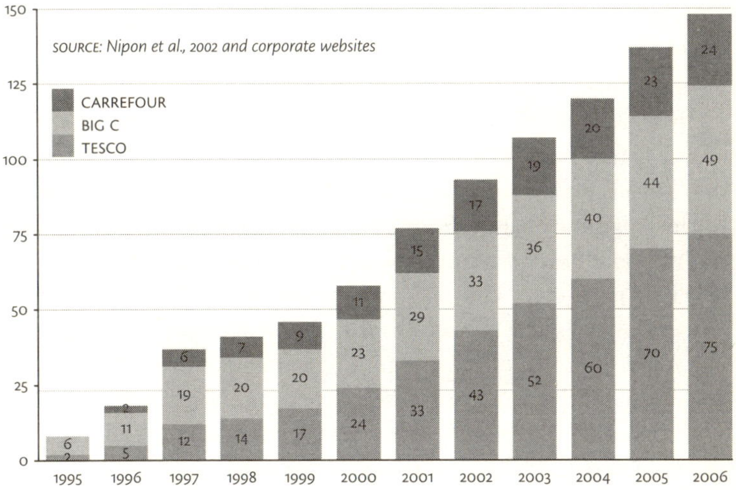

THE INSTITUTIONAL ENVIRONMENT IN THAILAND

What role did government policy, business environment, and consumer behavior play in the entry of the transnational chains into Thailand?

Government policy

One key characteristic of the Thai state is that it has remained very centralized and very top-down. Although the form of government changed over seventy years from an absolute monarchy through military dictatorship to a parliamentary system, the change in the distribution of power has been far from complete. The bureaucratic frame still exerts a strong grip over policymaking, especially economic policymaking.

Moreover, a big business elite has successfully adapted to each stage of political change. Politics is largely a negotiation between business and bureaucracy over the division of power and over the distribution of the benefits of economic growth (Seksan 2005; McVey 2000). Ordinary people have little access to power, with the result that social policy lags far behind economic development. Although small retailers are collectively a large group, and often have strong links to elected politicians in the localities, they have not had any significant impact on policymaking on the arrival of multinational retailing.

There is also a mindset embedded in the centralized state that one of its key functions is to deliver economic growth, and that failure to fulfill that function is one of the few ways it might become vulnerable to challenge and change. Further, over the last half century, this centralized state has more and more looked outwards for the ideas and resources needed to achieve growth. Particularly since the 1970s, the Thai economy has grown with the help of foreign demand, foreign capital, imported technology, and immigrant labor. The 1997 crisis was potentially a major threat to this centralized state. Naturally, the reaction of the bureaucratic frame was to restore growth as rapidly as possible, and to look outwards for the resources to do so.

Hence, there was no serious questioning by bureaucrats or politicians of the rapid expansion by the transnational hypermarket chains from 1997 onwards. The fact that government allowed the transnationals to circumvent the letter of the Alien Business Law was paradigmatic of the Thai state's attitude towards these firms. In the absence of any legal framework to manage the special issues raised by such stores, the chains were able to locate stores without any concern for the impact on the economy, environment, traffic, or community.

Over 1998 and 1999, some protests were lodged by organizations of local retailers. When he was drumming up support for his new political party in the late 1990s, Thaksin appeared to cultivate this lobby. He promised to protect and promote domestic capital in the teeth of globalization. In the 2001 election campaign, he presented himself as an example of a small entrepreneur who made good in a big way. The local retail lobby played to this sentiment by arguing that mom-and-pop stores were the classic way in which Thai-Chinese immigrant families accumulated capital in their first or second generation. From this perspective, the multinational chains were a threat to the very heart and soul of Thai capitalism. In rhetoric, Thaksin supported the retailers. After gaining power, he set up a committee to research ways to regulate the retail industry. For almost two years, there were consultations between government, representatives of local retail, and the transnational chains to develop legislation to install a proper legal framework. But in late 2002, Thaksin announced that the idea of legislating any protection for local retail had been abandoned. A minister explained that this decision had been taken "simply because we don't want to send a wrong signal to the foreign community." Thaksin added: "External trade is important to the Thai economy since it generates new investment and increases our productivity" (*The Nation*, 17, 18, and 20 November 2002). These statements made it very clear that Thaksin's government was following the long-run trend of seeking economic growth through foreign investment, and was no more sensitive to a local lobby such as the retailers than any of its predecessors.[2]

Business environment

By selling their major stakes in hypermarkets to the transnationals, the Central and CP groups did not exit from the sector. Indeed, they continued as business partners who significantly helped the multinational chains to succeed. They themselves benefited in the process.

The Central group helped Casino to find good locations for new Big C stores, including land that Central owned and made available in return for rental income. Central and Casino jointly helped each other to expand to other ASEAN countries, a major goal of Central group (*Phujatkan Raiwan*, 27 May 2004). Central also helped Carrefour to receive Board of Investment privileges in 1998 against the advice of the Ministry of Commerce (*Thai Post*, 25 December 1998).

---

2. Thaksin tried to soften the blow by setting up a government support service for small stores, but it never really got off the ground.

Similarly, CP helped the expansion of Tesco-Lotus. Sunthorn Aruna-nonchai, who had been in charge of the group's property company, CP Land, became the managing director of the company that managed the Tesco-Lotus stores. He used his experience and network in real estate to find good locations for branches, including land belonging to his own family for the branch in Chiang Rai (*Than Setthakit*, 22–24 October 2001). CP also benefited from learning new management technology, which was applied to the Lotus hypermarkets still owned by CP in China. Finally CP was able to supply chicken products to Tesco's European network to the tune of around 5 billion baht a year (*Than Setthakit*, 27–30 August 2000).

Within the retail trade, interests were fragmented (Jirapar 2003). Both the wholesalers and retailers were affected by the rise of purchasing through the hypermarkets. Some survived by accommodating to the new system. A new type of informal agent known as "gunmen" (*mue puen*) appeared in the distribution chain. They bought goods from the hypermarkets and sold them onwards to wholesalers, retailers, and vendors in occasional markets. Original suppliers found themselves in a weaker position because they were increasingly dependent on the hypermarkets and thus more vulnerable in price negotiations. Their margins were cut. The wholesalers, retailers, and vendors could buy from the "gunmen" and sell on to consumers at prices close to their old level. The hypermarkets offered consumers better prices, but many traditional stores could still compete by offering other advantages such as convenience of location.

As a result of such survival strategies, the resistance to the big stores was less concerted than it might have been.

Consumers

People have become so accustomed to the centralized state that it is reflected in their values. Inoguchi et al. (2005) conducted a survey of urban lifestyle and attitudes in ten Asian countries. In Japan and South Korea, they found that people had more trust in local government than in central government. In Thailand, the results were reversed, and

FIGURE 3.2 Accommodation of hypermarkets in the retail trade

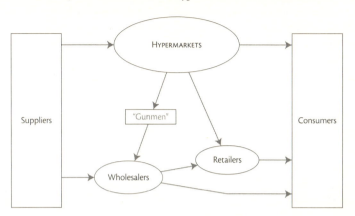

the proportion expressing trust in central government (86 percent) was much higher than in South Korea and Japan (below 33 percent). In other words, the dominating role of the centralized state has been internalized in the popular mentality.

Over several decades, Thai consumers had been educated to equate foreign branding with higher quality. Multinational consumer goods manufacturers had located factories inside Thailand. The language of product branding from the top of the market to the bottom had become English. Local competitors had usually been forced to the economy end of the market, and even there competed to sell their goods by imitating the attributes of international brands. In the mid-1980s, the Carabao band had lampooned this consumer behavior in the hit song, "Made in Thailand."[3] There had been no phase in Thailand equivalent to the years in Korea when local conglomerates sheltered by protection learned how to achieve international quality, and when consumers became accustomed to their locally named brands. Shopping from an internationally branded retailer was thus

3. "*Made in Thailand*. But when you display it in the shop/Attach a brand label 'Made in Japan'/ It'll sell like hot cakes, fetch a good price/We can tell ourselves it's foreign-made/Modern style from the fashion magazine/Nobody has to cheat us. We cheat ourselves!"

quite consistent with consumer expectations. There was nothing similar to Japan, where consumers were disappointed by French-owned retail outlets because they expected them to be "more French."

Timing was also important. Over the year following the onset of the crisis in mid-1997, total consumer spending dropped by a fifth. The ability of the hypermarkets to offer lower prices was a very convincing draw in this environment.

The fact that mom-and-pop retailing had become very much the preserve of first and second generation immigrant families also tended to work against them. The practice of such families was to accumulate through hard work and high savings, rather than through innovation or customer service. By and large, the consuming public showed little support for the local retailers' protests against the multinational chains.

Perhaps because the local Central and CP groups pioneered the first few years of hypermarkets and remained as partners of the multinational chains, the design of the stores made major accommodation to local tastes. Inside, there were many food outlets, and outside a section of the area that might have been used for car parking was typically given over to a vendor market selling foods, clothing, and sundries. These two innovations gave the hypermarkets some of the advantages and some of the atmosphere of traditional retailing.

PROVINCIAL EXPANSION

Over 1998 to 2001, the multinationals expanded their number of branches in Bangkok and the immediately surrounding areas. As this market became saturated, they moved further afield. Between 2002 and 2005, they opened sixty-three branches in forty-one of Thailand's seventy-six provinces.

With government non-intervention, partnership and accommodation from the local trade, and ready acceptance by consumers, the transnational retailers were quickly very successful in their initial expansion in and around the capital of Bangkok. But in the provincial areas, the experience of the multinational retailers was more mixed. In some provinces, conditions were not fundamentally different from the capital. But in others, they encountered more resistance.

Acceptance and cooperation

Naturally, one of the first places to be targeted was Thailand's second largest city, Nakhon Ratchasima or Khorat. In 2000, three multinationals (Makro, Big C, Tesco-Lotus), as well as the domestic The Mall department store chain all opened branches in the city. Local businessmen eagerly found good locations for them. Tesco-Lotus rented 30 rai in a prime location from Suchinda Cherdchai, head of a big transport firm, and member of one of the most powerful and long-established political families in the town (*Daily News*, 2 September 1999). Consumer behavior changed very rapidly. By 2004, it was estimated that Tesco-Lotus, The Mall, and Big C had each grabbed around a 20 percent share of local retail expenditure. Local shops lost heavily. There was no sentiment to favor local businessmen against the new arrivals. A leading local businessman, owner of a fruit market, remarked ruefully, "In the past, local shops had made so much profit by exploiting people" (INN, www.innnews.co.th, 29 June 2001).

This pattern was replicated in other places such as Chiang Mai, Pattaya, and Chachoengsao. A slight variant was found elsewhere. Here big local businessmen had already established their own large-scale retail outlets in good locations. Rather than be drawn into competition with new entrants, they chose to compromise. They leased space in their own stores for use by the multinationals. In this way Tesco-Lotus appeared in Big Jiang's store in Nong Khai, Sermthai in Mahasarakham, and Fairy Land in Nakhon Sawan. Similarly the Nok Hong group in Rayong and Naza group in Suphanburi leased space in their retail stores to Tops supermarkets owned by the Central group.

Localism

In certain other provinces, the entry of the multinationals was not so smooth. They faced resistance grounded in local sentiment. Businessmen were able to use organization, legal measures, and popular feelings to obstruct the entry of these powerful competitors. A key tool in their favor was a Town Planning Act enforced in 2003.

In 2003, Tesco-Lotus made arrangements to rent land for a store of 7,000 square meters in Chumphon. Fifty local businessmen formed an organization to oppose Tesco. Importantly, the protests was joined by five leading local figures—the chairman of the Provincial Administrative Organization, the city mayor, and the heads of the provincial chamber of commerce, provincial industrial association, and provincial association for retail and transport. They petitioned the governor to withhold permission from Tesco on grounds of the impact on traffic and local business. The municipality plastered the town with banners proclaiming, "Catastrophe is coming! Oppose Tesco in any form, eyeball to eyeball, tooth for tooth!" (*Prachachat Thurakit*, 30 June 2003). Campaigners protested when Tesco went to present its building plans. Local officials cooperated by insisting that the town development plan disallowed any building over 500 square meters within the city limits. Tesco had to accept defeat. Until June 2007, neither Tesco nor any other large retail chain has been able to open a store in Chumphon.[4]

In Prachinburi, there was a similar case. Because of protests by influential local leaders, the municipality simply refused to process the building application. But Tesco took the issue to the Administrative Court, and won on grounds that the municipality was exercising unfair discrimination.

In Chanthaburi and Kanchanaburi, Tesco's plans to open stores also faced concerted protests by local retailers. In both cases, Tesco negotiated with the local business community and made several concessions. Most importantly, it provided space inside the store for local retailers, and outside the store for vendors, at discounted rentals. It also undertook to promote local products, including fruit and local handicrafts. These concessions were enough to mollify the opposition and enable the stores to be built. Subsequently, the local business community pressed Tesco hard to ensure it delivered on these promises.

---

4. They might be discouraged by a large sign emblazoned, "You build. We burn." But Lotus has included Chumphon in plans to expand the number of its smaller convenience stores.

In Phrae, the resistance started in a similar way with businessmen using local laws, but eventually went further to involve more widespread popular sentiment.

In May 2003, Tesco-Lotus purchased 25 rai of land in Phrae for a store. The head of the provincial chamber of commerce consulted with local government heads to block the project but the local government body (TAO) had already given permission for the construction before the protest arose, and refused to reverse its order. The store opened in October 2003. The Chamber of Commerce then organized resistance among retailers and consumers with a campaign entitled "Unite to keep the profits in Phrae." They encouraged local shops to improve their service. They organized a coupon scheme under which people buying in any of the participating local shops received coupons that qualified them for discounts and raffle prizes. Local radio stations agreed to advertise the scheme for nothing.

In the first phase, ending in May 2004, ninety shops participated, two million coupons were distributed, and the shops' revenue increased by 300 million baht. In the second phase, the number of participating shops rose to 150, six million coupons were issued, and sales revenue grew by 600 million baht (*Siam Rath*, 21 April 2004; *Prachachat Thurakit*, 31 October 2005). The provincial chamber of commerce continued to organize such schemes on a regular basis.

Unlike many other provinces, Tesco-Lotus failed to dominate local retail in Phrae. It gained an estimated 30 percent share of the market, but local retailers survived, and at least until the end of 2006 no shop was forced out of the market by the multinational's arrival.

However, Tesco-Lotus has reacted against this local upswell. It has found a clause in the Building Control Act of 1989 which states that "anyone can build, adapt, dismantle, or move a building without applying for permission from local officials. They only need to inform the local official." Their lawyers cite this clause in cases of dispute. Also in cases where local governmental bodies refuse to process their applications for building permits, Tesco-Lotus petitions the parliamentary ombudsman to investigate these bodies for failing to carry out their duties.

A new Retail Business Bill has been submitted to Parliament. The bill prescribes principles and rules for new stores. The debate has revolved around who should apply these rules. The original draft gave the power to provincial committees. The Cabinet and the Ministry of Commerce want to relocate this power to the center. A committee of the Parliament argued, "If there were local politicians with a conflict of interest, there would be attempts to abuse power, which may be harmful to entrepreneurs." The transnational retail chains have avoided taking any public position on the bill, but have perhaps been sowing an argument, taken up by some Thai newspapers, that the bill is in the interests of Thai suppliers in the Sahapat group.

CONCLUSION

The influx of multinational retailers in the aftermath of the crisis is an extraordinary story. In a handful of years, these chains spread throughout the country, and grabbed a major share of the retail market. From just eighteen hypermarket outlets prior to the crisis, by 2006 the number had grown to 148 stores with a turnover of 173 billion baht (see table 3.1).

TABLE 3.1 Turnover of hypermarket chains, 2001–2006 (billion baht)

	2001	2002	2003	2004	2005	2006
Tesco	46.5	54.3	64.7	72.7	80.7	92.1
Big C	32.6	38.2	42.3	47.4	53.2	58.0
Carrefour	13.1	15.9	18.7	20.6	22.3	23.1
TOTAL	92.1	108.4	125.7	140.7	156.2	173.2

SOURCE: PricewaterhouseCoopers (2005); corporate websites; annual reports.

From 1998 to 2002, Tesco invested over a billion US dollars. Within six years, Thailand had become the second largest operation for Tesco outside its UK base (as measured by floor space).[5] After the hypermarkets,

---

5. In Thailand in 2004, Tesco's stores occupied 6.8 million square feet, with the next largest country

Tesco began opening convenience stores. By 2004, it had established around two hundred, and had plans to add a further two hundred over the following two years. These plans had to be suspended in 2006 after another wave of local protests.

The speed of the transnational entry was partly the result of the removal of artificial barriers, releasing the floods built up behind. But it would be naive to picture this rapid entry as simply the working of the free market. Markets are always constructed by the institutional environment, and conditioned by changing circumstances. The examples of Japan and Korea indicate that the institutional environment differs greatly across countries. In Thailand, the multinationals were so successful because the national government imposed no barriers, consumers were generally welcoming, and the business environment was, on balance, positive. To a very large extent, these "rules of the game" were shaped by Thailand's centralized polity and outward orientation. Local government was weak. Consumers had been educated by long exposure to international goods. There had been no phase of economic nationalism or developmentalism. But to some extent these conditions were shaped by the special conditions of the crisis. Government was even more than usually desperate for foreign investment. Pole-axed local businessmen were disposed to cooperate for short-term advantage. Consumers were more than usually sensitive to price. Land was cheap. Regulation was even more than usually lax. The multinationals were able to site stores without concern for laws, environmental consequences, and social costs in ways which would have been impossible in their home markets. The result has been to create a rather oligopolistic market, which does not sit well with free-market principles.

The inability of local retail capital to resist was partly a function of speed and timing. Both the big domestic capital groups in retail, and the local operators, were crippled by the crisis. Even in the best of circumstances, however, they would have found difficulty in rivaling the

---

(Poland) at 4.8 million (www.tescocorporate.com/asiadetailed.htm, figures for 2004, viewed on 9 March 2007). Tesco's 2006 annual report (p. 8) boasted that cash return on investment averaged 16 percent across its four major overseas markets, including Thailand.

scale of the resources that Tesco and other chains threw at the Thai market over a very short span.

At the national level, government was inclined to favor foreign capital in the belief it would achieve economic growth, rather than domestic capital in the belief it had a duty to provide some protection. Politicians showed little interest in retailers as a political constituency. Thaksin wooed the retailers but then betrayed them. Popular opinion could not be mobilized in the support of domestic retail under the flag of economic nationalism. Particularly in Bangkok, people were really just not interested.

The cases of resistance in Phrae and Chumphon were in the minority, but are interesting for the differences they display. In Chumphon, local business interests were able to keep the big retailers out and protect themselves against competition. In Phrae, local businessmen organized themselves to compete more effectively against a big store. In these provinces, local political leaders did see retailers as an important constituency, and were prepared to provide the coordination that made resistance effective. Local government was susceptible to the retailers' demands, and sometimes acted in ways that suggested local government had a responsibility to promote local capital. Regulations could be applied on grounds of controlling the environmental and social consequences. Popular opinion could be organized in the retailers' support under such blatantly localist slogans as "Unite to keep the profit in Phrae." In these places, the rules of the game were different.

"In the age of globalization, there are dimensions which connect us to the wider world. But no matter how far this connection would go, there is still an initial starting point which must begin right here within our society" (Nithi 2006: 41).

4

HELLO AND GOODBYE TO THE MOBILE PHONE

Ukrist Pathmanand and Chris Baker

MOST of the new wave of entrepreneurs who emerged in the great boom were in the service sector rather than industry. The families that headed the rankings of major holders on the Thai stock exchange were in entertainment, media, banking, property development, and telecommunications. After the crisis, when so much of manufacturing capital was transferred to the multinationals, the service sector seemed even more to be the last refuge of domestic capital. The Alien Business Act of 1999 opened up manufacturing almost completely to foreign ownership, but still formally limited foreigners to a minority stake in most service industries.

From 1990 onwards, the star segment of the service sector was telecommunications. Within telecommunications, the star product was the mobile phone. For one family, this device created within five years a fortune that, according to an admirer, would normally have required two to three generations of accumulation. For a handful of other families, telecoms offered a fast route from relative obscurity to the front rank of Thai business. And Charoen Pokphand (CP), arguably the nation's most sophisticated corporation, nominated telecoms as the focus of its future growth. For around fifteen years, this sector created more wealth for Thai entrepreneurs and shareholders than any other. It also had a huge impact on politics by underwriting the extraordinary political career of Thaksin Shinawatra.

In the space of five months over late 2005 and early 2006, the two leading mobile phone firms were both sold into foreign ownership. The sale triggered a political crisis. It also raised new questions about the ability of Thai capital and enterprise to survive in the globalized world.

This chapter traces the rise and eclipse of Thai capital in the mobile phone industry. It looks at how the mobile phone business came to be a pot of gold; how that pot of gold was defended over the 1997 crisis; and why the pot of gold suddenly disappeared.

THE CONCESSION ERA

The early technology for mobile phones arrived in Thailand at the same time the economy took off into the great boom, and the politics shifted jerkily from military rule to parliamentary democracy. The coincidence of these three things shaped how the telecoms sector would evolve.

Telephony was the preserve of two government agencies. The Telephone Organization of Thailand (TOT) provided domestic services and the Communication Authority of Thailand (CAT) provided overseas services, but the two agencies competed bitterly where their spheres overlapped. Because of bureaucratic inefficiency, telephones were always in short supply, and waiting lists long. After the great boom started in 1986, the unmet demand soared. In 1988, the politics took a shift towards democracy. Cabinet ministers with a business background promoted the idea of subcontracting telecom services to private suppliers, both as a way to meet the demand and as a way to generate some corruption revenue (Sakkarin 2000).

In 1990 both TOT and CAT granted concessions to private companies to provide mobile phone services. The most promising of the two was the CAT concessionaire, Ucom. The firm had been founded in 1956 by the Bencharongkul family, and had a long history of supplying communication equipment to the Thai armed forces and government agencies. It had expanded into a mini-conglomerate with investments in insurance, finance, and hotels. The patriarch, Boonchai, had wide contacts in government agencies.

By contrast, the TOT concessionaire was a firm recently founded by a novice to the sector. Thaksin Shinawatra hailed from a Chinese immigrant family that over the previous two generations had distributed its progeny between commerce and the uniformed services. Thaksin initially entered the police, but then tacked across to business. He launched a series of failed ventures that racked up a mounting pile of debt. Then he hit a formula. He wrote a plan to provide computers to his own police department, bid against his own spec, and won the contract from a board which included his father-in-law. The contract gave him only moderate profits, but vital learning. He expanded the computer agency to other government departments, and acquired the important skills in dealing with government officials. An aide later explained that he "has no problem dealing with senior officials because he knows how to show respect" (Sorakon 1993: 83–4). Thaksin confessed that the normal kickback on government projects was 10 percent but could drop to 3–5 percent on large deals (Pasuk and Baker 2004: 42–3).

CAT and TOT each had a vested interest in helping their particular concessionaire gain a larger share of the market and hence a larger revenue to be shared with the agency. A year earlier, Thaksin had won a paging concession from TOT. To ensure an advantage, TOT levied a charge from the rival CAT concessionaire for each access to the landline telephone network that it controlled, while sparing Thaksin from an equivalent charge. With the mobile phone concession, TOT built in the same advantage. This little kink practically ensured Thaksin's market advantage, and he defended it tenaciously for the following seventeen years.

The mobile phone service debuted as the economy hit double-digit rates of growth. With the large pent-up demand for phone services, both operators could charge a very high premium. With his cost advantage granted by TOT, Thaksin had funds to invest in high-intensity marketing, and cornered over half of the market. The profits of his Advanced Info Services (AIS) rose steeply to reach 3 billion baht in 1995. Thaksin launched four of his companies onto the stock market between 1991 and 1994 while the index was being wafted to unreal heights by the great boom. The market value of AIS rose from 16 billion in 1992, to 105 billion three years later. In five years Thaksin had, from nothing, become one of the richest entrepreneurs in the country.

Ucom also made a comfortable profit on this expanding and highly profitable business, and also listed on the exchange in 1993. The two telecom agencies and other government bodies auctioned several other concessions for services in telecoms and related areas. Thaksin won several, including those for a cable TV service and a satellite. Several other firms climbed on the bandwagon. TelecomAsia of the CP group and TT&T/Jasmine under the Thai Farmers Bank group became major suppliers of landlines, while Shinawatra and Ucom specialized in wireless operations. Together these formed the Big Four of the telecoms sector.

As the technology was constantly changing, and the market evolving, there were constant reasons for these firms to negotiate with government agencies to modify and extend their concession arrangements. These negotiations were also occasions for firms to attempt to create some advantage over their competitors. Thaksin had constantly to defend his in-built cost advantage against Ucom. As parliamentary politics became better established after 1992, the telecom firms became closely involved with politicians and political parties. CP TelecomAsia was close to the New Aspiration Party; Ucom aligned with the Democrat Party; and TT&T/Jasmine floated between the Democrat, Chat Thai, and Chat Phathana parties. Thaksin took a step further and entered politics personally, serving three brief stints as a minister under the Palang Tham Party over 1994 to 1996.

There was no intrinsic reason why the telecom sector should have generated such enormous wealth. All the technology came from elsewhere. The Thai firms were mainly acting as importers and marketers. The high level of profits was created by the novelty of the technology, by the rapid rate of economic growth, and especially by the creation of a duopoly under political tutelage. The involvement of all the firms in politics was totally rational on commercial grounds.

DEFENDING SUPER-PROFITS

In the later 1990s, however, this cozy market situation seemed set to change for three reasons: competition, liberalization, and regulation.

The large profits of AIS and Ucom excited the envy of their rivals, prompting many new projects to invade the mobile phone market. With their privatization now mooted (though, as it turned out, distant), CAT and TOT were interested in launching new mobile phone ventures in which they would be shareholders and managers rather than just licensers. In mid-1996, CAT entered into a venture with Loxley and

IEC to start a new mobile phone network. The partners in the venture, which came to be called WCS, bought some unused bandwidth owned by Ucom, contracted Canada's Northern Telecom to construct the network, and were preparing to launch it in mid-1997. CAT made another deal with the Samart group and Telekom Malaysia, which also bought unused bandwidth from Ucom and launched its network under the name DPC in May 1998. CAT made a third deal with a subsidiary of the Hong Kong company, Hutchison, which launched another network under the name Tawan Mobile in April 1998. In addition, TOT licensed its fixed-line supplier TT&T to plan the launch of a PCT network in 2000, and the communications minister in the Chuan government, Suthep Thaugsuban, directed TOT to launch another network known as ACT Mobile with the specific purpose of undercutting the inflated price levels of the duopoly. The contracts were signed in the dying days of the Chuan government in January 2001.

The high pricing of mobile phone services, and the high profits of the telecoms companies, also came in for criticism from consumers, economists, and technocrats. Over 1996 to 1998, plans emerged to overhaul the sector. CAT and TOT would be privatized as service providers competing with the telecom firms. A new regulatory body, the National Telecommunications Commission, would take charge of issuing licenses and making rules. The old concessions would be abolished, making way for an open market with fair competition. These plans were enshrined in the 1997 Constitution, a 1997–2006 National Telecommunications Masterplan, and commitments to the WTO.

The mobile phone duopoly was threatened with regulation, market liberalization, and five new competitors. But the prospects of such a dramatic transformation were erased by the 1997 crisis and the subsequent rise of Thaksin to the premiership.

THE MOBILE PHONE SECTOR IN THE 1997 CRISIS

As in other sectors, the crisis created both winners and losers. All the telecom companies had raised funds through the stock market, but like other corporations, they had also been seduced by low-interest foreign loans and were badly hit by the baht fall. The level of the debt and the ability to cope with restructuring varied greatly across the Big Four.

Dealing with debt

The Shinawatra group fared much better than its rivals. According to the group's own figures, its exchange losses in 1997 were only 1.1 billion baht compared to 26.1 billion baht for CP TelecomAsia, 11.1 billion for Jasmine, and 17.7 billion for Ucom (Athiwat 2003: 159). The total liabilities of AIS (and other Shinawatra companies) increased in 1997, but much less than those of the others in the Big Four (see table 4.1). Thaksin claimed that the Shinawatra companies suffered less than competitors because they had hedged their foreign loans six months before the baht was floated (Athiwat 2003: 159). But some have suspected that other reasons came into play. It was rumored that Shin Corp had repaid or converted large amounts of US dollar debt shortly before the flotation of the baht on July 2, 1997.[1] At the time of the float, Thanong Bidaya was finance minister.[2] Thanong had arranged Thaksin's first loans from Thai Military Bank in 1986, and joined Shinawatra as financial overseer for 1989–1992, before returning to the bank as president. He was Thaksin's foremost financial adviser and had been a director of Shinawatra companies. He was part of the decision made to float the baht, a week before it was announced. After ceasing to be finance minister, he served on Shin Corp's internal audit committee (Wingfield 2002: 281).

The Shinawatra group was hardly damaged. AIS's profit dipped in 1998, but rebounded strongly in 1999. Armed with such figures, the group was able to raise funds from the stock market by offering new

1. See *Thaicoon*, January 1999. The exact amount of the Group's US dollar liabilities still remains confidential. Also unknown are the reasons why Shin Corp repaid its foreign debts before the due date, and why the company decided to cover some of its foreign debts against currency exchange risk, while other companies did not.

2. Thanong became finance minister on November 25, 1996, and resigned on October 24, 1997, just twelve days before the Chavalit government fell on 6 November.

TABLE 4.1 Total liabilities of telecom companies (million baht), 1996–2002

	1996	1997	1998	1999	2000	2001	2002
AIS	10,974	23,373	26,751	18,339	31,045	72,517	74,844
TelecomAsia	62,304	94,415	85,346	86,020	79,757	81,577	86,049
TT&T	30,595	48,453	44,878	44,339	47,726	34,357	32,681
Jasmine	12,784	19,871	20,440	21,743	19,382	17,009	16,129
Ucom	48,740	101,787	79,455	68,178	15,070	13,108	13,130

SOURCE: *Company reports*

shares at a time when few other companies could hope to succeed in such a tactic. In 2000, AIS had the resources to invest in a new GSM network, wireless application protocol, and international roaming service, improving its technical advantage over rival networks. The Shinawatra group also had the funds to buy up damaged rivals (see below), as well as investing in a range of new business ventures including television, retail, property, leasing, and publishing (FEER, 28 December 2000).

The others of the Big Four fared much worse. The TT&T/Jasmine group staggered from the government debt restructuring machinery into the bankruptcy court, repeatedly drawing up restructuring plans it was unable to complete (*The Nation*, 4 February 2004). Its strategic partner, Nippon Telegraph and Telephone, declined the offer to increase its stake. In effect, the Thai Farmers Bank group concentrated on saving its core banking business, and allowed its telecom interests to remain hamstrung by massive debt, and to fade from the front rank of the telecoms sector.

Ucom fared little better under the highest liabilities among the telecom groups (102 billion baht, see table 4.1). In early 1998, the group hired Union Bank of Switzerland and Lehman Brothers to help restructuring in which the stake of the Bencharongkul family was reduced from 45 percent to 26 percent, while a British investment bank, Somers, became the largest shareholder with a 46 percent stake. In contrast to AIS, Ucom's mobile phone business made a loss from 1998 to 2000. Ucom had no funds to invest in expansion, and lost about 10 percent share of the market to AIS over these years.

CP TelecomAsia was also forced into a restructuring and recapitalization under which its biggest creditor, Kreditanstalt fur Wiederaufbau
Bank, acquired a 24 percent stake. But the CP group had deep pockets and had nominated telecoms as a core business, so the damage was
contained to some extent.

Competition contained

Much of the threatened new competition in the mobile phone market
disappeared in this carnage. The WCS venture between CAT, Loxley, and
Northern Telecom floundered. TT&T's plan to launch a PCT network
on a TOT concession was abandoned. Other potential competition was
thwarted by the combined financial and political power of the Shinawatra group once Thaksin became prime minister in 2001.

After the 2001 election but before formally taking office, Thaksin
announced he would review Suthep's price-busting ACT Mobile network. On his first day at work, the incoming minister of communications ordered the review, and six weeks later the project was suspended
(*Bangkok Post*, 15 and 22 February 2001, 30 March 2001). In May 2001,
the Council of State ruled that the project was improper as it had not
been licensed by the National Telecommunications Commission (which
had not yet come into existence; see below). CAT and TOT protested
that they needed such a project for their revenues beyond privatization,
and threatened to continue defiantly. For the next year-and-a-half the
project floated in limbo while the government repeatedly revised the
privatization plans for the two agencies. Eventually it was launched in
November 2002 but without a technical advantage or marketing budget to give any hope of success. By June 2004, it had lost 900 million
baht (*Bangkok Post*, 14 June 2004).

The Hutchison project, Tawan Mobile, was launched despite the
crisis but had no money for marketing. A year later it had only four
thousand of its projected fifty thousand subscribers. To provide some
market advantage, Hutchison invested in a CDMA network. Shortly
after taking office, Thaksin twice rubbished its CDMA technology in
public. He said CDMA was failing worldwide, and the project should

be scrapped (*The Nation*, 20 November 2001). Like ACT Mobile, the project then floundered while CAT's future was repeatedly recast. It was eventually revived in January 2002 as a 65:35 joint venture between Hutchison and CAT, and was launched in February 2003. The real reasons for rubbishing the technology then became apparent. The network provided faster downloads which made it attractive for fashionable novelties like transmitting photos. By the end of 2003, Hutch had gained half-a-million users and was rated the second most preferred network (*The Nation*, 28 February 2003, 15 January 2004). However, the venture was constantly dogged by the uncertainty over CAT's privatization, and failed to grow its market share beyond that point. It remained a very minor player.

The Samart/Telekom Malaysia DPC project was launched despite the crisis but was unable to offer any serious competition. In February 2000, Shin Corp bought out Samart's share, then forced out the Malaysian partner in July 2001 (*Bangkok Post*, 7 February 2000, 19 July 2001). Subsequently the network was merged with AIS, and DPC continued life as a Shinawatra subsidiary.

In sum, of the five new networks promised on the eve of the crisis, two had collapsed, two had been launched into limbo, and one had been bought over by AIS. The duopoly was still in place, and AIS had become even more the stronger of the two.

Arrival of the multinationals

But the crisis had also introduced a new factor. Several international firms had sought ways to buy into the Thai market while the local firms were desperate for financial assistance. Singtel, the Singapore government telephone monopoly, contributed to the AIS recapitalization in 1999 and eventually held a 19.6 percent stake.[3] With Shin providing such aggressive and effective leadership, Singtel was content to be a sleeping partner. Two other cases were different.

---

3. In February 1999, AIS sold 360 million baht of new shares to Singtel, which then had an 18.63 percent stake.

Telenor, the government-majority-owned Norwegian mobile phone company, began prospecting for an entry opportunity soon after the crisis struck. It initially approached AIS, but without success. Between May and August 2000, Telenor bought a 24.8 percent share in Ucom and provided the funds for a recapitalization of its mobile phone subsidiary in which it became a 30 percent shareholder. The branding of the mobile phone business was switched from Ucom to DTAC, and a Norwegian marketing executive soon emerged as the driving force and public face of a more aggressive company.

The third foreign entrant was the French company Orange. In early 2000, TelecomAsia bought the WCS project, a CAT concession that had been on the cusp of its launch program when the 1997 crisis struck. The project had never been launched, and was sold first to Ucom and then to CP TelecomAsia. Six months later, TelecomAsia announced that Orange would take a 49 percent share and provide the technology, while British Verizon would also become a partner. The service was launched in late 2001 with high expectations that Orange's success in other markets would make a difference.

In April 2002, DTAC and Orange launched an attack against AIS's dominant position on two fronts. First, they sparked a price war that undercut the massive profit rate in the segment. Second, they refused to pay the discriminatory interconnection charge that gave AIS its key market advantage.

AIS parried this attack. The price war severely reduced the cost of owning a mobile and greatly expanded the market from 7 million users in 2001 to three times that number two years later (see figure 4.1). AIS followed the pricing downwards, while investing in saturation marketing, which secured the majority of the new subscribers. From 2001 onwards, AIS was one of the nation's largest spenders on advertising. Its full marketing budget was 1 billion baht in 2001, and 2 billion in 2002 (*The Nation*, 4 January 2001, 11 February 2002).

From his position as prime minister, Thaksin personally reprimanded the two firms for daring to challenge his family firm's discriminatory market advantage. TOT held firm to their boss, and threatened to block calls from DTAC or Orange to a TOT landline if they persisted in withholding the connection charge. Faced with this possibility, the two rivals crumbled and agreed to pay the charge.

AIS increased its share of the market from around half in 2000 to over two-thirds three years later. Its profits also spurted from 3.8 billion baht in 2001 to 18.5 billion in 2003 (see figs. 4.1, 4.2). DTAC held onto a one-fifth share and adequate profitability, but after a massive marketing investment TA Orange had gained only 1.9 million subscribers, far short of the scale needed for profitability. The foreign partners

FIGURE 4.1 Growth and shares of mobile phone market, 2000–2006

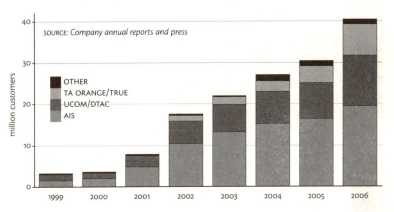

FIGURE 4.2 Net profits of mobile phone firms, 2001–2006

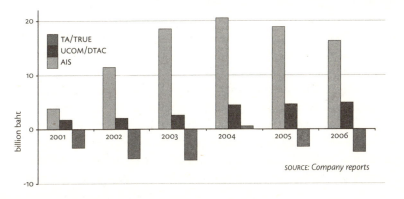

lost their stomach for such an uneven battle. Verizon sold its 10 percent stake in July 2003, and Orange sold 39 percent of its 49 percent stake in March 2004, probably incurring a huge loss (*Bangkok Post*, 18 July 2003; *The Nation*, 10 March 2004). The venture in effect reverted to CP ownership, and was re-branded as True in 2004.

Defeating regulation

The process for selecting members of the new regulatory National Telecommunications Commission, established under the 1997 Constitution, began in 2000. Under the enabling act, a selection committee was formed of senior figures from various categories of public life. This committee prepared a short list sent to the Senate for final selection. On paper this procedure sounded smooth. But the airwaves over which this commission would hold sway were very valuable. Those currently enjoying that value were unlikely to let the procedure take its own course. They formed a pressure group and plotted to pack the selection committee and the nominee list with military efficiency. But this strategy failed on one key point: the enabling act forbade any conflict of interest between the selection committee and its nominees. Besides, the plotters seemed so used to this sort of rigging that selection committee meetings were attended and even chaired by military men who were not committee members. A rejected candidate challenged that the procedure had been flawed; the Senate voted by an overwhelming majority that it had been "illegal, non-transparent, and unfair;" and the Administrative Court invalidated the whole process (*Bangkok Post*, 5 May 2001, 7 and 8 February 2002). A round of appeals added further delay. The government showed no interest in speeding things up.

In 2001, a Telecommunications Business Act was passed to provide a framework for the commission when it finally appeared. During the bill's passage through Parliament, the Senate inserted a clause limiting foreign shareholding in any new telecom venture to 25 percent. While Shin's AIS conformed to this rule, DTAC and Orange did not. While the limit applied only to new licenses, it would create problems when the existing concessions were transformed into licenses. Despite a howl of protest, the legislation was passed in this form. The government subsequently agreed informally to alter the limit to 49 percent, but made no move to pass the legislative amendment (*Bangkok Post*, 15 May 2002).

Since they had become part of the concession market and slated for privatization, CAT and TOT had lost any semblance of providing regulation. Besides, in time-honored fashion, the ruling party had recomposed the boards of these agencies with chosen nominees (*The Nation*, 24 July 2002). Moreover, while their privatization had been mooted since 1995, the timing was constantly delayed and the methods repeatedly revised. The Thaksin government instructed the two agencies first to privatize separately, then to merge, then to separate again, then to shelter under a common holding company, and then again to go their own ways. As these agencies constantly drafted and redrafted their business plans, they fell further and further behind their future rivals.

The effective source of regulation, thus, was the minister in charge. The disgruntled executive of a rival company remarked: "We've been playing in a football game where some of the players have referees' whistles in their pockets" (*The Nation*, 19 December 2003).

The immediate problem for regulation was unwinding the concession structure. Plans for the sector's future envisaged CAT and TOT evolving into companies that competed with the other players who currently were their concessionaires. That would mean breaking the licenser-licensee relationships, and finding ways to share revenues for services that criss-crossed between networks. Given the chaotic way the original concessions were evolved, this was not a simple matter.

The first task was to decide how to deal with the revenue-sharing payments that the concessionaires made to CAT or TOT. The concessions mostly had ten to fifteen years still to run, and the concessionaires had to share 15 to 25 percent of revenues. The Chuan government (1997–2001) had commissioned the TDRI think tank to consider the problem. TDRI took the principle that any new arrangement should not change future expectations of revenue flows. It thus summed the estimated revenue each concessionaire would have to pay from 2006 to the end of the concession period, converted it into a capital sum, and proposed the concessionaires pay this amount by 2006 and then be free of all obligations. The telecom companies howled this proposal down. The heavy upfront payment, they claimed, would make them financially vulnerable in face of incoming foreign competition. After the advent of the Thaksin government, another study was commissioned from a university institute which passed the task onto a subsidiary run by a cousin of Thaksin's justice minister (*The Nation*, 16 January 2002). This IPI study proposed the concessionaires pay until 2006 and then simply stop, free of any future obligation. The difference between the TDRI and IPI proposals was between 70 and 290 billion baht by different estimates (*The Nation*, 16 and 20 January 2002). Critics said the concessionaires would profit under the IPI plan at public expense. Thaksin retorted: "I'm convinced no private companies are so thick-faced as to seek billions of baht extra profit.... Nobody would think of doing something so shameless" (*Nayok Thaksin lem 2*, 98).

There the matter deadlocked. In the bureaucratic reform of October 2002, the telecom sector was moved under the new Ministry of Information and Communication Technology headed by Surapong Suebwonglee. He first wondered whether each concessionaire should negotiate its own settlement with its licenser. Then he proposed replacing the revenue sharing with an excise tax. Reputedly, this idea had originated inside Shin Corporation (*Bangkok Post*, 24 May 2003). Certainly Shin's head, Boonklee Plangsiri, welcomed it enthusiastically as the "best way out for everybody" (*The Nation*, 26 December 2002). Certainly also the shareholders of the concession firms liked it. The sector's shares jumped at the initial announcement, and jumped again when the proposal was finally implemented (*The Nation*, 26 December 2002, 22 and 29 January 2003). Thaksin justified the proposal on nationalist grounds. After privatization, CAT and TOT could be acquired in some part by foreign investors, and then the revenue-sharing payments "will have to be shared with [foreign] investors. In such a scenario, the government will not get the full amount, so it's better to have private telecom operators directly pay the Excise Department" (*The Nation*, 26 January 2003). The proposal was enacted through an executive decree, a procedure normally used only in an emergency.

In fact this arrangement was only a very partial solution to the problem. Concessionaires now paid 10 percent of their revenues as excise to the Finance Ministry, and continued to pay the balance of the original revenue sharing to CAT/TOT. What would happen at privatization was still moot. The excise tax level could easily be adjusted downwards, though Thaksin accused critics who raised this point of "overreacting" (*The Nation*, 26 January 2003). Effectively, this arrangement killed off the TDRI proposal, while leaving the government with lots of flexibility. It also helped to block future competition. Any new entrant would have to pay the same excise tax while competing against existing players whose networks were already established and substantially amortized (Somkiat 2003). Stock investors certainly appreciated this point: from this moment, the trajectory of AIS's share price separated from that of the market as a whole and climbed upwards.

COMPETITION, REGULATION, DIVESTMENT

By 2004, some seven or eight years after expectations that the mobile phone market would become more open, competitive, liberal, and regulated, it remained a triopoly dominated by a strong market leader, with even weaker regulation, and new barriers against entry. The concession structure remained in place, and profits were highly dependent on politics.

Over the next two years, however, many things changed.

First, the pace of market growth slowed once prices leveled out. After adding 14 million users in two years, the market grew more modestly. Then, with the advent of fierce competition in 2002, margins were shaved and revenue growth stalled. In mid-2005, the firms competed so hard to attract custom through discounting usage prices that networks overloaded and many calls were lost. Revenues were forfeit, and the stock prices of the three firms all fell. AIS came out to call for a marketing truce (*The Nation*, 17 June 2005). True made substantial losses every year except 2004 when it turned a narrow profit. AIS's profit peaked in 2004 (see table 4.2, figure 4.2). There were powerful signs that the golden days were over.

Second, the mobile firms faced a difficult decision over future investment. A new, "third generation" (3G) of technology was becoming available. All the firms queued up to apply for licenses to offer this new technology, to avoid allowing their competitors to gain an advantage. But the jostling showed more apprehension than urgency. The new technology would require high investment.[4] It would take time (possibly three years) to develop the content and peripherals before any payback could be expected. If 3G were to be implemented in a phase when profit margins were narrowing, the affect on the bottom line would be severe.

Third, after a long delay a new regulatory framework began to take shape. After the first attempt to form a National Telecommunications Commission was aborted in early 2003, a new process began later in the year. The nominees included several of the same names as before, as well as new names that attracted the same criticism of being too closely tied to vested interests in the sector. Despite objections, the Senate finally selected the seven members of the commission in August 2004.[5] The commission started work tentatively, spending most of its first year establishing its own internal systems and policies, and addressing immediate short-term issues. In mid-2005, it began to lay out guidelines and policies for proper regulation of the sector. These included a code of fair competition under which the commission could prevent "dominant players," defined as a company with at least a 35 percent market share, from unfair competitive practices such as loss-leader pricing and over-exploitation of consumers (*The Nation*, 2 and 20 December

---

4. AIS estimated the cost at 8.2 billion baht (*The Nation*, 22 October 2005). An independent analyst predicted something nearer 100 billion (*The Nation*, 6 January 2006).

5. Post and Telegraph Department director-general Rianchai Reowilaisuk; Chulalongkorn University electrical-engineering professor Prasit Prapinmongkolkarn; Public Relations Department director-general Suchat Suchatvejapoom; King Mongkut's Institute of Technology North Bangkok Professor Artorn Chantawimol; Chulalongkorn University law professor Sutham Yoonaitham; former Post and Telegraph Department director-general Sethaporn Kusripituk; and retired army general Chuchart Promprasit, who became chairman. Direk Charoenpon, former deputy director of the TOT and former deputy minister at the Transport and Communications Ministry in the Chavalit government, who was criticized as a stooge for Thai Rak Thai, was dropped at the final round of selection, along with Koson Petchsuwan, a former board member of TelecomAsia (*The Nation*, 23 and 25 August 2004).

2005). It also began the process of replacing the concession structure with new licenses and a fairer fee structure.

In sum, regulation and competition had begun to change the market.

TABLE 4.2 Revenue and profit of mobile phone firms, 2001–2006

		2001	2002	2003	2004	2005	2006
Revenue	AIS	59.2	80.2	89.5	96.4	92.5	91.4
	DTAC	22.1	25.2	30.3	37.5	43.1	48.5
	TA/True	20.6	25.8	27.9	32.3	44.1	51.9
	TOTAL	101.9	131.2	147.7	166.3	179.7	191.8
Net profit	AIS	3.9	11.4	18.5	20.5	18.9	16.3
	DTAC	1.8	2.1	2.6	4.5	4.6	4.9
	TA/True	−3.4	−5.4	−5.7	0.6	−3.3	−4.2
	TOTAL	2.3	8.1	15.4	25.6	20.3	17.0

SOURCE: Company reports

The sell-off

In October 2005, a Telenor affiliate paid 9.2 billion baht to raise its stake in Ucom from 40 to 65 percent, and thereby increased its stake in the DTAC subsidiary to 48.5 percent. A year earlier, the Bencharongkul family had rejected a similar takeover bid, but now succumbed to the fact that Ucom could not match the additional investment that Telenor was prepared to make to install the 3G technology and sustain the necessary level of marketing. Boonchai Bencharongkul said he had withdrawn because the mobile phone business was becoming exclusively reserved for global players. The chief executive of Shin Corp commented, "The transaction [of Telenor] signals that the local telecom operators are weakening, given that they have to continue considerable investment in business expansion in this capital-intensive industry." The head of True admitted that he had also been approached by several foreign telecom operators, and that he might need go into a partnership to raise the funds for the 3G expansion (*The Nation*, 21, 22 and 25 October 2005).

Within weeks, rumors spread that the Shin telecom interests would be sold to China Telecom. The head of the National Telecommunications Commission noted that several overseas firms were prospecting to enter the Thai market. Thaksin's wife retorted, "We have no plan at all to do that. No way. We have never even thought about it" (*The Nation*, 3 and 5 November 2005). Within days, however, it emerged that the true buyer was Singapore, either in the form of Singtel, or the government investment arm, Temasek Holdings. On January 23, 2006, the family's 49 percent share in Shin Corp was sold to Temasek Holdings for 73.3 billion baht. Subsequently Temasek made an offer to buy other outstanding AIS shares. Rumors spread that True would also sell a stake to Telekom Malaysia, but for the moment that did not emerge.

In the space of four months, controlling interests in the two firms with 84 percent of the mobile phone market had been sold for a total sum of 83 billion baht.

The fall-out

The political power that had once been used to protect AIS from competition and regulation was now used to facilitate the sale and maximize the return. Only days before the transaction, the Telecommunications Law was modified to extend foreign ownership from 25 to 49 percent. The Revenue Department reversed an old tax ruling, and reimbursed a taxpayer, to remove a precedent that would have made the capital gains tax-liable (Ma Nok and Dek Nok Krop 2006).

The fact that such a massive sale incurred virtually no tax unleashed a wave of emotional disgust that led eventually to Thaksin being deposed by coup on September 19, 2006, and to his family being later served with demands for back-taxation on this and other deals. One sub-theme in the criticism of Thaksin which exploded over the sale showed disappointment that he had risen to power promising to promote the interests of domestic capital and protect it from foreign competition, but had ended up being responsible for the single largest sell-out to foreign owners in the country's history. Critics argued that Shin Corp had risen by being entrusted with "national assets" such as its satellite concession and mobile networks. Some in the armed forces claimed that the transfer of these assets jeopardized national security, as the new foreign owners would be able to eavesdrop on military communications and personal conversations.

This disappointment also fuelled anger at the nominee structure, which enabled the new owners of Shin (and DTAC) to have majority ownership, exceeding the 49 percent stake permitted by the letter of the law. Under the Shin deal, Shin Corp was nominally owned by holding companies that were defined as "Thai." But, as the Temasek website boasted for a time until the information was swiftly removed, its true ownership in AIS was around 93 percent, disguised by a pyramid of holding companies and a web of nominees (Ma Nok and Dek Nok Krop 2006). Thousands of other companies had used this method to work around the law, and the method had long been considered conventional. Anger against the symbolic significance of the Shin sale prompted the post-coup government to initiate a reform in the law that placed these many thousands of corporate arrangements in jeopardy.

CONCLUSION

Behind the local excitement generated over the Shin Corp sale a much larger, global process was at work.

On a world scale, the mobile phone industry was becoming a mature industry in which rents due to novelty or market distortion were being erased by open competition, and in which survival required sufficient scale to fund continuous heavy investments in technology. That scale implied a cross-country reach. Singtel and Telenor were very similar in one key respect. Both were government-invested companies based in small countries (Norway 4.7 million, Singapore 4.5 million). Both had made strategic decisions early on that they had to expand across the world in order to survive. The Thai firms had dabbled with projects in neighboring countries during the 1990s, but had virtually completely withdrawn under the impact of the 1997 crisis. Telenor and Singtel could view the 3G investments in a broader and longer-term framework than the Thai firms.

For Thaksin, there was an additional reason to make the sale. Over its fifteen years under Shin management, AIS generated 97 billion baht of net profit (74 billion under Thaksin's premiership, see figure 4.3). The value of his family firms had been greatly boosted by his ability to defend their market shares and increase their profits by using political power. Investors admired this ability so much they added a "Thaksin premium" to the price of shares in the Shin group. In late 2005, a flurry of foreign buying in the Thai stock market had given the Shin stocks an especially large boost. He could sell at the top.

FIGURE 4.3 AIS net profit, 1992–2006

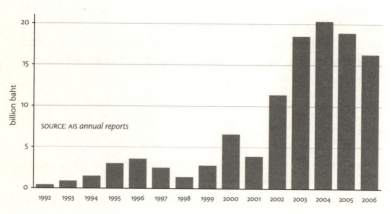

The value of this political underpinning could be seen by what happened once it was removed—by the sale of the company, and then by the removal of Thaksin from a position in which he might be able to provide after-sales service. Over the following year, AIS's share of the mobile market dropped from around two-thirds to a half. In the first quarter of 2007, the firm's profits dropped by 31 percent as a result of the heavy marketing investment required to prevent an even larger fall in market share (*Bangkok Post*, 14 and 19 May 2007). The stock price of AIS fell from 104 at the time of the sale to 90 in May 2007. In the same quarter, Shin Corp registered a net loss for the first time since the crisis. The price of Shin Corp shares dropped from 49.25 at the time of sale to 28.75 in May 2007, a reduction of its market value by around US$1.7 billion. That was the measure of the "Thaksin premium."

Possibly also there was an added political dimension behind Thaksin's decision to sell AIS. He had shown that, as long as he was prime minister, he could defend the family's mobile phone business against competition and against regulation. For that very reason, AIS had increased its market share, and multiplied its profits since 2001. At the same time, the Shin group had become more involved in telecoms on a regional basis through its satellite business, with deals in India, Burma, China, Vietnam, and Australia. Thaksin had blatantly used his position as prime minister to help this regional expansion (Ukrist 2005). Perhaps if Thaksin had felt confident in his political position, Shin could have taken a positive view of the globalizing trend in the mobile phone business, and become a bigger player in the region, possibly in partnership with Singtel or any of the other suitors. Perhaps, then, the decision to sell the family business was based on a realization that he was losing his grip on power, and hence likely to lose his power premium if he delayed the sale. Besides, were he to be deposed, it would be better to have cash that could be used quickly and flexibly in his own defense, rather than other assets, which would be easier to seize.

The mobile phone industry had developed from infant status to a mature sector within two decades. In Thailand, this history fell into three stages. In the first, the combination of novelty, cartelization under government concessions, and a background of economic boom created economic rents on an unprecedented scale for a small handful of entrepreneurs. In the second stage, political involvement by a few key players prevented the market from moving towards more open competition and better regulation, ensuring that the increased profits generated as the market moved from niche to mass were even more concentrated in a few hands. In the third stage, following the entry of world-class firms in the aftermath of the 1997 crisis, the market became subject to the trend of concentration on a global scale, forcing the Thai firms to withdraw.

The lesson of this history for Thai capital is clear. In a new market segment, huge rents can be made with the assistance of political influence, but the time span will be short term.

SURVIVORS

5

KHUN CHAROEN AND THE LIQUOR INDUSTRY
THROUGH CRISIS AND LIBERALIZATION

Nualnoi Treerat

WHILE the crisis left many fortunes in ruins, it made Charoen Siri-vadhanabhakdi spectacularly rich. He defied not only the economic trend of the crisis, but also the enthusiasm for market liberalization. He made his money from a monopolistic liquor concession that was slated for liberalization in 1999.

In 2005, Charoen was the richest man in Thailand on the Forbes list of the world's billionaires. He ranked 194th[1] with assets of 120 billion baht (around US$3 billion), almost half as much again as the 88 billion baht of his nearest Thai competitor, Chalieo Yoovidhya, owner of the Kratingdaeng or Red Bull drink brand. On the eve of the crisis in the mid-1990s, Charoen figured among the richest businessmen, but not head-and-shoulders above the rest. A decade earlier in the mid-1980s, he did not appear in any survey of Thailand's leading businessmen.

His rise in the throes of crisis and liberalization has many causes. Because many people drowned the sorrows of the crisis in alcohol, the liquor industry that he dominated scarcely faltered through the crisis and its aftermath. While 1997 was primarily a crisis of credit, Charoen did business very much in the old-fashioned way with cash. But most of all, the liquor industry was based on government concessions, and profits depended on special skills to manipulate the monopoly rents created by such concessions, not on the skills required for market competition. The fact that Charoen, the maestro at gathering such monopoly rents, became the richest man in the country over the crisis and its aftermath, that he did so despite liberalization of the industry he

---

1. In 2006 he had slipped to 214th with a slight rise in his estimated worth to US$3.2 billion.

dominated, and that he captured another near-monopoly to boot, tells a lot about the realities of the era.

THE LIQUOR INDUSTRY

Across Southeast Asia, there is a long tradition of making and drinking liquor made by fermenting and distilling rice. The base materials are cheap, the process simple, and the resulting production cost very low. In Thailand, this white or clear liquor was joined by a brown type made from sugarcane waste and known as "Thai whisky," although technically it is rum.[2] In the late nineteenth century, government raised a major part of its revenue by auctioning tax farms for liquor, opium, and gambling. The tax farmer won the monopoly right to run the business in a defined area. In the early twentieth century, government stopped the opium and gambling taxes on moral grounds, but continued liquor on essentially the same tax-farming system. These concessions became one of the great engines of primitive accumulation for Thailand's early capitalism. The list of families that have held these concessions reads like a who's who of the *chao sua* (merchant lords) of the post–Second World War era: Tejapaibul, Lamsam, Sarasin, Iamsakunrat, Phatraprasit, Chaiyawan, Tantiwiwatphan, Srifuengfung, Ratanarak, Kanchanalak, Laochinda, Mahakhun, Narongdej, Pisanbut, Assarat, Wichitbunyaset, Chiwasiri, and even Sophonphanich.

In 1933, the Bhirom Bhakdi family persuaded the government to grant a concession to build a first brewery for beer. The product form was not traditional in this market, and the ratio of price to alcohol very high compared to local liquor, so beer remained a niche market confined to the urban areas. As with liquor, government preferred to manage this sector like a concession, and the Bhirom Bhakdi successfully dissuaded the government from making any significant change

---

2. Known as *sura khao*, white liquor, and *sura phasom chiangchun*, blended liquor. Mekong is a variant of the latter, technically termed, *sura prung phiset*, specially distilled, but different mainly by being branded where the white and brown liquors are commodities.

in their virtual monopoly for six decades. The Singha beer produced by their Boonrawd Brewery had no serious rival.

The art of making money from such concession arrangements was the art of maximizing rents. Government auctioned the concession for a fixed amount. The profit was the sales revenue less the production costs, bid amount, and other costs involved in maintaining the concession. The production costs were small and insignificant. The profit depended on the other two—the dues paid to government, and the cost of ensuring those dues were modest. Most important of all was to manage competition over the bidding so the auction did not raise the price too high. This required skills to share the rents with rivals who were too powerful to ignore, the abilities to intimidate rivals who were not too powerful, and the judgment to discriminate between the two. These negotiations were deeply bound up with the relative strengths and mutual relations among the business dynasties in any area, and sometimes could explode into open warfare.

THE CONCESSION WARS

The liquor business underwent a major change after the Sarit military regime took power in 1957. This change was part of a major increase in the power of the central state as a result of military power, US funding, and new infrastructure. Sarit reorganized the liquor concessions in order to increase the revenues of the central government, but also in order to bring local godfathers into a direct relationship with the state, and thus facilitate control.

At the time, there were thirty-three distilleries all over the country. The largest was Bangyikhan on the outskirts of the capital. It produced white liquor, brown liquor, and the "special" brown liquor that had become the favorite tipple of urban men under the branding as Mekong Thai Whisky. The distillery had come under the Ministry of Industry during the era of economic nationalism in the 1930s, and like many such enterprises made regular losses because of bad management and systematic fleecing. The other thirty-two distillers were smaller units in provincial areas producing white and brown liquor. In the rearrangement of 1959, concessions were auctioned for each of the thirty-two small distilleries to produce and sell white and brown liquor as a monopoly within a defined area (usually one to three provinces). The concession for Bangyikhan carried a similar monopoly on white and brown liquor for the Greater Bangkok area, plus the right to sell Mekong all over the country. Sarit's Cabinet did not hold an auction for Bangyikhan, but presented a concession for ten years (1960 through 1969) to Sahat Mahakhun in return for a fixed annual charge of 41 million baht.

Sahat Mahakhun had migrated from China as a teenager in the 1910s. He owned a large construction firm, and was a close friend of Sarit.[3] It was an outright crony deal. But Sahat had neither enough funds nor expertise so he brought in three other business families as partners. The most important was Uthane Tejapaibul, head of one of the biggest business dynasties of the postwar era. His family had held the concession for a distillery in Nakhon Sawan, and had experience in running liquor sales networks in several provinces. Uthane was also the founder and major shareholder of Sri Nakhon Bank. Uthane became chairman and managing director of the new Sura Mahakhun company, and brought in his younger brother Sumet to run production and procurement. The second partner was Bancha Lamsam, founder and major shareholder of the Thai Farmers Bank, the third largest bank, and center of an expanding network of companies in finance and agricultural trading. Bancha supervised finance and general administration. The third partner, Thaloeng Laochinda, was a close friend of Sahat who had expertise in liquor trading and who took charge of sales.

The company was a gold mine, largely because the annual concession fee was fixed, while the sales of Mekong boomed as the urban economy grew under US patronage and development planning. The profits not only accrued to the shareholders, but were widely redistributed among the military cliques in power. As the moment for renegotiating the con-

---

3. Sarit had a stake in several of Sahat's companies, including his bank. Sahat was head of the Taechieu Association and of the Chinese Business Association for many years. He died in 1961 (Cremation volume, 22 November 1961).

cession approached in 1969, however, the shareholders began to squabble. The Laochinda and Mahakhun families felt they had benefited less than the Lamsam and Tejapaibul. Their strategy to gain greater control was to promise a greater share of the cake to the ruling generals who would decide on the next concession. They formed a new company (Boworawong) and gave shareholdings to the five most important generals in government since Sarit's death in 1963, including the prime minister, Thanom Kittikachorn.[4] They diluted the holdings of the Tejapaibul and Lamsam by forcing them to sell shares, while raising the registered capital and making their new company a partner. In 1969, the Thanom government renewed Sura Mahakhun's concession for another ten years, while raising the annual charge to 51 million baht and an additional 25 percent share of the profit. Under the new arrangement, the Mahakhun and Laochinda families took a larger role in the management, pushing the Lamsam and Tejapaibul into the background.

Enter Charoen

In such concession businesses, there are two main strategies for extracting rents. The first is to minimize payments to government. This is achieved by managing competition over the auction of the concession, but also by reducing or evading demand for other taxes and dues. The second is by leaching profits away from the enterprise before they appear in the books. Shareholders and executives find ways to make individual profits through leveraging the advantages of their position. For example those in the sales chain may demand kickbacks from agents, and those in procurement may demand kickbacks from suppliers.

Procurement is especially important in both strategies. A simple way to reduce the enterprise's book profit and hence tax liability is to inflate production costs by over-pricing inputs through the collusion of suppliers, who also transfer the margin into an individually extracted rent through kickbacks. In Sura Mahakhun, the practice

---

4. The others were Praphat Charusathian, Prasoet Ruchirawong, Thawee Chulasap, and Krit Srivara.

was so prevalent that suppliers gave kickbacks as a matter of custom without being asked. In the internal revolution of Sura Mahakhun in 1969, Thaloeng Laochinda displaced Uthane Tejapaibul's brother Sumet from control of procurement.

Kiakmeng Sae Sow or Charoen Sisombunanon was born on May 2, 1944, as one of the eleven children of a Chinese immigrant who rose from being a street vendor of fried mussels to restaurant-owner in Bangkok's old Chinatown. Charoen completed four years of primary education before leaving school to help out in the family business, and make money by petty trading. He caught the eye of Kungju Sae Jiw, a comprador of Bangkok Bank, and supplier of bottle caps to the Bangyikhan distillery, and ended up marrying his daughter. Through the procurement business, Charoen got to know Thaloeng, and by the mid-1970s was working as Thaloeng's aide and fixer.[5]

When the liquor concession came up for renewal in 1979, the politics had changed. The generals no longer had independent control, but were gradually having to share power with elected politicians under the formula dubbed semi-democracy. The industry minister in charge of the bidding was Kasem Chatikavanij, a prominent technocrat. He made the process more transparent and more competitive. He asked bidders to propose an annual fee that had to be at least 30 percent of the value of retail sales. On top they would have to pay tax levied on each bottle, renovate the old distillery, and invest from 700 to 900 million baht in a new one. In return, the concession would last fifteen years up to 1995.

The two factions inside Sura Mahakhun, now headed by Sumet Tejapaibul and Thaloeng Laochinda respectively, girded for battle. Sumet had the advantage of being close to General Kriangsak Chamanan, the prime minister. He also collected several major upcountry liquor agents[6] as his partners in a new company, Sura Mahachon.

---

5. The exact history is difficult to disentangle from legend. Some sources say he went to sell supplies to Bangyikhan, was adopted by Thaloeng, and given a job in the distillery. Others say that a relative who was head of the Taechiu association got him a job through Sahat Mahakhun. Others say he worked with Kungju Sae Jiw, his future father-in-law.

6. Especially Wisan Phatraprasit from the lower north, Wanit Chaiyawan from the south, Komen Tanthiwiwatthanaphan from the northeast.

Thaloeng made an alliance with two businessmen in the Social Action Party, which had been formed during the brief liberal era in 1973–1976 and would become one of three major parties of the semi-democracy era. Pong Sarasin came from a very prominent family in business and politics. His father had been prime minister under Sarit's patronage, and their business interests included the Coca Cola franchise. Prasit Narongdej belonged to a branch of the Phornprapha family, leaders in the automotive industry. Thaloeng bought the Thara distillery that Pong and Prasit owned in Nakhon Chaisi. By the time for the decision on the liquor concession, Prasit Narongdej had become minister of industry.

Seven companies bid, of which three were serious, including Sumet and Thaloeng. Rumors flew around about massive bribes being paid. Even though the matter was technically in the charge of a committee under the Ministry of Industry, the prime minister, Kriangsak, insisted on personally overseeing the opening of the bid envelopes. Sumet won by offering 45.67 percent of the sales revenue, as against 36 percent by Thaloeng.

But that did not end the war. Thaloeng's camp judged that Sumet had paid too much for the concession and hence would be vulnerable. Also, the new era of semi-democracy created a little space for competition within the concession framework. The Thaloeng camp bought another distillery located in Ayutthaya with a concession to sell in eight provinces stretching northwards from Bangkok.[7] Together with the Thara distillery in Nakhon Chaisi they had a ring stretching at least half way round the capital. Thaloeng lured his friend Chun Kanchanalak, who had been the blender credited with crafting the success of Mekong, to leave Bangyikhan and create a clone of Mekong called Saengsom (Moonlight), and a clone of Bangyikhan's second brand Kwangthong (Golden Deer), called Hongthong (Golden Swan). Their clone products had lower taxes than the Bangyikhan products and hence could be sold for less. By working a little magic inside the Excise Department, the Thaloeng camp was able to sell these products

---

7. Ayutthaya, Singburi, Angthong, Lopburi, Saraburi, Nakhon Ratchasima, Uthai Thai, and Chainat.

outside their designated concession area in direct competition with the Bangyikhan products, even in Bangkok.[8] The phrase, "A Golden Swan can fly anywhere" entered the culture as a proverb that captured the ability of money to overcome regulation.

Even though the Thaloeng camp's strategy was technically illegal, it was helped by several government actions. Over 1980–1982, a sibling of Pong Sarasin[9] became director of excise, and issued several orders that seemed to prejudice Mekong and favor its rival. In 1984 a new minister of industry, Ob Vasuratna, insisted that Bangyikhan should raise the prices of Mekong and Kwangthong, prompting a senior official in the ministry to object that this would clearly benefit the rival products of the Thaloeng camp. Somehow the objecting official was placed under an investigation and subsequently removed, while the prices were raised. In 1985, the Ministry of Finance adjusted the tax rates in a way that further increased the price disadvantage for the Bangyikhan products. All these maneuvers indicated how the manipulation of rents in this concession business had become a more complex and competitive matter involving senior bureaucrats and politicians. The battle also became a focus of public interest, with the press and rumor mill regularly passing on stories about vast sums of money changing hands to persuade bureaucrats and politicians to use their influence.

Around this time, leadership changed in the Thaloeng camp. After losing the concession battle and while preparing to fight the undercover war of competition, Thaloeng cut Charoen and blender Chun in as partners in a new company titled with their initials, TCC. Soon after, the ageing Thaloeng sold some of his shares to Charoen (who was backed by his father-in-law), and withdrew from the frontline of management. Chun also took a back seat (and died in 1987). Charoen was now in charge.

---

8. Before the bidding for the provincial distilleries, the Cabinet inserted a clause banning the winners from making such clone products to compete with Mekong, but somehow the Excise Department did not seem to acknowledge this rule.

9. Banthit Bunyapana, like Pong, was a son of former prime minister, Pote Sarasin. He rose to be the permanent secretary of the Ministry of Finance, and died while holding that position in 1993.

The birth of the cartel

In 1983, the Excise Department set up a bid for all thirty-two of the provincial distilleries under its control. The distilleries were grouped into
twelve zones, each of which was auctioned separately. The successful
bidder in each zone would have to pay the first year's tax immediately
after winning the bid, build a new and larger distillery to replace the
old plant, and surrender the distillery back to the government at the
end of a fifteen-year concession period. Charoen set up a new company,
Surathip, in partnership with Pong Sarasin to bid for all twelve zones.
Their bid won by a mile, but the bankers judged they had bid too high
and every bank except Bangkok Bank refused to advance loans.[10] On
the day for signing the contract, Surathip could offer the advance payment for only five zones. The Excise Department held a second round
of bidding for the other seven zones, but did not disqualify Surathip,
which won all seven at a reduced offer. Six other banks then agreed to
stump up the necessary loans.

Surathip now had the right to sell their products throughout the
country except in Bangyikhan's concession area of Bangkok. The two
groups were now toe-to-toe. The marketing war that had begun in 1980
ratcheted up to another level of intensity.

But competitive ambitions had outrun financial logic. Surathip
needed to pay the advance for all twelve zones, invest in new plant, and
buy up the existing stock of the prior concessionaires. A devaluation in
1984 increased the cost of imported machinery needed for the revamp.
The total expenses, earlier estimated at 2.8 billion baht, ballooned to 4
billion. Charoen needed more loans, taking the number of his creditor banks up to fourteen. In 1984–1985, the Thai economy slumped,
and liquor consumption shrank. Both Charoen and Bangyikhan were
making losses. By 1986, Charoen owed 14 billion baht to the banks,
and 6 billion in unpaid dues to the government. To all intents and
purposes, Charoen and TCC were bankrupt.

---

10. Charoen had a special relationship through his old patron, and through the Iamsakunrat,
another old liquor family which became allied to the TCC camp in the 1980s.

This crisis made Charoen into the undisputed king of Thailand's liquor business. Neither the banks nor the Excise Department could afford for him to fail. The loans that he had received from virtually every Thai commercial bank were project loans without collateral, guaranteed by personal guarantees. Charoen had been able to secure these loans through his special affinal relationship with Bangkok Bank, his close association with Pong Sarasin, and his contacts with other political figures, often through the network of old liquor families who had diversified into many sectors of business. Were Charoen to fail, the shock waves would shake institutions and fell families. Nor could the government allow Charoen to fail because the liquor concession contributed 4 percent of government revenue, and because tax collection was especially sensitive at a time the economic slump had dumped the budget into a huge deficit.[11] The Bangyikhan camp had also been hammered by the marketing war, and offered similar risks for both government and the financial industry. To forestall disaster, the bankers' association formally requested the prime minister to step in.

The result was that the government and the banks brokered a truce on March 7, 1986, under which the two sides merged into a single national monopoly, generally known as "the cartel." Sura Maharat, the company running Bangyikhan, was restructured as the mother company owning both Bangyikhan and the provincial distilleries. The two sides each held 49 percent of Sura Maharat, with the balance of 2 percent controlled by the creditor banks.

As part of the deal, the banks agreed to provide additional loans, and restructure the terms to reduce the annual burden, while the government agreed to receive a fixed annual amount for the remainder of the concession period (until 1999). This amount was calculated according to the *minimum* output level envisaged in the original concession agreement.[12] With competition under control, the financial burden lifted, and the liability to government capped, the cartel was set to make a

---

11. The treasury deficit in 1985 was 39 billion baht, equivalent to 25 percent of government revenue (Bank of Thailand, *Quarterly Bulletin*, table 25).

12. A fixed tax payment of 2,611 million baht, plus 5,394 million baht as a share of profits.

fortune. Although the period from 1980 to 1986 was very messy, it ultimately resolved the problem of competition, and produced the perfect
result for the extraction of rents—a near 100 percent monopoly blessed
with sweetheart deals from government and finance.

Charoen was soon in control. Sumet Tejapaibul complained that
the merger had come about because others had not played by the rules,
and he would not work with Charoen. He sold his shares to his elder
brother, Uthane, withdrew from the cartel, and set up his own company to import liquor. Uthane had many other businesses, and took no
prominent role in management. Three other old liquor families[13] allied
to the Tejapaibul had holdings in Sura Maharat as part of Bangyikhan's
portion, but these were minorities. Charoen had by far the largest single shareholding at 49 percent. The cartel was effectively his. In 1987
he changed his surname to Sirivadhanabhakdi.

Almost as the merger deal was made, the Thai economy took off
on a ten-year boom, and liquor sales rose along with GDP. As the tax
liability was capped under the merger agreement, all increases in sales
revenue went straight to the bottom line. Charoen concentrated on
streamlining the production and distribution systems to eliminate
costs. He continued to drag his feet on tax and loan repayments. He
made his dealers provide the working capital by forcing them to pay
one month in advance for their supplies. Uthane had introduced this
system in 1960 when his company was short of cash to meet its dues
to government, but Charoen was able to make it systematic because
his full monopoly situation gave him great power over the trade. Over
the period 1987 to 1996, the annual sales value was estimated in the
region of 50 billion baht, or roughly 137 million baht a day.

Charoen's strategy was to share enough of the benefits of the monopoly with others who might threaten this highly profitable arrangement.
His main targets were potential business competitors, bureaucrats, and
politicians.

He found ways to accommodate the old liquor families that would
discourage any thoughts of mounting competition. Besides Sura Maharat

---

13. Phatraprasit, Chaiyawan, and Tanthiwiwatthanaphan

itself, the cartel consisted of over a hundred companies connected by a dense lattice of cross holdings. Charoen set up a holding company with the name Saengsom in which he had a 70 percent stake. This company then took a 25 percent stake in various other companies set up to manage production, distribution, marketing and other activities, while other business partners including members of the old liquor families held the other shares in these companies and thereby benefited from the cartel.

Among bureaucrats, Charoen became famous for his generosity. By the mid-1990s, his "public relations budget" was said to be 2 billion baht a year. In departments of critical importance to his business, his generosity was said to extend from top to bottom. His Golden Swan was ready to fly to any government department party and celebration. He especially cultivated long-term relationships with senior officials from the industry and finance ministries. The boards of his companies filled up with former high officials and a sprinkling of generals. He was known as someone who "must always repay the kindness shown to him" (*bunkhun tong thot thaen*).

Major politicians were subject to similar attentions. An oft-told story may be apocryphal but sums up his technique. When a new prime minister was appointed, Charoen made enquiries and discovered he loved shark's fin soup. Every day, Charoen had the soup prepared in his house, and drove over to the prime minister's residence to deliver the soup. The premier refused to see him, but Charoen waited outside. He came back the next day, and for several days after that, with the same result. One day, Charoen decided to while away his time by finding a hose and watering the flowers. At that point, the minister caved in.

A financial journalist later wrote,

> Each day at his office, many people wait to see him. Interestingly these are not ordinary folks but all senior figures from the highest levels of society.... He is ready to help anyone who asks, no matter whether the person is an ordinary man or a politician at a very high level. He seems conscious that any money he distributes will be returned to him either in this life or the next. (*Dok Bia*, 3–9 December 2001)

Even with such generosity, the monopoly delivered Charoen an enormous profit which he began to diversify into other businesses. He bought into property, banks, insurance, and hotels. Often these deals were part of maintaining business relationships. In 1987 he bought the prestigious Senanivet property development from the banker Chuan Ratanarak, reputedly as a favor in return for support that Charoen had received from the Ratanarak family's Bank of Ayudhya during the concession wars. Similarly, he bought into Siam City Bank when the bank was in trouble. In 1994, he acquired the Imperial Hotel group when it was threatened with bankruptcy. When the project to build a tollway to Bangkok's airport got into financial trouble, Charoen made an offer. By 1996, the value of Charoen's investment portfolio was estimated at 47.2 billion baht (Wilai 2002).

LIBERALIZATION

In 1992, the Anand Panyarachun government proposed to liberalize the liquor industry. After discussion, it was decided to delay liberalization of distilled liquor until the end of the current concessions in 1999, but to proceed with liberalization of beer brewing immediately in 1993.

In 1998, government announced the outline of the liquor liberalization. First, all the government distilleries would be auctioned off, including land, buildings, and equipment. Second, any company could thereafter apply to the Excise Department for a license to produce liquor but would need to conform to certain prescribed laws and standards.

Charoen plotted to retain the monopoly intact despite liberalization. His first priority was to retain control of all the government distilleries. He used several strategies to block or deter potential competitors. He made a bid for the only two glass companies making liquor bottles, but was turned away. He bought interests in several sugar factories, which were the source of one key ingredient. He accumulated a massive stock of liquor on which tax was already paid (see the inflated production in the late 1990s, especially 1999, in figure 5.1). As Charoen himself had faced in 1985, any new owner would have to buy up this stock, which significantly raised the upfront cost. If any new entrant appeared as a competitor, Charoen could release this stock into the market at a discount, delaying the time the competitor could hope to make a profit, and so again raising the upfront cost. At some distilleries, Charoen was said to have bought the surrounding land and access, as a further deterrent. Besides, any new player would have to confront Charoen's grip over both the sales channels and suppliers

FIGURE 5.1 Liquor production, 1987–2006

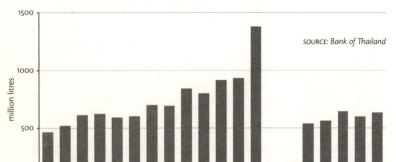

SOURCE: Bank of Thailand

Charoen used the accumulated stock in another, creative way. He issued bonds using the stock as collateral and thereby raised 18 billion baht. He thus used the stock to deter competitors while financing his own bid. Later he petitioned the Finance Ministry on grounds that the product had deteriorated in storage, and secured a rebate of one billion baht in tax. A Senate committee ruled that the official who had certified the product deterioration had failed to perform his duty and caused government to lose a billion baht, but the case was somehow smothered.

Finally Charoen repeated the 1985 strategy of bidding preemptively high. At the auction in September 1999, Charoen and his allies secured all the twelve government distilleries, including Bangyikhan and the Mekong brand. The only competitor was the Boonrawd brewing empire, and Charoen's offer for Bangyikhan was over three times as high as theirs.[14]

Subsequently Charoen preserved the monopoly largely intact by managing competition. He continued the old tactic of persuading potential competitors to become part of the monopoly and profit from it, rather than attacking the golden goose. Chalieo Yoovidhya proposed to leverage the franchise of his hugely popular Kratingdaeng (Red Bull) sports drink by extending the brand name into liquor. Charoen set out to persuade Chalieo to change his mind, and ended up buying up Chalieo's liquor company.

One of the old liquor families, Chiwasiri, owned United Winery, which principally made wine and wine cooler but also had a small independent distillery. After liberalization, Paisan Chiwasiri applied for a license, and announced plans to produce liquor under the name Paithong at a price that would undercut Charoen's products. On the eve of Paithong's launch, Charoen dropped his prices to two-thirds of its usual level, while simultaneously extending an invitation to Paisan to join his group. Eventually Charoen took over United Winery, and Paisan became a shareholder in Charoen's holding company.

Thus after liberalization, no single major competitor entered the market. However, a movement appeared among small producers. Many villages still made illegal moonshine on a small scale. Local activists argued that government should support this activity as part of its promotion of local manufactures (OTOP). They also claimed that the regulations and standards set as part of the 1999 liberalization had been deliberately made too stringent in order to favor large-scale producers. For example, the regulations specified minimum size for factory, output, and capital.[15] In 2003, government relaxed these regulations for small

---

14. Charoen's company bid 8,252 million baht for Bangyikhan, and Boonrawd 2,544 million. The total bid for eleven other distilleries was 7,210 million baht.

15. A new factory was required to produce liquor of at least 28 degree, with minimum production capacity of 90,000 litre a day, be situated in an area not less than 350 rai (140 acres), and be at least two kilometers away from waterways. These regulations were stricter than those applied in 1985. By 2004 only one company, Sinsurang, had applied for a license to produce white liquor on a plot of 400 rai with more than a billion baht investment.

local producers. Subsequently over six thousand small producers and community enterprises registered to enter the market. Most, however, were either unable to make a profit, or unable to meet the regulations, and soon fell by the wayside. The remainder took an estimated 10 percent of the white liquor market, leaving Charoen with 90 percent.

BEER: LEVERAGING ONE MONOPOLY INTO ANOTHER

While successfully defending his own effective monopoly in the local distilled liquor market despite liberalization, Charoen attacked the beer market after liberalization and utterly devastated the old near-monopoly.

Since gaining a license to open a brewery in 1933, the Bhirom Bhakdi family of Boonrawd brewery preserved their monopoly almost unscathed for six decades. The Tejapaibul family secured a rival brewing license but never made a serious attempt to challenge Boonrawd and its dominant Singha Beer brand. Instead the Tejapaibul developed a niche primarily among foreign residents and tourists, leaving Boonrawd with around 90 percent of the market.[16]

Perhaps because of the lack of competition, and the absence of any re-bidding process every few years, the Boonrawd family never cultivated the sort of relationships with bureaucrats, politicians, and other businessmen that Charoen amassed. Indeed, the family was tinged by the aristocratic origins of its founder, and viewed as rather aloof from the business world.

The liberalization of the beer market came in 1993 at the height of the decade-long boom. With rising incomes and growing urbanization, beer consumption multiplied eight times over the boom decade (see figure 5.2). Several international brewers were keen to enter this market, led by Carlsberg and Heineken. They were aware of the importance of establishing the right political and business linkages. Heineken allied

---

16. The Tejapaibul brewing interests collapsed along with the whole group in the crisis. In 2002, the Kloster brand was transferred to Boonrawd. In 2004, their Thai Amarit brewery was sold to San Miguel.

FIGURE 5.2 Beer production, 1987–2006

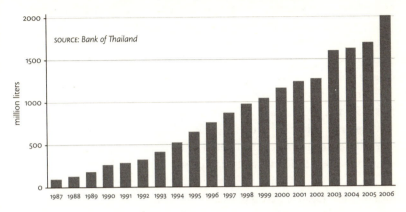

itself with the Sarasin family. The patriarch of the family, Pong Sarasin, had played an important part in the early rise of Charoen, but, more to the point, the family had an unparalleled span across business, bureaucracy, and politics. Heineken was positioned as an upmarket brand, and very successfully created a small but profitable premium market without confronting Singha.

In 1991, Carlsberg allied itself with Charoen. The international brand was launched in 1993, and positioned like Heineken as a more upmarket product than Singha. But while Heineken flourished, Carlsberg withered. The Carlsberg company had only a 10 percent stake in the joint venture, and struggled to influence its direction. Charoen and Carlsberg eventually fell into dispute, Charoen bought out the Carlsberg share in the brewery in 1999, and Carlsberg beer disappeared from the Thai market in 2003, before reappearing under a new and separate company.

Charoen's experience in the liquor business was in the mass market, not upmarket segments. In March 1995, he launched Beer Chang, made in the brewery Carlsberg had kindly built for him, and positioned not just to challenge Singha, but also to undercut it at a significant price gap. Chang was sold at 35 baht or three bottles for a hundred, whereas Singha was around 50 baht or two bottles for a hundred.

Charoen achieved this gap using a method he knew very well. The

Excise Department set different tax rates for the economy, standard, and premium segments, and assigned brands to each segment. Heineken was allocated to the premium segment, paying 20.87 baht tax per bottle; Singha to the standard segment, paying 20.32 baht; and Chang to the economy segment, paying 14.96 baht.[17] Charoen claimed that Chang was made more cheaply through innovative use of local rather than imported raw materials (mainly sticky rice in place of barley), but this would not have made a difference of more than a couple of baht. The main ingredient in his massive price advantage over Singha was an 5.36-baht difference in tax mandated by the Excise Department, with which Charoen had long worked so closely in the liquor business.

Charoen's other strategy was to leverage his influence in the distribution trade. Dealers were required to stock Beer Chang as a condition of securing Charoen's liquor products. Outside Bangkok, liquor sales were far larger than beer sales, and a good source of steady income, so few dealers could resist this bundling. Beer Chang's distribution quickly rivaled that of Singha, and then surpassed it. With its low price and the extra reach of Charoen's liquor sales network, Chang extended the reach of the beer market.

Boonrawd complained bitterly about the tax differential, and in 1999 challenged the bundling of Chang with liquor as an unfair trade practice under new anti-monopoly legislation. It was a measure of Charoen's far superior network in bureaucracy and politics that neither of Boonrawd's attempts at resistance went anywhere. Chang's sales grew rapidly as it both extended the beer market and savaged Singha's dominant share. Ironically even the 1997 crisis helped because many long-time Singha consumers were prepared to trade down to Chang when their incomes were cut. In just six years, Singha's share of the

---

17. Excise tax was nominally set at 55 percent of the "final price," meaning the estimated production cost plus the tax. In fact, this is a 122.222 percent tax on the production cost. To prevent brewers under-reporting their production cost in order to reduce their tax liability, the Excise Department created this three-tier structure based on its estimate of average production costs. When Boonrawd submitted its costing for a new variant to counter Chang, the department initially allocated it to the economy segment, but only weeks later changed its mind and put it in the standard segment. The product then had no chance of competing with Chang on price, and was soon withdrawn.

FIGURE 5.3 Beer market shares, 2002–2004

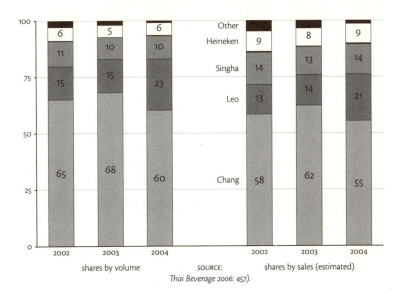

shares by volume   SOURCE: shares by sales (estimated)
Thai Beverage 2006: 457).

total beer market by volume fell from around 90 to around 31 percent, while Chang grew from nothing to 64 percent. Thereafter Boonrawd regained a little by launching its own cheaper brands including Leo, but Charoen had become a clear market leader (see figure 5.3).[18]

CHAROEN IN THE CRISIS

When the stock market had taken a downturn after the coup of 1991, Charoen had opportunistically bought stakes in some seven or eight banks, especially Bangkok Metropolitan, and in a few finance companies, especially Mahathanakit Finance. When the crisis hit in

---

18. In this chart, the data for Chang also include Archa, another economy brand from Charoen's Beer Thai Company; Leo includes Thai Beer, both economy brands from Boonrawd; Carlsberg is included in "Other."

1997, Bangkok Metropolitan Bank was seized by government, and Mahathanakit was among fifty-six finance companies which the government closed down. Charoen was reportedly greatly hurt by the collapse of his banking investments, and there was even a rumor that he attempted suicide over it (Yipphan 2002: 175). Possibly he had acquired these banking interests in preparation for financing his schemes to manage the liquor liberalization.

His main business was relatively unharmed by the crisis. Liquor sales were relatively untouched, partly because people dulled their worries with drink, but partly because many drinkers downtraded from expensive choices such as imported whisky to Charoen's lower-end offerings. Beer Chang went on growing through the crisis, aided by such downtrading. Moreover, the crisis probably helped Charoen over liberalization. In 1998, when overall consumption in the country had just plummeted by 20 percent and when the timing of recovery was still unknown, few entrepreneurs had the stomach or the resources to mount a challenge against such a strongly entrenched business empire. In the beer market, too, the crisis probably helped Charoen by delaying market entries to compete in the economy segment that Chang had begun to create. Singha offered some limp opposition, but Heineken delayed any move until 2004, by which time Chang was unassailable.

Charoen does not seem to have been saddled with the foreign-currency denominated loans that were the prime cause of loss and bankruptcy in the crisis. As already noted, Charoen raised most of his working capital from liquor dealers by requiring them to make advance payments. A great deal of the internal transactions of his empire, including salaries paid to some executives, were still made in cash, possibly to avoid records. Foreign financial institutions were reluctant to lend to Charoen because his business was not transparent. Any loans that Charoen did require were negotiated through local banks as part of the long-term relationships he cultivated in the business community.

Hence while the crisis left most businessmen desperate for new capital and desperate for cash flow, Charoen was among the very few who were not greatly damaged. He still had a steady flow of cash from the liquor cartel to the tune of several tens of millions of baht a week. This fact made Charoen very popular. A few months before the crisis, when companies had already begun to crumble, an American banker commented, "If you want to know which Thai company is in trouble, all you need to do is sleep at Charoen's gate. They're all coming to see him" (*The Nation*, 1 March 1997).

Over the crisis, Charoen acquired stakes in countless businesses, and many tracts of land. Often in the immediate term his investments were acts of friendship to save fellow businessmen from disaster. Some of such investments undoubtedly came to nothing. But many blossomed in the recovery and contributed to Charoen's transformation from rich businessmen before the crisis to the richest man in the country after it. In 1999, the *Asian Wall Street Journal* (28 January) described him as "richer than god." Many of his acquisitions are invisible, but several were in the form of property. The collapse of the property market began from 1995, before the crisis hit. In this period, Charoen bought a major stake in the prestigious North Park project of Land & Houses. By the aftermath of the crisis, Charoen's property company TCC Land was known as "one of the largest landlords in Thailand."[19] In 2004, it entered into a 60:40 joint venture with Capitaland from Singapore to develop five retail condominiums worth 17 billion baht.[20] Besides the Imperial Hotel group bought in the mid-1990s, Charoen also acquired the Plaza Athenee Hotel in New York in 1997, built a hotel of the same name in Bangkok in the early 2000s, and added a hotel at Angkor Wat managed by the Meridien chain, and another in Chiang Mai.

In the wake of the crisis and liberalization, Charoen reorganized his companies in preparation to go public. Given the clannish, closed, secretive nature of the liquor industry in the past, the proposal to go public represented a considerable change of style. Probably there were several reasons. Although Charoen had weathered liberalization by using old-fashioned methods, with a little help from the crisis itself, he knew that in the medium term he would face competition from big international players in the liquor industry. Indeed Charoen had tried tentatively to

19. *Bangkok Post Year End Economic Review 2005*, p. 40.

20. http://www.capitaland.com/en/files/CL.newsrelease.EmpirePlace.8Dec05.pdf.

make alliances with some international liquor firms on the same model as his alliances among the old Thai liquor families, and had bought distilleries in Scotland in 2001. Listing on the stock exchange would offer Charoen a means either to raise the funds to fight international competitors, or to bring them into alliance through shareholding. In addition, his family business was approaching a change in generations. Charoen's eldest son returned from a US education in 2001[21] and began training to take over the business. Finally, Charoen understood that his main brown and white liquor business would decline with economic growth, social change, health concerns, and government regulation. He was interested in the possibilities of replicating his old business model in neighboring countries where development lagged behind Thailand. He hoped to transform Chang Beer into an international brand, and concluded a sponsorship deal with Everton Football Club to gain some international exposure. A public listing offered a way to raise the funds for such expansion. He hired new executives with experience working for multinational liquor companies.

In 2003, Charoen set up Thai Beverage to act as his holding company. He and his wife Wanna held 28.7 percent of the shares directly and another 12.21 percent indirectly. Charoen made preparations for listing the company on the Stock Exchange of Thailand, but faced a hitch. Morality campaigners, led by Chamlong Srimuang, opposed the listing on grounds that liquor was socially unacceptable and outlawed by Buddhism. The protest campaign was able to raise fifty thousand people for street demonstrations outside the stock exchange building. The exchange authorities repeatedly delayed taking a final decision on the listing in order to avoid being seen taking sides. Ultimately in May 2006, Charoen listed Thai Beverage on the Singapore exchange, where it raised US$863 million, the third (second in some reports) largest IPO

---

21. Thapana had studied finance at Boston University. Charoen had two other sons. Thapanee also studied finance at MIT and Harvard, and returned to work in the finance side of the business. Phanot studied computers and returned to work on the IT side. Charoen also had two daughters. Walnapha became head of the land company.

in Singapore, but less than the billion dollars the company had been expecting.[22]

CONCLUSION

For some neoliberals in 1997, the Asian crisis was a punishment for old-fashioned crony capitalism. It is a huge irony that the Thai entrepreneur who emerged from the crisis more successfully than any other should be such a prime example of old-fashioned cronyist business.

Charoen's rise is a classic of primitive accumulation. He made his fortune from a monopoly government concession left over from the ancient era of tax farming. He developed his super-profits by investing in the politicians and bureaucrats who made the rules governing taxation. He escaped the worst of the crisis because so much of his business was still cash-based. Charoen rose to dominate the liquor business in part because of his extraordinary talent for managing and manipulating the monopoly, and in part because many of his potential rivals abandoned the business as too old-fashioned. As Thailand prospered and modernized in the great boom, selling rotgut liquor to poor people seemed very unglamorous. The new generation of the old liquor baron families transferred their interest to shopping malls, condominiums, hotels, and insurance companies. But, as one commentator noted "Charoen started with liquor and will continue to step forward with liquor, the last monopolistic business of Thailand" (Yipphan 2002: 167). Prior to the crisis, he was viewed as something of a dinosaur within a business community that prided itself on becoming modern. After the crisis, his extraordinary wealth commanded more respect. In the early 2000s, Charoen bought the mansion of an old noble family, one of the few grand compounds left in the heart of Bangkok's business district,

---

22. "Listing our stock in Singapore is to enlarge the overseas market, which is possible through alliances. It is necessary to have the same standard as the prospective alliance partners, almost all of whom are listed companies. We aim to become the biggest brewer in the ASEAN region over the next five years" (*The Nation*, 5 May 2006). Charoen still hoped to make a parallel listing on the Thai exchange.

and renovated it as a showpiece for corporate entertainment. The fried oyster vendor's son had truly arrived.

The crisis helped Charoen in many ways. He survived relatively unscathed because his core business was cash-based with little debt, was immune to the sudden fall in consumption, and was unaffected by the slump in the currency. He commanded a massive cash flow at a time when so many other entrepreneurs were prepared to sell assets cheap in order to survive. The destruction of so much capital, and the poor prospects for the economy, deterred rivals from challenging his scheme to retain the liquor monopoly despite market liberalization. He leveraged the market slump to shift beer-drinkers into the new economy segment he created with Chang.

Though both the beer and liquor markets are now liberalized, his monopolistic command of both markets is still underwritten by government rules—the regulations which deter small liquor producers, and the bizarre tax structure on beer. Since the crisis, rivals have challenged these arrangements, but without any success.

But Charoen has also used the massive increase in wealth gifted him by the crisis to modernize, aided by an increase in the management resources within the family following his children's return from their studies. He has shifted the structure of his business away from the tangle of interlocking companies that characterized the cartel, towards a more streamlined divisional pattern. He has listed the holding company and thus submitted himself to the disciplines and disclosure of the stock market. He has also begun to look beyond Thailand, including an ambitious plan to make Beer Chang a transnational brand.

BIBLIOGRAPHICAL NOTE

As almost all the sources for this chapter are in Thai, we have omitted almost all footnotes. Readers who want to follow up the sources are directed to the Thai version of this chapter. The main sources are: *Background on the Thai liquor market* from Phra Phisan Visalo 1993; Chanthra 2002. *On Charoen's background and the concession wars*, Sorakon 1994; Chirawat 2004; Yipphan 2002; Songkiat 2002; Bunchai 2003, 2005; Sonthi 2002; Athiwat 2002; Jun 1987; Sahat 1961. *On monopoly business*, Deunden et al. 2002; Niphon 2004. *On the beer industry*, Runai 1998; Nopphon 1999; Sombun 2002a. *On the liberalization of liquor*, Renu 1999; Piyawan 2001; Sombun 1998a, 1998b, 1999, 2001a, 2001b.

6

THE CROWN PROPERTY BUREAU
FROM CRISIS TO OPPORTUNITY

Porphant Ouyyanont

AMONG the business conglomerates that dominated Thailand's urban economy in the pre-crisis era, one is very distinctive. While the others are family businesses that trace their roots back to immigrants who arrived from China between the mid-nineteenth century, the Crown Property Bureau (CPB) is an institution that manages the assets of the ruling dynasty.

In many other respects, the CPB resembled the other conglomerates. One of its key investments was a bank. It had expanded into industry, joint ventures with multinationals, and speculation in stocks and property. Hence the CPB was hit by the crisis just like the other conglomerates. Its major subsidiaries had taken foreign loans and faced bankruptcy or recapitalization. Its income stream dropped precipitously for several years. But for the CPB, these problems had extra significance because its income was used for the support of the monarchy.

Ultimately, however, the CPB did not just survive the crisis but emerged far stronger than it had ever been. This chapter examines how this came about. To understand the specialness of this case, we need to go back to the origins of the CPB and how it developed through the twentieth century.

ORIGINS OF THE CROWN PROPERTY BUREAU

Under the absolute monarchy, the Privy Purse financed the expenses of the royal household, including the living expenses of the king and his family, payments to a vast array of immediate relatives, and maintenance of such assets as the royal palaces. In 1890, as part of the overall modernization of administration, these royal expenses were formally separated from the government budget, and placed under the management of a revamped Privy Purse Bureau (PPB) within the Ministry of Finance. Around 15 percent of total government revenue was assigned to the PPB (Chollada 1986: 34–41).

Over ten years earlier, government had begun a reform and centralization of the revenue machinery that resulted in a massive increase in the resources available to the central administration. The income of the PPB rose on this trend, growing from 1.5 million baht in 1892, to 6.1 million in 1902, 8.7 million in 1912, and 9.0 million in 1922 (Chollada 1986: 35, 38). The allocation to the PPB allowed a surplus after current royal expenses. This surplus was investing in acquiring assets that became the financial foundation of the modern monarchy.

Three pillars

These assets were of three main types. The first was land. Bangkok had begun to grow rapidly on the back of an expanding colonial-era trading economy and the foundation of modernized government. The PPB acquired land on which it built hundreds of shophouses along new roads cut to accommodate the capital's growing population and business activity. The PPB also acquired market sites in Bangkok and in several upcountry towns, and became the country's largest landholder. In 1902, the PPB's holdings in the capital totaled 6,458 rai (1 rai = 0.16 hectare). Some of these plots were around the royal center on Rattanakosin Island. Others were along roads that ran southwards down the east bank of the Chaophraya River. In later decades these roads became the main thoroughfares of the Chinatown area, which was the main business district for the first half of the twentieth century, and of the modern business district which developed after the Second World War. In each of these periods, the PPB was the owner of the most valuable commercial land in the kingdom (Chollada 1986: 72–192; Tasaka and Nishizawa 2003: 163–180; Anon 1971: 124–125).

The second sphere of the PPB was banking. The PPB lent from its surplus to many entrepreneurs including noble property developers and Chinese rice millers. Prince Mahit, the king's half-brother who served as minister of finance from 1890 to 1906, had the idea of founding a bank to compete with colonial banks, which "squeezed the blood from our traders" (Brown 1988: 128). This was first done semi-covertly by opening an institution called the Book Club, which did some banking business from a PPB-owned building. In 1906, the Book Club was reconstituted as a commercial bank, and shortly afterwards renamed as the Siam Commercial Bank (SCB). Of the 3,000 shares issued in 1906, 1,300 shares were taken by Prince Mahit and his Book Club partners (who were mainly Sino-Thai merchants), and 300 shares were directly owned by the Privy Purse Bureau. A further 540 shares were taken up by German and Danish banking interests. Of the management board of seven, one was a PPB appointment and three others were Prince Mahit's Book Club associates. Thus from the outset the royal family and the PPB were involved directly and substantially in the bank. The bank's credentials were further established by depositing surplus government funds, and issuing a royal charter. Even so, in 1913 the bank was almost undermined by collateral damage from a fraud in the related Sino-Siam Bank. The assets had to be written down to almost zero, and the bank reconstructed with 3 million baht of new capital of which 1.6 million came from PPB (Brown 1988: 127–44). From this point onwards, the PPB became the dominant shareholder of the bank.

The third sphere of PPB business consisted of investments in various projects related to the growing commercial economy. Many of these projects grew out of lending activity by the PPB or SCB. By 1918 the PPB owned around half of the sixty rice mills around Bangkok, many acquired by foreclosure during the downswings of the world rice trade. The PPB also invested in saw milling, tramways, importing, mining, and electricity generation, and financed construction of the first railway line to Khorat. As in the case of banking, some of these ventures were launched with the aim of reducing dependence on foreign business. This was the motive behind the establishment of the Siam Cement Company in 1913, and the launch of a shipping venture in 1918. The PPB, with the backing of the king, provided half of the cement venture's total capital of 1 million baht. The king also approved the loan of a further 220,000 baht to secure shares in the name of Chaophraya Yommarat (Pan Sukhum, 1862–1934), minister of the capital (1907–1922), and his associates, against the mortgage of the shares. In this way, nearly three-quarters of the initial capital of the Siam Cement Company came from the PPB. From the outset, therefore, a close connection was established between the Siam Cement Company and royal finances (Brown 1988: 153–5). As the capital of the company was increased (to 4 million baht by 1940), the Privy Purse maintained its interest and remained the principal shareholder. With a monopoly on domestic production of cement at a time of steady urban expansion, the Siam Cement Company became the third major pillar of the PPB beside its property and bank.

Under King Chulalongkorn, the PPB had become "a kind of proto-investment bank which exclusively served as the core organization to undertake private business on behalf of the king" (Suehiro 1989: 91). This had been possible because of the crown's flow of tax revenues and ability to assert control over land. The king was motivated by the need to maintain the sprawling royal household (he had over seventy children) and the splendor of the institution, and also by a desire to counterbalance the inroads of colonial capital.

Contraction and stagnation

This triple foundation of the PPB was laid between 1890 and the 1910s, after which there was a phase of contraction. King Vajiravudh (Rama VI) spent on nationalist projects, travel, and royal display rather than commercial investment. The PPB still received around 15 percent of the government budget (Suntharee 1990: 108), but in many years was in deficit. From 1919, the PPB accumulated debts that amounted to 15 million baht, while the king amassed personal debts that had reached 5.5 million baht by 1925–1926 (Greene 1999: 169).

Nothing was added to the property holdings, and at least 293 plots had to be sold to defray debts. No more shophouses were built. Many earlier investments were liquidated. All the rice mills passed to other owners. The shipping project, called Siamese Steamship Company, beset by unrealistic ambitions and bad management, folded in 1926 (Suehiro 1989: 55–57; Thaweesilp 1985: 141).

Moreover, by this time competition for the use of government revenue had become intense, and the large allocation to the PPB was a focus of political resentment. King Rama VII (r. 1925–1935) reduced royal expenses from 11 million baht in 1924 to 4 million baht in 1931 in an attempt to balance the budget as the economy faltered towards depression and as anti-royalist sentiments rose (Batson 1984: 92). After the 1932 revolution ended the absolute monarchy, the annual allocation to the PPB was further reduced to 440,000 baht (Chollada 1986: 38). In 1935, the civilian government set up a commission to divide the royal properties between those belonging to the king personally, those deemed state property such as the palaces, and those used to finance the institution. This latter category, which included the landed properties and the investments in SCB, Siam Cement, and other companies, was placed under the control of a new body, the Crown Property Bureau, within the Ministry of Finance (Sakuna 2000: 42, 84). The directors of the CPB were appointed by government. These properties were now managed by the state.

The CPB assets suffered some further decline. After King Rama VII abdicated in 1935 and went into self-exile in England, he transferred some overseas properties and bank accounts into his own name, but the government sued for their return. In Siam, politicians with influence in the government were found to have sold some CPB properties to themselves in suspicious circumstances (Suphot 2002: 42). Politicians tapped the funds of the CPB to help finance some state enterprises founded in the late 1930s and 1940s as part of a war economy and economic nationalism. They also used CPB funds to finance private businesses. None of these ventures proved to be permanent. The private projects were dissipated during the political infighting and economic chaos of the era immediately following the Second World War. The state enterprises fared badly as a result of the postwar economic slump and poor management. They were closed down or sold off as the government abandoned economic nationalism in the 1950s.

As a result of the consolidation in the sixth and seventh reigns, and the stagnation following the 1932 revolution, the major assets of the CPB in the postwar era were exactly the same three pillars as in the 1910s: landed property, the Siam Commercial Bank, and Siam Cement. One small addition was Deves Insurance, founded in 1947 to insure the CPB's assets.

FROM 1948 TO THE ASIAN CRISIS

In 1948, in the wake of the first of a string of royalist-military coups that reestablished the political role of the monarchy, the CPB was transferred back from the state to the crown. This allowed the assets again to be managed for their commercial worth. Over subsequent decades, the CPB became one of the conglomerates at the core of the expanding urban economy.

Crown Property Act of 1948

The Crown Property Act of 1948 reconstituted the CPB as a juristic person with considerable independence within the overall framework of the government. It also gave control back to the palace.

The minister of finance continued to serve as chairman of the CPB board, but other board members, including the director, were chosen by the king. The role of the director, who had great independence to manage the CPB's assets, became of paramount importance. While prior to 1948 there had been frequent changes of management, over the next six decades there were only three directors, which gave great continuity. The two distinguishing characteristics of these directors was that they were well educated and palace insiders. The first, Thawiwong Thawansak, was educated at Cambridge University and served as a page to King Rama VI. He was succeeded in 1970 by Phunphoem Krairirk, who had been educated at Stanford University and had earlier served as head of the royal pages and secretary of the palace. Dr Chirayu Isarangkun na Ayuthaya became director in 1987 after taking a doctorate at the Australian National University, teaching at the prestigious National Institute for Development Administration, holding the post of minister of industry during the 1980s, and serving as grand chamberlain of the royal household.

The 1948 Act had some other important characteristics. It specified that the use of the CPB's resources and income "depends totally on the royal inclination." It laid down that the CPB's landed assets could not be seized or transferred. It absolved the CPB from tax on its income (a provision introduced in 1936). It constituted the CPB as an absolutely unique entity that was difficult to define in terms of Thai law. In the course of subsequent legal processes, the Council of State had to give rulings on the nature of the CPB on four occasions. Not one of the rulings was unanimous, and the four rulings conflict. The Council agreed that the CPB was not a private company, government department, or state enterprise, and ultimately in 2001 ruled it was a "unit of the state," whatever that meant (Somsak 2006: 67–93).

Following the 1948 Act, the CPB again had the institutional ability to become a major corporate player. Thailand was entering a period of economic growth and urban expansion after decades disrupted by depression and war. Planned development and American patronage boosted the upswing. But the CPB did not resume the role that it played from the 1890s to the 1910s as a pioneer of domestic capitalism. Until 1987 the CPB remained a rather passive investor. The rents on its landed properties remained low, often fixed at prewar rates despite subsequent inflation. There was little internal reorganization of the bureau, and no steps taken to involve it more actively in the affairs of the Siam Commercial Bank or Siam Cement (Siriporn 1996: 3–4, 47–48; Suprani 1992: 194–197; Crown Property Bureau 2006a: 24–31). As Chirayu later explained (interview, 2 February 2005), the bureau deliberately preferred a more understated role:

> The fact that CPB is the investment arm for the monarchy, with a long-term and continuous reputation for reliability, induces Thai and foreign investors to seek joint ventures. Hence CPB is invited to take a minority stake as a passive partner.

As a result, the bureau's assets in this era were essentially unchanged from what they had been in the first phase of the bureau's existence, namely the three pillars of landed property, the Siam Commercial Bank, and Siam Cement. In this era of industrialization, diversification of the Thai economy, and rapid growth of Bangkok, the three existing pillars of the CPB empire all prospered in their own right.

The three pillars in the postwar era

From the 1950s to the 1980s, commercial banks were at the core of Thailand's economic expansion. They scooped up the savings of an expanding agricultural sector, and parceled them out to investors who exploited growing trade and urban growth. For twenty years, the assets of banks expanded at the extraordinary rate of 20 percent a year. SCB was a major participant in this trend. Although it grew less precipitately than three other commercial banks owned principally by Thai-Chinese families, it still multiplied its deposits almost thirty times in twenty years, and in 1981 was the fourth largest commercial bank (Suehiro 1989: 248). The CPB at this time held a 50 percent share. Along the way, SCB established several subsidiaries, mostly in related areas such as finance and insurance.

Siam Cement, in which the CPB held a share around 44 percent in the postwar era, also grew steadily on the back of urban expansion and the investments by the US military engaged in the Vietnam War (Anon. 1971: 124). Until 1955, it remained the monopoly domestic supplier of cement. Even after Siam City Cement and Jalaprathan Cement were founded in 1956 and 1968 respectively, the cement market was still very much an oligopoly with Siam Cement as the largest supplier, controlling around 70 to 75 percent of domestic sales in 1980 (Wirat 2000: 267).

Siam Cement prided itself as a pioneer of professional management in Thailand. With its steady income, strong reputation, and splendid backing, it became the first Thai company able to tap overseas financial markets from 1965 onwards (Wirat 2002: 9, 13). With these resources, Siam Cement founded or acquired many new companies, and matured into one of the first and largest of the Thai business conglomerates.

Some of this expansion was into areas related to its cement business such as ceramics and plastic construction materials. But Siam Cement also acquired several companies when they were faring badly and vulnerable to takeover. Some of the first acquisitions were in resource-based industries such as marble, rubber, and plywood. But gradually Siam Cement moved into manufacturing by acquiring Siam Kraft, the sole producer of industrial paper, Siam Navaloha, the largest iron and steel foundry, a battery company, plywood venture, and sanitaryware firm (Suprani 1992: 205–206; Suehiro 1989: 241; Pavida 2001b: 53–57; Paisal 1985). A senior banker was quoted as saying, "Siam Cement resembles a vulture capitalist group, prone to oligopoly. It doesn't monopolise; but it's clear most of its diversifications are in areas having few competitors" (Paisal 1985). In the early 1980s, after natural gas was found in the Gulf of Thailand, Siam Cement took a major strategic decision to branch into petrochemicals. As a result of this expansion, Siam Cement and its subsidiaries were reorganized as the Siam Cement Group (SCG) with Siam Cement as the holding company. By the eve of the great boom, SCG was the largest industrial conglomerate not only in Thailand, but also in Southeast Asia (Suehiro 1989: 239).

Property also contributed to CPB's growing income. At the end of the Second World War, the CPB held around a third of the land within the official city limit of Bangkok. In 2004, the total CPB land in the city was 8,835 rai, with another 31,270 rai upcountry (*The Nation*, 12 April 2004).

The growth and prosperity of Bangkok ensured that the bureau's landholdings became increasingly valuable and attractive to developers. The CPB took no active part in developing this land in a manner analogous to the construction of shophouses during the fifth reign. Instead, the CPB became a partner in projects by providing the land in return for a lease income and some share in the overall venture. In an early and typical version of such deals, the CPB became a partner in the Dusit Thani, Bangkok's first modern hotel and first high-rise building which rose on CPB land at a junction which became one the major crossroads of the modern city. Through similar ventures, by 1970 the CPB had shares in over thirty companies including the Dusit Thani Hotel, Siam Intercontinental Hotel, Thai Danu Bank, and Siam City Bank. Over the next two decades, and especially after the onset of the great boom in 1986, the number of such projects, and the value of the CPB's land invested in such partnerships, both increased. The CPB acquired shares in other hotels such as the expanded Oriental, Regent, and Royal Orchid, and in many commercial projects on prime land including the Sermmit Tower, Sinthon Tower, and the ambitious World Trade Center (Suprani 1992: 211–212).

But under the deliberately passive style of CPB management, much of the land was used in ways that did not reflect its real value. Many tracts were in old areas of the city with long-standing tenants, including several slum communities, and the CPB made no effort to redevelop such sites to reflect their rising commercial value. Other tracts were leased to government departments or state enterprises, often at peppercorn rents. Not far from the Dusit Thani Hotel, for example, a large tract of CPB land was occupied by an army cadet school. Not too far away again, another even larger plot hosted the cigarette factory of the government's Tobacco Monopoly. And a little to the north was the police headquarters, again on a large tract of CPB land, and paying rent of a thousand baht a year. The cadet school and the tobacco factory had been founded when the surrounding area was still rural, but now they were incongruous neighbors to the office blocks, megastores, and luxury condominiums of the new city. In all, around 30 percent of CPB land was leased to government departments and state enterprises (*Post Today*, 13 April 2004).

CPB in the great boom, 1986–1996

Once the great boom began after 1986, this pattern of expansion changed in speed though not in shape.

Chirayu became director of CPB in 1987, and took the first steps to modernize the institution by introducing a more commercial outlook, especially with regard to property rents and land development.

SCG invested heavily in new cement plants to keep up with the breakneck pace of urban expansion, and continued to diversify into other construction-related materials to meet larger and more sophisticated demand. The company had a 65 percent share of the Thai market in

1986, and a 48 percent share of a greatly expanded market in 1997 (FEER, 12 July 1990; Pavida 2001b: 54).[1] SCG also rapidly expanded its petrochemical interests.

In addition, many multinational companies flocked to Thailand after 1986 to take advantage of the liberalizing environment and participate in the boom in export-oriented manufacturing. Most sought local partners, sometimes because investment regulations required it, but more often simply to find a way over the bureaucratic hurdles and gain some influence on political decision-making. SCG was very attractive as a partner because of its financial stability, its reputation for competent and honest management, and its unique political connections. As a result, SCG became a partner in many joint ventures with multinationals. Among the first were the Japanese Obayashi construction company, Fuji copying, Kubota diesel, and YKK textiles. Several others were related to the group's petrochemical and construction businesses, but many others were in the sub-sectors of electrical goods and automotive parts that boomed in this era. Its subsidiaries and affiliates numbered around 120 companies.

Siam Commercial Bank was also caught up in the wave of diversification associated with the boom, foreign inflows, and the financial market liberalization that began in the later 1980s. By the eve of the 1997 crisis, SCB had seventy-seven subsidiary and associated companies in which it had shareholding of more than 10 percent. These subsidiaries ranged across asset management, real estate, industry, warehousing, mutual funds, insurance, mining, sugar, construction, entertainment, and vehicle production.

As SCB thus changed from a bank to a conglomerate, the CPB share was diluted, but remained 26 percent on the eve of the crisis. Similarly the CPB stake in SCG declined from around half but remained a dominant 35 percent.

Besides the investments through its two main subsidiaries, the CPB expanded its own shareholdings using the surplus that its boom-era income delivered after deduction of royal expenses. Most of this surplus

---

1. In 1997, Siam City Cement and TPI Polene controlled 25 and 17 percent of the market, respectively.

was reinvested through the Stock Exchange of Thailand, which became more active from the mid-1980s. The CPB targeted new sectors of expansion in Thailand's maturing economy, especially media, manufacturing, and energy. In 1996, the CPB became the major shareholder in ITV, the first television channel under private ownership, as well as ventures in press and radio. The Bureau acquired a crucial 2 percent "balancing" stake in the National Petrochemical Corporation and Thai Oil, the largest oil refinery (Paisal 1988). The bureau also joined in an electronics venture with Japan's Minebea group, the largest foreign investor on the upswing of the boom.

By the closing stages of the great boom, the CPB had become a sprawling conglomerate. According to estimates, the CPB had direct interests in around ninety companies, and indirect interests in another three hundred. Of these, forty-three were listed on the stock exchange. Of ninety-two companies in which CPB and its subsidiaries figured among the major shareholders (over 10 percent), forty-one were in manufacturing, eighteen in finance, seven in insurance, eight in hotels, six in property and construction, and twelve in media. The CPB's interests stretched across the spectrum of Thailand's modern urban enterprise.

Pre-crisis income and wealth

Because of the CPB's unique status, it is not bound by the rules of disclosure governing a state enterprise, a listed company, or even an ordinary unlisted company, which is required to report its annual profit and other details to the Department of Commercial Registration. Hence estimating the CPB's income is difficult.

Over the boom, the profits of the CPB's two main companies increased rapidly. In 1996, the Siam Cement Group had assets of 180 billion baht and profits of 6.8 billion baht, both figures having roughly doubled over the prior three years. The Siam Commercial Bank returned profits which averaged 6.4 billion baht between 1992 and 1996, and peaked at over 9 billion baht in 1996.

On the eve of the crisis, no less than 60 percent of the CPB's total income came from the dividends of SCB and SCG (Chirayu quoted in

Anon. 2003a: 38), which rose from just under 1 billion baht in 1984 to 1.7 billion baht in 1995. The next largest portion of the CPB's income came from land rents, estimated to be somewhere in the range of 300 to 600 million baht a year (Suprani 1992: 204, 218; Yipphan 2004: 68). The remainder came principally from shares in other companies, mostly held through the stock market. The largest such contributors were Dhana Siam Finance and Securities and Thai Farmers Bank, but also included Nakhon Thon, Krung Thai, and Siam City banks, Siam-Sanwa Industrial Credit, Thai Glass, Siam Rubber, and Christiani & Nielsen construction company (Suprani 1992: 204; Ellis 2003: 1–2; *Post Today*, 13 April 2004; Crown Property Bureau 2006a: 18–19; Anon. 2003b). The total dividends in 1994 are estimated at 870 million baht. Allowing for other undisclosed sources of income, the total income of the CPB immediately prior to the crisis was around 3 billion baht a year.[2]

The CPB owned one of the largest (perhaps *the* largest) corporate groups in Thailand. In 1997, *Forbes* magazine estimated its asset value at US$1.8 billion. In 1999 Michael Backman gave an alternative estimate closer to 8 billion US dollars,[3] and this range of 2 to 8 billion was quoted in *Time* magazine (Backman 1999: 249; Horn 1999).[4] In baht terms, this would be between 90 and 350 billion baht.

CPB IN THE 1997 CRISIS

When the economic crisis broke in July 1997, the Crown Property Bureau was heavily dependent on two companies. The crisis struck with such

2. This was the figure later cited by Chirayu (see *The Nation*, 4 March 2005), but he may have been underestimating a bit.

3. That is the figure that Backman headlined, but his calculation is actually US$9 billion. He estimated that the shareholdings were worth US$4.079 billion. As for property, he calculated that the holdings in central Bangkok amounted to 2.5 million square meters with a value of US$2,000 per square meter pre-crisis, giving "a long-term market value of approximately US$5 billion" (Backman 1999: 250–251).

4. Suehiro (2003) estimated the assets of the CPB (excluding land) were worth 475 billion baht in 1997, but this figure includes the full value of corporations (like SCB and SCG) in which the CPB had a controlling stake.

severity that both concerns made large losses, were unable to pay dividends, and needed to raise new capital. In turn their losses undermined the income of the Crown, and their need to recapitalize threatened to undermine the CPB's controlling share in these enterprises.

CPB's vanishing income

The Siam Commercial Bank paid no dividend for three consecutive years, and the Siam Cement Group paid none for five consecutive years (see table 6.1). Most of the other financial and industrial companies within the bureau's portfolio were also forced to suspend dividend payments. Thus, at a stroke, the bureau lost some 75 percent of its income and was forced to borrow heavily to cover royal household expenses. Chirayu later reported that this borrowing amounted to 6 or 7 billion baht. Others estimated the sum at US$200 million, equivalent to over 8 billion baht (Ellis 2003). In addition, the balance sheets of the two principal companies were wrecked. As Chirayu later reported, "every morning when we woke up and found the currency had dropped by another 1 baht, it meant the debts had risen by 2.5 billion baht" (Anon. 2003a: 41). Correcting the balance sheets would require recapitalization, raising the possibility that the CPB's dominant share might be undermined. The CPB faced the problem of how to continue financing the expenses of the monarchy, and how to survive.

Siam Commercial Bank was hit in both its income statement and balance sheet. In keeping with all banks, SCB found it impossible to recoup payments from stricken customers, especially those who were its own subsidiaries. The bank's proportion of non-performing loans rose to 34 percent in 1998, and in the following year the bank had to write off 64 billion baht of bad debts.[5] Also in keeping with other banks, SCB had borrowed money in dollars (around 20–22 percent of its liabilities) and lent it onwards in baht, resulting in huge losses after the baht

---

5. As a result, NPLs fell to 23.0 percent in 1999, 19.3 percent in 2000, 18.5 percent in 2001, 24.2 percent in 2002, 17.5 percent in 2003, 13.1 percent in 2004, 3.4 percent in 2005, and 5.0 percent in 2006 (SCB annual reports).

TABLE 6.1 Income, profit, and dividend of SCG and SCB, 1996–2006 (billion baht)

	SIAM CEMENT GROUP			SIAM COMMERCIAL BANK		
	INCOME	NET PROFIT	DIVIDEND PER SHARE*	INCOME	NET PROFIT	DIVIDEND PER SHARE*
1996	110.7	6.8	20	25.1	9.0	9.0
1997	122.6	−52.5	10	31.8	3.2	3.5
1998	105.2	19.3	−	22.7	−15.6	−
1999	101.8	−4.8	−	19.1	−35.6	−
2000	128.1	0.0	−	27.2	3.6	−
2001	120.4	7.6	1.0	24.6	0.4	−
2002	128.2	14.6	3.0	28.5	−12.5	−
2003	148.9	20.0	6.0	31.0	12.5	1.4
2004	192.4	36.5	15.0	43.0	18.5	2.0
2005	218.3	32.2	15.0	42.1	18.9	3.0
2006	258.2	29.5	15.0	52.3	13.3	2.0

SOURCE: *Siam Cement Plc annual report, various years; Siam Commercial Bank Plc annual report, various years. SCG had a ten-way share split in 2003, and the dividend from 2001 reflects this new valuation.*

* Unit in baht

depreciated. Under IMF conditions, the bank was forced to find new capital to square its balance sheet and meet more stringent standards of banking prudence.

The crisis caught the Siam Cement Group in a phase of investment expansion in both cement and petrochemicals to meet the accelerating demand of the prior boom. The group had contracted US$6.6 billion in debts, mostly in foreign currency and mostly unhedged. In addition, the crisis halved the turnover of the construction industry,[6] and hence slashed demand for the group's products.

Both companies experienced heavy losses during the crisis. SCG did not regain its 1996 level of profitability until 2001 (the positive profit

6. The contribution of the construction industry to GDP, in billion baht, from 1996 to 1999 was: 197, 144, 88, 84.

in 1998 was achieved by selling off assets to increase liquidity). SCB did not record profits as high as 1996 until the year 2003.

Heavy losses and bankruptcies were found throughout the CPB's affiliated companies, especially in the financial sector. Siam City Bank, Nakhon Thon Bank, Bangkok Metropolitan Bank, Dhana Siam, and Siam Industrial Credit all effectively went into liquidation. Other banks in the portfolio paid no dividends for five years.[7]

The crisis forced major changes in the CPB's outlook and strategies. The changes included new policies with regard to the running of Siam Cement, Siam Commercial Bank, and other companies with affiliations to the Bureau.

An early measure was the appointment of Chirayu, the director of the CPB, as chairman of both SCG and SCB. These were, of course, appointments designed to restore confidence in both companies by linking them directly with the power and prestige of the bureau. They also signified more attentive control.

Restructuring the Siam Cement Group

Siam Cement underwent a major restructuring. The group decided to concentrate on the three core businesses of cement and construction materials, petrochemicals, and paper. New talent was drafted onto the group's board, including experts in finance (Pridiyathorn Devakula, Panas Simasathien), retired technocrats with expertise in industry (Sivavong Changkasiri, Sumet Tantivejkul), and businessmen with experience and contacts in the core business of petrochemicals (Yos Euarchukiati). In 1999, SCG tried to raise capital for restructuring from the international markets, but the attempt failed miserably. Instead it raised money primarily by selling off the joint ventures contracted

---

7. For aspects of the crisis and the impacts to the CPB's affiliated company, also see Backman 1999: 249–254. On the eve of the economic crisis, Christiani & Nielsen construction company, one of the CPB's affiliated companies, experienced losses of 954 million baht in 1995 and 2,634 million baht in 1996 because of over-rapid expansion into China, Vietnam, Malaysia, and Germany. Many of company's subsidiaries were sold off, and the company had to enter the rehabilitation process of the Stock Exchange of Thailand.

with multinationals over the boom decade, especially ventures in auto-motive parts, electrical goods, iron and steel.[8] In all, SCG raised 49 billion baht by selling off stakes in 57 of its 124 subsidiaries (*Bangkok Post Mid-year Economic Review 2007*: 22). The CPB share in SCG fell from 35.6 percent in 1996 to 30 percent in 2004.

Siam Cement turned a profit in 2001, and thereafter the profit grew steeply. Initially, while the domestic construction industry was in slump, little of this profit came from its cement and construction materials busi-ness. However, the paper factory, which still had a virtual monopoly for industrial paper products, continued to show a profit through the crisis, and was the major contributor to SCG's income until 2002 (see table 6.2). Petrochemicals was the next relevant sector to recover. As a result of the fall in the value of the baht, Thailand's exports of petro-chemicals soared, multiplying over eleven times from 18 billion baht in 1996 to 206 billion baht in 2006. SCG's net profit from petrochemicals expanded rapidly from 2.6 billion baht in 2001 to 20.5 billion baht in 2004. SCG not only enjoyed these profits, but also found the resources to increase its investment in this sector, especially by taking higher stakes in existing ventures such as NPC and Aromatics. Although the group still went by the name of a cement company, petrochemicals became its largest segment both in profits and assets (see table 6.2).

In 2003, profits from cement also revived. Siam Cement was able to export increasing amounts of cement and construction materi-als, principally to China, which entered a construction boom and faced a lag before domestic production could catch up with demand.

---

8. To finance this restructuring, extra capital was raised, and the SCG board agreed to allow the foreign share to rise from 25 to 40 percent (Brooker Group 2001: 148–155, Siam Cement annual report, 2000 and 2001). Many non-core businesses were sold including Siam Magot-teaux (to Magotteaux International of Belgium), Siam Guardian Glass (to its US-based partner Guardian Industry Corp) and Tianjin Cement Thai Gypsum Products (to KNAUF GmbH of Germany). In addition SCG reduced its equity in other non-core business such as Siam-Hitachi Construction Machinery, Thai Engineering Products, Siam AT Industry, Nawaloha Industry and Siam Fuchs Lubricants in 1999 and TileCera distributing Inc (all shares of both to Florim Ceramic of Italy) in January 2000 (Brooker Group 2001: 149). Over 2000–2001, SCG issued two sets of debentures in the local market, and used the proceeds to convert virtually all its remaining foreign debt.

TABLE 6.2 Financial results of the Siam Cement
Group, 2001–2006 (billion baht)

	2001	2002	2003	2004	2005	2006
PETROCHEMICALS						
assets	54.2	57.7	67.2	75.1	78.6	105.0
net sales	38.1	38.1	50.7	75.1	86.0	122.6
net profit	2.6	2.6	7.7	20.5	16.5	17.6
CEMENT						
assets	59.6	60.6	56.3	54.8	55.9	57.8
net sales	24.1	27.2	30.5	36.6	41.6	44.1
net profit	0.8	2.0	5.3	6.5	7.9	6.7
PAPER AND PACKAGING						
assets	25.8	28.7	32.8	39.1	38.5	40.7
net sales	26.9	29.3	33.5	38.2	40.3	42.6
net profit	3.2	4.0	4.2	4.1	3.6	3.6
BUILDING PRODUCTS						
assets	16.0	15.3	15.7	18.0	20.2	20.6
net sales	13.0	16.1	18.1	20.5	22.2	22.7
net profit	0.4	1.5	2.2	2.7	3.0	1.9
DISTRIBUTION						
assets	7.8	6.8	6.6	7.7	8.5	10.6
net sales	53.3	52.1	56.5	68.5	76.9	81.5
net profit	1.0	0.9	0.2	0.5	0.6	1.0
OTHER						
assets	25.9	19.2	18.5	18.1	22.3	12.0
net sales	6.7	0.5	0.4	0.4	6.0	3.0
net profit	2.2	5.0	3.3	3.7	4.5	1.1
TOTAL						
assets	189.3	188.3	197.1	212.8	224.0	221.9
net sales	162.1	163.3	189.7	239.3	273.0	258.2
net profit	10.2	16.0	22.9	38.0	36.1	29.5

SOURCE: *Siam Cement Plc, annual report, various years*

Domestic demand for cement and other construction materials also revived with the recovery of the building industry and renewed government spending on infrastructure, especially the new Bangkok international airport.

From 2001 onwards, the group was able to expand by buying up companies in trouble, expanding capacity, and founding new ventures overseas. The paper division bought majority stakes in Phoenix Pulp and Paper in 2001 and Thai Cane Paper in 2003, besides increasing its stake in United Pulp and Paper in the Philippines and building a plant in Vietnam in 2006. The cement division bought a 20 percent stake in the largest cement producer in Bangladesh in 2001, and built a plant in Cambodia in 2005. The petrochemicals division increased its holding in many local companies, and bought stakes in companies in China, Iran, and Indonesia in 2005.

Restructuring Siam Commercial Bank

In 1999 Chumpol NaLamlieng retired as head of SCG and was inducted to advise SCB on a similarly aggressive makeover. Olarn Chaipravat, a former academic, resigned as head of SCB to take responsibility for the bank's losses. He was replaced by Jada Wattanasiritham, who had earlier been head of the central bank's research and planning division before spending two decades in SCB. The bank also hired Vichit Suraphongchai, who had earlier been a rising star and managing director in Bangkok Bank, before leaving because of internal friction and serving briefly as a government minister in 1995. McKinsey was hired as consultants to advise SCB on restructuring.

SCB was also obliged to recapitalize. Initially, it attempted to raise capital from foreign banks with which it had some association, especially the Sanwa Bank and Long-term Credit Bank of Japan, but this was only partially successful.[9]

As all the major commercial banks faced a similar problem, on August 14, 1998, the government launched a scheme in which government would

---

9. Sanwa's stake in SCB rose from 0.58 percent before the crisis to 13.12 percent in February 1999.

provide counterpart funding against additional capital raised by the banks themselves.[10] This scheme considerably raised the attraction for outside investors to take a holding in Thai banks. SCB first attempted to raise funds for this scheme on the local stock market, but failed miserably. In early 1998, the bank took a roadshow overseas, and raised US$675.7 million from the US and Europe.[11] As *Time* reported, "Of course, being known as the King's bank didn't hurt. Says Chumpol: 'I'm sure investors were confident they would get fair treatment from the royal family'" (Horn 1999). CPB put in US$202.7 million, and the government matched the total with US$878.4 million. Under this arrangement, the CPB's share was diluted from 25.3 to 11.05 percent,[12] while the Ministry of Finance became the largest shareholder with 38.8 percent.

Most other surviving banks were wary of taking advantage of this scheme because they feared it would make them subservient to government direction, and vulnerable to a state takeover. They preferred an alternative scheme that was less robust and ultimately more costly. Only the Thai Military Bank and Tisco finance company followed SCB's route. SCB was thus not only the first of the surviving Thai commercial banks to recapitalize, but also the most robust.

SCB returned to profitability in 2003 (see table 6.1). But already by 2001, as a result of the recapitalization under the August 14 scheme, SCB had enough funds to contemplate expansion. On the exit from the crisis, all the surviving commercial banks reoriented themselves to some extent towards consumer banking. From 2001, SCB was among the most aggressive in this respect, hiring expert marketing staff, and investing heavily in new systems and a redesigned branch network. From 2002 to 2006, it increased its branches from 483 to 793, and ATMs from 1083 to 3028. By 2006, retail banking contributed almost 60 percent of profits (*The Nation*, 8 May 2007). In 1996, prior to the crisis, SCB's share of the banking market, measured by assets or deposits, was around 9 percent.

---

10. Tarrin Nimmanahaeminda, the finance minister who designed this scheme, was a former president of SCB.

11. UFJ Bank took 12.6 percent. Other participants included State Street Bank and Trust, and HSBC.

12. CPB's share fluctuated between 11.05 percent in 1999 and 12.5 percent in 2003.

A decade later, that had risen to around 13 percent. In 2006, SCB captured almost a quarter of the total profit of commercial banking.

In 2000, the SCB board took a decision to divest many of its affiliated companies other than those that contributed to their core banking business.[13] At the onset of the crisis, the bank had stakes in forty-seven companies worth 4.6 billion baht. Several were closed down or sold off over 1999–2001. But by 2001, the bank felt expansive again. It revoked the policy to invest solely in financially related businesses in favor of a "focus on long-term investments in businesses with high growth potential or high dividend yields" (SCB *Annual Report* 2001: 26). SCB entered into negotiations to merge with the Thai Military Bank in order to create Thailand's largest commercial bank, but ultimately this plan came to nothing. In 2006, SCB still had stakes worth 23.4 billion baht in twenty-five subsidiary and affiliate companies.[14]

Possibly SCB was less wary than other commercial banks of the August 14 scheme because, as later reported, "there was an agreement allowing the CPB to repurchase the stock once market conditions turned favourable" (*The Nation*, 10 April 2004). In 2004, the CPB arranged to buy shares back from the Ministry of Finance at the original price plus interest, which amounted to 13 billion baht. This purchase was achieved by transferring to government a tract of 485 rai of CPB land in central Bangkok (Phaya Thai) on which several government institutions had been built (*The Nation*, 10 April 2004). This deal was unique. No other bank enjoyed similar treatment. The deal raised the CPB share in the bank back to a dominating 24.0 percent (*The Nation*, 10 April 2004; Songkiat 2004: 34–41).[15]

---

13. "In the past, it was the Bank's intention to invest in various businesses in order to facilitate the operation of the Bank and distribute risk through investment in various businesses, directly and indirectly .... The emphasis is now to focus mainly on the investment in financial businesses that are complimentary to the commercial banking business and in businesses that can support or add value to banking services." (SCB Annual Report 2000: 26)

14. These were principally its financial subsidiaries, but also included Christiani & Nielsen construction and some property companies. It was planning to reduce the number to sixteen.

15. Under laws designed to dissipate concentrated family control, the Commercial Bank Act no. 2 of 1979 placed an upper limit of 5 percent on any individual shareholding in a bank. This law did not apply to CPB.

CPB *share portfolio*

The CPB sold some of its significant holdings in non-core companies, but seemingly without the pressure of distress sales. In 2000, its stake in ITV was sold to the Shinawatra group for US$60 million. Given that ITV had consistently lost money, some commentators have judged that this was a very friendly price. The stake in Dusit Thani (10.28 percent), one of its oldest and largest non-core holdings, was also sold, but not until 2002 after the economy had recovered from the crisis.

Far-reaching changes also took place in the organizational structure and strategies of the bureau. In 2001 a new entity, the Crown Property Bureau Equity Company (Thun Laddawan, in Thai), was formed to look after the CPB's share dealings. The registered capital was 11.621 billion baht, with CPB holding 99.99 percent. CPB Equity set out to manage the share portfolio to maximize revenues and capital gains through more active dealing (Anon. 2002a: 54–57).

From 2000 to 2002, CPB Equity was mostly disposing of bad investments and booking the write-offs as losses. Its assets fell from 15.1 billion

TABLE 6.3 CPB Equity Company, 2000–2005 (million baht)

	2000	2001	2002	2003	2004	2005
Assets	15,151.6	12,932.1	9,289.7	22,376.3	24,601.9	24,036.9
Securities investment						
-Short-term	1,420.3	1,927.4	6,119.1	7,747.5	9,129.2	9,264.8
-Long-term	12,585.5	10,493.4	3,697.3	6,821.9	6,911.7	6,752.3
Dividends	72.4	164.7	210.9	249.6	560.6	1,099.5
Interest earned	1.8	1.7	2.7	25.0	190.3	192.1
Profit/loss on securities	(2,061.9)	(1,457.7)	(239.0)	3,523.6	232.7	(579.3)
Profit/loss on exchange	0.0	0.0	133.1	191.5	0.0	(276.2)
Fees and operating costs	(18.5)	(75.9)	(106.4)	(104.2)	(114.6)	(80.7)
Interest paid	(136.5)	(428.9)	0.0	(181.4)	(434.5)	(475.6)
Other	0.0	8.0	7.8	8.6	211.5	19.9
Net Profit	(2,142.7)	(1,788.2)	9.0	3,712.7	646.1	(100.2)

SOURCE: *Department of Business Development, Ministry of Commerce*

to 9.2 billion baht. But low interest rates and rising GDP growth lifted the Thai stock market slightly in 2002, and then dramatically in 2003. CPB Equity rode this trend. Between 2001 and 2005, the company switched most of its portfolio from long-term holdings into short-term trading (see table 6.3). The combined income from dividends and trading rose from a net loss in 2001 and 2002 to a gain of 3.7 billion baht in 2003. The value of its assets more than doubled to 24 billion baht. In 2005, the company again made a loss because of high interest payments, and losses on both securities dealing and exchange.

Landed property

To manage its landed properties, CPB set up another new entity called CPB Property Company (Wang Sinsap, in Thai). Again new executives were hired, headed by Yos Euarchukiati, member of a prominent banking and industrial family, and including people with experience in finance and real estate.[16]

The management of the CPB's property portfolio was also restructured and reoriented to become more commercial and aggressive. The initial aim was simply to increase the cash flow as rapidly as possible. Private tenancies were renegotiated on an individual basis, and shortly after the crisis there were rumors of long-standing commercial tenants being asked to pay greatly inflated rents. The CPB insisted that the hikes were large because earlier rentals had not kept up with the rising value of the land. The Dusit Thani Hotel objected strongly to the scale of its rent hike, and the negotiations were not settled until 2003 (*The Nation*, 24 March 2003). Soon after, CPB sold its entire stake in the Dusit Hotel company, possibly because of the soured relationship with one of its oldest business partners. Complaints were also heard

---

16. Others were Dr. Vichit Suraphongchai, MR Disnadda Diskul, Michael David Selby, Bodin Asavanich, Sirin Nimmanahaeminda, David James Mulligan, and Santi Grachangnetr. Selby had formerly been an adviser to Jefri, the "Prince Playboy" of Brunei at the time when Jefri was sacked by the Sultan (his brother) as minister of finance in February 1997. Jefri was sued for embezzling US$15.4 billion from the Brunei Investment Agency, but the charges were dropped in 2006 (*Asiaweek* 12 and 26 September 1997, 24 August 2001).

from long-standing tenants in old areas of the city such as Chinatown, who were displaced to make way for more profitable commercial ventures (Our Correspondent 2007).

Some prime tracts were transferred to more commercial and rewarding uses. For example the army cadet school was given notice to quit the prime plot of 120 rai in the city center. Part of the plot was allocated for foreign embassies, and the Japanese embassy became the first tenant. Part was leased in 2001 to a contractor at 700 million baht a year for creating a "night market" to attract tourists—a way to increase the revenue with little investment or lead-time (*The Nation*, 16 October 2001).[17] In 2007, this market was closed and the plot leased to the Central group to build a large commercial complex. Similarly, unused CPB land in older areas of Bangkok, such as the Sampheng Chinatown district, and around Ratchadamnoen Avenue, were earmarked for extensive development (*The Nation*, 5 October 2002, 11 February 2003, 11 March 2003).

Large commercial clients who had been bankrupted by the crisis and who had stopped paying rents were pursued through both legal process and private negotiation. One of the largest was the massive World Trade Center commercial complex in the city center. The Tejapaibul family, which had been the major promoter of this project, had suffered badly in the crisis. In 2002 the Central group agreed to take over the project and pay 200 million baht annually in rent and other costs to the CPB in return for a 30-year lease (*The Nation*, 24 December 2002).[18]

Many plots that were occupied by long-standing tenants or slum communities could not be managed so aggressively but still provided opportunities for revenue increase. On sixty areas which housed local markets and slum communities, CPB prepared to invest 200 million baht in improving the environment, employment opportunities, and quality of life (*The Nation*, 4 March 2005). To avoid criticism for raising

---

17. This usage of the land provoked anger among the displaced army cadets (Our Correspondent 2007).

18. SCB sued the holding company of the World Trade project for bankruptcy, but the suit failed. Subsequently the project was taken over by the Thai Asset Management Corporation, the government's debt-restructuring agency, which helped to conclude the deal with Central (*The Nation*, 26 September 2001).

rents on long-established communities, the CPB adopted a policy of subcontracting redevelopment work to intermediary companies. This policy was applied to a residential area and market area in Chinatown (*The Nation*, 12 April 2004).

For state-related institutions, which were often paying peppercorn rents, CPB set out a policy of gradually raising the annual rental up to 2 percent of the property valuation for government agencies, and 3 percent for state enterprises, by 2006 (*Bangkok Post*, 12 April 2000). As a result of these new arrangements, rents from government agencies increased from 70 million baht in 2000 to 300 million in 2002, and those from state enterprises doubled from 422 million baht in 2003 to 845 million in 2005 (*Bangkok Post*, 20 March 2003; Yipphan 2004: 68–69).

In one case, CPB was able to deploy land in an unusual way. In 2001, a plot worth 1.2 billion baht in the Dusit district was transferred to the Ministry of Finance in exchange for shares that became available under the partial privatization of the state petroleum company, PTT. Over the next three years, the value of these shares multiplied almost five times (Songkiat 2004: 39). The use of land to buy such shares through the intermediation of the Ministry of Finance seems to be unique.

In 2003, according to one report, CPB's rental income was 1.7 billion baht (Chirayu quoted in *The Nation,* 12 April 2004). According to data from the CPB, the rental income was in the range of 2.2 to 2.3 billion baht a year between 2003 and 2005. Estimates of the CPB's pre-crisis rental income were in the region of 300 to 600 million baht. Although this might be an underestimate, it seems likely that the CPB managed to hike its property income in the immediate aftermath of the crisis by anything up to five or six times in the same number of years.

Prospering after crisis

The revenue of the CPB before the crisis was 3 billion baht a year. Chirayu reported that during the crisis, this fell to 2 billion baht (*The Nation,* 4 March 2005). Possibly this figure is an average of several years. From 1997 to 2000, the income from the dividends of SCB and SCG was virtually zero, and the share portfolio would have yielded little. The regular income may initially have fallen to the estimated 300 to 600 million baht from property.

Subsequently, income was raised by increasing the property income rapidly, and selling off properties, stakes in joint ventures, and shareholdings. Then from 2001, and more convincingly from 2003, SCB and SCG returned to profitability. Indeed, strengthened by the internal restructuring, buoyed by China's extraordinary demand for cement, boosted by the recovery of the local construction industry, and helped perhaps by the collapse of some competitors, SCG returned record profits.

In 2002, the CPB reported that it was already able to pay off its 6 billion baht debt incurred at the onset of the crisis (*The Nation*, 6 August 2002). With its SCG dividend and increased property income, the CPB income in 2003 was nearly 8 billion baht—that is, up to 2.7 times its peak pre-crisis level.[19] Over the next two years, as SCG's profits continued to soar, and SCB returned to profitability, the CPB income increased again to around 9.3 billion baht in 2005, around three times its pre-crisis income (see table 6.4).

The two traditional core holdings of the bureau, the Siam Commercial Bank and the Siam Cement Group, continued to contribute the largest share of bureau income. Together they accounted for three-quarters in 2005, with the Siam Cement Group alone contributing around 65 percent.

CPB's worth

What was the total worth of the CPB after the crisis?[20] The value of the holdings in SCB, SCG, and Deves Insurance can be estimated from the

---

19. Chirayu told reporters that the CPB income in 2003 was 4 billion (*The Nation*, 12 April 2004), and in 2004 was 5 billion (*The Nation*, 4 March 2005).

20. There are several ways to estimate the value of a corporate group. Suehiro (2003), for example, sums the value of all the companies in which the group has a controlling interest. By that method, CPB's worth would include the total worth of SCG and SCB and several other companies in which it has a controlling stake. Suehiro estimated this figure as 475 billion in 1997, and 1,172 billion in 2000. Here, the method assesses the value of the assets were they to be liquidated today. Hence for the corporate holdings, the figure is the value of the shares at current value.

TABLE 6.4 The Crown Property Bureau's estimated income,
2003–2005 (million baht)

	2003	2004	2005
Siam Commercial Bank	0	140.3	1,022.2
Siam Cement Group	1,980.0	3,240.0	6,120.0
Deves Insurance	23.9	26.9	26.9
CPB Equity*	3,712.6	646.1	(101.1)
Rents and fees**	2,168.8	2,255.9	2,253.7
TOTAL	7,885.3	6,309.1	9,321.7

SOURCE: Dividend income from company reports; CPB Equity from the company filing at
Department of Business Development, Ministry of Commerce; rent and fee income from
unpublished files of the Crown Property Bureau, provided by CPB.

* This row shows the profit/loss of the CPB Equity Company, but there is no evidence to show what
sum was delivered to the CPB as dividend, hence this figure must be treated with some caution.

** These figures may underestimate the revenues from rents as there seem to be some major
omissions, and it is a little bit surprising that rents and fees were rather static between 2003 and 2005.

value of the shares. For the holdings under CPB Equity, the asset value
provides a reasonable approximation. The segment that is difficult to
assess is the landed property. While the total area owned by the CPB
in central Bangkok is known to be 8,835 rai, there is no information
available on exactly where this land is located.

However, from historical data we know that most of the holdings
were on Rattanakosin Island, in the Chinatown area around Yaowarat,
in the business district around Silom, and further west towards Wireless Road and Sukhumwit. In other words, the plots are widely spread
across many areas of central Bangkok.

Prices of land in different zones of Bangkok are published by a
private consulting firm, the Agency of Real Estate Affairs (2006). To
estimate the value of the CPB properties, twenty-two of the Agency's
total of seventy-eight zones were selected on the basis of historical and
contemporary information that there are CPB plots in these areas. As
the exact distribution of the CPB properties is not known, a simple

average was made of the 2005 price in these twenty-two zones.[21] This is more likely to underestimate than overestimate as the CPB has large tracts in high-priced zones such as Yaowarat (640,000 baht per square wa, the highest), Silom (525,000), Sathon (425,000), Wireless Road (425,000), and lower Sukhumwit (320,000). The simple average gives a figure of 279,409 per square wah or 111.8 million baht per rai. At this rate, the CPB's Bangkok land is worth a little short of one trillion baht. The CPB also owns 31,270 rai outside Bangkok, but as the whereabouts of this land is unknown, it is impossible to calculate the value.

TABLE 6.5 Estimated worth of CPB, 2005

	METHOD	BILLION BAHT
Siam Cement Group	30 percent of market capitalization of 292.8 billion	87.8
Siam Commercial Bank	25 percent of market capitalization of 94.1 billion	23.5
Deves Insurance	25 percent of market capitalization of 1.3 billion	0.3
CPB Equity	Value of assets	24.0
Land in Bangkok	8,835 rai at 111.8 million baht per rai	987.4
TOTAL		1,123.0

Summing these items gives a total worth of 1.1 trillion baht (see table 6.5). Obviously the estimation of the land value has a large margin of error, so this should be taken as a rough order of magnitude. At the end of 2005, the baht was exchanging at around 41 to the US dollar. At that rate, this worth translates as US$27.4 billion.

With these figures we can evaluate Backman's pre-crisis estimate of the CPB value of US$8 billion. At the end of 1996, the CPB shareholdings

---

21. The zones and prices per wa were: Charoen Krung Soi 1, 300,000; Charoen Krung (Thanon Tok), 155,000; Yaowarat, 640,000; Phayathai (department of livestock), 275,000; Rama I (Siam Center), 550,000; Si Phraya, 195,000; Silom, 525,000; Sathon, 425,000; Rama IV, Bon Kai, 300,000; Rama IV, Kluai Nam Thai, 170,000; Trok Chan, 145,000; Phahonyothin (beginning), 235,000; Wireless Road, 425,000; Sukhumwit 21, Asok, 275,000; Sukhumwit 63, Ekkamai, 205,000; Sukhumwit, Times Square, 320,000; Ratchawithi Suan Oi, 102,000; Pinklao Road (beginning), 160,000; Charoen Nakhon Road, Khlong San, 160,000; Rachadaphisek, Huai Khwang, 260,000; Bangsue market, 135,000; Krung Thonburi Road, 190,000.

were worth around 3 billion baht, lower than Backman's estimate of 4.09 billion.[22] Backman under-estimated the extent of the CPB's Bangkok land by a factor of almost six, and also slightly under-estimated the average price.[23] Hence his estimate of US$5 billion for the land should be corrected to around US$38 billion, giving a total CPB value of US$41 billion, again around a trillion in baht terms.

External links

CPB not only emerged from the crisis bigger and stronger, but also changed in another way that exemplifies one of the themes of this book. It became less parochial, more international.

From 2001 onwards, SCG launched a slew of projects across Asia from Iran to China. In addition, SCG became much more dependent on income from exporting, and hence much more sensitive to market forces beyond the national boundaries. SCB was also affected. It went overseas to raise capital, and had to adjust to living with around 40 to 45 percent of its shares owned by foreign entities, and with foreign-owned banks as competitors in the domestic market.

Within this general internationalization, Singapore acquired a special role, which initially had more to do with Singapore than with CPB. The Singapore government took a strategic decision to promote outside investment to overcome the limitations of the country's size. In the backwash of the 1997 crisis, Singapore capital took special interest in opportunities in Thailand. Corporations associated with the Singapore government were inclined to link up with Thai businesses that also had

22. The CPB had a 35.6 percent share of SCG which had a market capitalization of 93.6 billion at the end of 1996, and a 26.2 percent share of SCB which had a market capitalization of 65.948 billion at the end of 1996. These sum to 1.972 billion baht. Using the same capital/income ratio as for SCB and SCG, the value of the other CPB shareholdings would be 1.019 billion, giving a total of 3.012 billion.

23. Backman estimated 2.5 million square meters, equivalent to 1,563 rai, and a price of US$2,000 per square meter. The Agency for Real Estate Affairs (2007: figure A03) reckons the index value of Bangkok land was 30.3 in 1996 and 30.9 in 2005. Adjusting the estimated 2005 price by this index and by the different exchange rate gives a figure of US$2,700 per square meter.

a special link with the state. The relationship that developed with CPB was two-way. After helping to oversee the restructuring of SCG and SCB, Chumpol NaLamlieng was hired as chairman of Singtel, the Singapore government telecom company. In the other direction, Singapore's state-owned investment arm took a stake in SCB and placed a representative on the SCB board.[24] The associated property company, Capitaland, went into a joint venture with CPB under the name Primus for property development in Thailand. And when the Singapore government's Temasek Holdings took the decision to buy another government-related Thai company, the Shin Corporation of the family of prime minister Thaksin Shinawatra, the Siam Commercial Bank took the primary role in structuring the deal, as well as providing much of the finance.

CONCLUSION

The Crown Property Bureau not only survived the crisis but also emerged far stronger. Although the figures are uncertain, it is possible that CPB's annual income in the mid-2000s was around three times the peak level it had achieved prior to the crisis. Some of this extraordinary record can be attributed to excellent management and strategic restructuring. Some of it is due to the fact that CPB, like other survivors of such a shake-out, gained from the failure of its former rivals. But much can be attributed to the very special nature of the CPB.

Critical to the CPB's survival and success was its deep pockets. At the onset of the crisis it was able to borrow a sum variously reported from 6 to 8 billion baht, equivalent to between two and three times its former peak annual income. We do not know where or how this money was raised. Some was undoubtedly borrowed through SCB, indicating the value of having a bank at the core of the corporate group. Some may have been secured against its reserves of land, or even borrowed

---

24. Peter Seah Lim Huat became a director of SCB in June 1999. He headed various government-related corporations in Singapore including the Government of Singapore Investment Corporation, and Singapore Technologies.

on the special strengths of the institution. This funding was critical to the ability of the CPB to continue to meet its expenses. It was also critical to the ability of the CPB to undertake such dramatic internal restructuring. The CPB also sold off many assets to improve cash flow, but relatively few in the immediate aftermath of the crisis when pricing was at its lowest. Most other corporate groups did not have recourse to such backstopping credit. They had to sell more assets at worse prices, and were slower or less robust in facing the task of restructuring.

The second crucial asset of CPB was its vast reserve of landed property in prime areas of the city, plus the fact that much of it was previously exploited in highly suboptimal ways. By simply applying more com-mercially minded management, the CPB was able to raise its income from property by possibly as much as five to six times over the same number of years. In addition, it may also have been able to borrow cash against its extensive land bank. In some cases, such as the two instances of exchanging land with the Ministry of Finance, the CPB was able to realize quick income from its land in ways that were not available to others. As with the ability to borrow, the existence of such reserves of land, and the special ways they could be used, marked CPB apart from others facing the same crisis.

These two factors meant that the CPB suffered less damage, had more resources to fund restructuring, and emerged from the initial impact of the crisis much faster than other corporate groups. By 2001, CPB was already in a position to invest in expansion, and was able to profit from the tardier recovery of its rivals.

The organization of the CPB was restructured from top to bottom. At the top, the CPB exercised tighter control. The two pillar compa-nies were refocused on their core businesses. Non-strategic businesses were sold off, or collected under a holding company to be managed like a share portfolio.

That much was by the book, but CPB's restructuring also had some special features. The organization was able to recruit high-level talent to serve as board members and top executives. These included some of the most admired technocrats of the past generation, and several business executives in their prime. Among the latter, some had become available precisely because of the crisis. In all cases, CPB could attract such talent because it offered some intangible rewards of status. This new talent brought not only expertise but also networks of contacts stretching through the upper levels of the technocracy, and into other business groups.

There is yet another factor behind CPB's brilliant recovery which is a little more subtle. In the pre-crisis era, CPB had become a large, sprawling business empire. Its interests were not different from other corporate groups, but rather typical. Hence the policies that the post-crisis government adopted to revive business as a whole were precisely the policies that favored the CPB. Government identified the collapse of the property market as central to the collapse of thousands of firms, and hence launched policies including low interest rates, tax breaks, and special credit windows to revive this sector. As a result, the property and construction market recovered by 2001, and with that the demand for the cement and other construction materials that the Siam Cement Group produced. Government also identified banking as a critical area for sparking revival and made a policy decision to ensure that at least some of the larger banks were preserved from foreign takeover. SCB benefited most from the resulting policies, especially the August 14 scheme, perhaps because it was uniquely reassured that it would not risk government takeover. Government also intended rising exports to drag Thailand out of the crisis, and the resulting low exchange rate helped SCG to expand from rapidly rising exports of cement and petrochemicals.

BIBLIOGRAPHICAL NOTE

Dr. Chirayu Isarangkun na Ayuthaya kindly provided a written comment on an earlier Thai-language version of this research (this note is cited as Crown Property Bureau 2006b). His comment included data on the rental and dividend income of the CPB (used for table 6.4), as well as explanation of business strategy. Information on the accounts and strategies of SCB and SCG comes from their annual reports, and from data published by the Stock Exchange of Thailand.

LOCALITIES

7

CRISIS FALLOUT AND POLITICAL CONFLICT IN RAYONG

Chaiyon Praditsil and Olarn Thinbangtieo

THE impact of the crisis was fiercest in the capital and the modern business sector that was directly exposed to the forces of globalization. But the effects spread far beyond. In Thailand's provinces, most business was still very locally focused. Prominent entrepreneurs tended to be involved in agricultural processing and trade, construction contracting, and local services such as hotels and department stores. Most had not been swept up in the enthusiasm for cheap dollar-based loans. Most did not have businesses that were greatly sensitive to the value of the currency. The immediate effects of the crisis had a limited impact.

Yet all provinces felt the secondary effects with varying degrees of severity. Land prices fell. Government budgets for public works shrank. Fewer people from the capital had money to spend on tourism. Remittances from rural-urban migrants fell away. The falls in employment and consumption reverberated nationwide.

This chapter traces the impact of the crisis on entrepreneurship in one province, Rayong. Even more than at the national level, business in the provinces is inseparable from politics. Political influence is needed to make wealth and protect wealth. Wealth is needed to gain political influence. Hence in this chapter, the economic impact of the crisis is inseparable from its effect on politics and political rivalry.

By the 1990s, people in the province could easily identify three families of exceptional prominence because of their wealth and influence. They were located in different corners of the province, and had accumulated wealth in very different ways over these two phases of the local economy. But they shared one thing in common. They had all become deeply involved in local politics. Indeed, political activity was an integral part of their business. The political environment had also gone through two phases that roughly matched the economy. The first phase was characterized by informal power and influence; the second, by the coming of elective institutions.

We will first sketch the commercial base of these three camps, then examine their fortunes in the 1997 crisis, and finally trace their rising political conflict in the aftermath.

BAN PHE

Fishing and informal politics

The head of the first family is Kim Haw.[1] Her father emigrated from China between the wars and settled in Ban Phe, a small fishing village on the eastern coast. He married a local woman, and made a living from sewing and petty trading. Kim Haw, born in 1941, was the eldest of their sixteen children. She left school after four years and earned money by growing vegetables, picking fruit, and doing laundry. By her teens, she had become an accomplished food vendor, specializing in fishcakes. She progressed from there to small-scale trading in fish, first as assistant to a merchant, then on her own account in a family business under the *kongsi* system.

She acquired her own small boat by borrowing money from relatives, and helping with the construction. At first, she rowed the boat herself, but later could afford a motor. She gradually passed the responsibility for fishing to her younger siblings, and concentrated more on trading in the fish caught by her family and their neighbors. She also designed and built fish traps to increase the catch. Over two decades she gradually expanded from the initial small boat to a fleet of around a hundred larger boats which fished all over the Gulf of Thailand and in the waters of Vietnam and Indonesia. She invested the profits in building fishing

---

1. This account is based on our team's interviews with Kim Haw and others in Ban Phe, supplemented with material from Ockey 1999. All unattributed quotes are from our interviews.

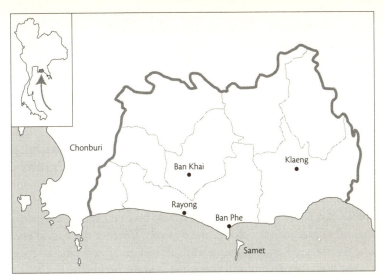

FIGURE 6.1 Map of Rayong province

piers, starting a factory for fishmeal, running a fish market, and selling petrol to other fishing boats. As the small fishing village expanded into a much more substantial town, she was at the center of its dynamism, employing an estimated six hundred people and controlling an estimated 80 percent of the town's economy by the mid-1990s.

In the 1980s, the economy of the town began to change. To promote the Eastern Seaboard project, government built new highways that connected the province more closely to the capital. The town and its surrounding area had a new lease on life as a center of tourism. The price of land rose. The population increased. Kim Haw moved into land speculation, construction, and tourist development. She built another pier to accommodate ferries running to the nearby resort island of Samet. She invested in new shops, shopping centers, markets, restaurants, and a hotel. She was able to expand by sharing out management of the business with five younger brothers.

Business led into politics. Although it is possible to point to successful business families in the province who have studiously evaded involvement in politics, there was strong pressure to push and pull

Kim Haw into political activity. Especially in the informal era, before the proliferation of local government institutions, successful business families came under pressure to provide some public goods, ranging from sponsoring the local temple festival, through building public facilities, to providing some crude forms of welfare. Kim Haw gained a reputation as a generous patron. The fishcakes she once made as a teenage vendor became a trademarked gift to social occasions such as temple ceremonies, ordinations, wedding, and *kathin* (presenting robes to monks). Kim Haw also sought connections with officialdom, in part as a defensive strategy. Police and local officials took opportunities to obstruct her business in the hope of being bought off. Rumors spread that Kim Haw was using her fishing boats for smuggling goods, including marijuana, a charge she denied. Whether the rumor was true or not, the best response to such attacks and to bureaucratic predation was to make political connections at the highest level. One of her brothers explained, "we seek some power, some positions, for self-protection, so that other people cannot harm us."

The family sought connections both in the informal and formal hierarchies of the region. She established links with Kamnan Po, the acknowledged godfather of the neighboring province of Chonburi, who had also begun his career in fishing, and risen by riding the upswing of the new urban economy in a much more prosperous location. Kim Haw also gained access to officialdom by becoming a village head, the bottom rung on the Ministry of Interior's hierarchy. In 1979, she also joined the village scouts, an officially sponsored vigilante organization formed in the 1970s to combat radicalism. Through this organization, local notables like Kim Haw gained access to powerful local officials such as the governor and provincial police chief, while officialdom gained access to the notables' informal networks of influence in the locality. The provincial governor called on her services several times to help disperse local protests. Kim Haw was a generous donor to the organization ("20 million baht was not enough") and became the provincial head of the village scouts which provided training for 100,000 recruits in Rayong. She also organized a welfare fund to provide funeral expenses for members of the organization.

Kim Haw became known as *mae phra khong changwat*, the province's Madonna,[2] as *pa phu ari*, kindly auntie, and as *chao mae*, literally godmother, the female variant of the more common *chao pho* (godfather) applied to powerful figures in the locality (McVey 2000). Kim Haw denied using the violence often associated with such figures, but other local people doubt this. The police suspect that some members of the family have gunmen for protection but disguise them as drivers or other retainers.

Elections, tourism, and urban development

As electoral politics became more established, Kim Haw was drawn into the networks of party politics. Electoral hopefuls contacted her, in part for donations, in part to tap her networks of influence to deliver votes. She became associated with Sawet Piempongsan, a prominent political figure in the province since the 1930s (see below), and said publicly she respected him enough to be his slave. Through him she made contacts in national politics, especially in the Democrat Party. She was reluctant to enter politics herself, in part because her educational qualifications were inadequate (something she could get around, and did so later). She did however run for village headman, rose from that to being *kamnan* (head of a sub-district) and later chairman of the village heads association in the district (*amphoe*). She subsequently had to resign as *kamnan*, but recognized the importance of the local government bodies that began to appear from the 1980s.

One of her brothers, Yongyot, became head of the local *sukhaphiban* (a semi-urban official territorial division, sometimes translated as sanitary district, since abolished). In 1985, another brother stood for election to the Provincial Administrative Organization (PAO) and secured the largest vote in the province. In 1992, Chatichai Choonhavan, former prime minister and head of the Chat Phatthana Party, asked her to submit a candidate for the general election. The same brother stood and won uncontested. At the next election in 1995, Kamnan Po persuaded

---

2. *Mae phra*, roughly "holy mother," is a term used among Catholics, principally as the title for Mary.

the family to shift to the Chat Thai party, where Yongyot won again. Through the 1990s, the family rode the expansion of electoral politics. Four of Kim Haw's brothers became respectively MP, head of the PAO, mayor of Ban Phe, and member of the municipal council. Kim Haw usually refused to stand for such offices on the grounds that "I'm not expert and I'm too busy." According to one of her employees, Kim Haw was "the MP in all but name, since she does much of the campaigning, including the financing, and many voters elect her brother because of their respect for her" (Ockey 1999: 1046). In 1999 she was elected head of the municipal council, but as with her spell as *kamnan*, she subsequently resigned in 2002, saying, "Before I entered politics, villagers all loved me, but now more people are criticizing me." Later, she enrolled in the local Rajaphat University, secured a B.A., and was planning to stand for the Senate, but her daughter dissuaded her.

Entering politics was partly a strategy to defend the family's business interests against gatekeeping and other predatory activity by policemen and bureaucrats. But political influence also served as a tool for expanding the family's business interests, especially in the new economy of urbanization.

Kim Haw wanted to build a tourist resort on land along the bank of a local canal. The land was occupied by squatters. Kim Haw offered them money to relocate, but they refused on grounds the money was too little. The squatters were then told, "Do you want money, or something else?" The squatters promptly moved, knowing that the police had previously arrested gunmen believed to be working for the family. The resort was built.

One of the brothers invested in a consortium to build a new pier for ferrying tourists to the resort island. Later there was a dispute over the sharing of the revenue from the pier. One of the partners was shot dead. Kim Haw denied any involvement in the shooting but the pier subsequently came under the sole control of the family.

Kim Haw took control of a stretch of beach to build a pier and a souvenir market to cater to tourists. Such land is technically public property and hence cannot be owned by anyone. The ability to use such land is a function of local political influence. The family was publicly accused of acting improperly. Kim Haw's response was to counter that making use of the beachfront in such a way might be illegal but was also absolutely customary, and that the accusations were just part of a campaign by her political opponents. One of her brothers was mayor of the territory containing this beachfront. He organized four hundred others involved in such illegal land occupation to resist the authorities until changes in local government laws gave his municipality powers over local zoning. After that, he was able to legalize the situation.

One of the main activities of the new local government bodies is the distribution of contracts for the construction of various local facilities. The PAO alone had a construction budget of around 400 million baht a year. Those controlling these budgets can either charge a commission, usually reckoned as 20 percent or above in this province, for allocating the contracts, or can set up their own construction companies and reap a higher margin through profit. As head of the PAO, Kim Haw's brother was able to secure control over a large portfolio of construction contracts, and this was valuable patronage for binding other families to their side. In order to evade charges of profiteering from this easy route, Kim Haw claimed that the family had no construction contracting business. But the family owned construction equipment, and it was locally believed that they owned two construction companies which were registered in other names, and which carried out contracts for the PAO.

The first stage of Kim Haw's rise belongs to the era of primitive accumulation based on natural resources, hard work,[3] a high rate of saving, and entrepreneurial flair. As the family accumulated capital, they needed to make personal links with figures of both informal and formal power networks in order to protect themselves from predators. With the coming of a new urban economy in the 1980s, the family shifted their economic base towards land dealing, retail, construction, and tourism. In 1994, Kim Haw was named an "Outstanding Entrepreneur" by the Gender and Development Research Institute in Bangkok. The family also moved aggressively into the new framework of elective

---

3. When this research team visited Kim Haw she was in the middle of doing a large pile of laundry by hand.

bodies at the local and national level. These positions gave them the influence not just to protect their assets, but also to multiply them by bending laws and intimidating people in ways which were not always available to their commercial rivals. By the 1990s, their political influence stretched over three districts in the southwest of the province. Their political expenses averaged a million baht a month, mostly in donations to various local projects and activities.

BAN KHAI

Pioneer agriculture and protective generals

The Hakka founder of the Pitudecha clan migrated from Guangzhou in the early twentieth century, and married a local woman from a family with a small fruit orchard. He worked as a common laborer and porter until he had enough capital to start a small trading business, buying goods from the local town for sale in village markets.

After both the couple fell sick, their son, Sakhon, left school before completing the elementary level, and worked as a rubber tapper to feed the family and send his sister to school. He earned enough and learned enough for the family to take up rubber planting on a small scale after his parents recovered. In the 1950s, when Sakhon was in his early twenties and just married, the plantation of sugarcane began to spread across the eastern region along new highways. Sakhon set up a grocery shop in front of a local sugar factory and came to know many of the growers and millers in the industry. When the mill went bankrupt, he went into sugar planting. In this era, illegal loggers took advantage of the new roads to clear-cut huge areas of pristine forest. Sakhon joined the ranks of pioneer farmers who moved in behind the loggers, and put the new land under cash crops. He started planting sugarcane in a small way but gradually expanded to several thousand rai.

This pioneer expansion operated outside any framework of law or regulation. The occupation of forest land was technically illegal, and Sakhon's control over land was enforced by informal means rather than documentation. According to the local proverb, ownership extended from where a gun was shot to the point where the bullet fell to the ground. Sakhon excelled in this milieu. He was the law, and openly admitted that on occasions he had eliminated local thieves and other criminals. He said there were three stages to settling a dispute: first, by talking; then, if that failed, by offering a financial settlement; and finally, murder. He showed more respect for his peers than for the letter of the law. On one occasion, he occupied a thousand rai of land. As this land was situated in a forest reserve, the occupation was technically illegal. That fact did not deter him at all, but something else did. Around half of the land, which had been sold to him by another local strong man, was already claimed by another influential land pioneer from a neighboring province. Sakhon circumspectly ceded the land to his powerful neighbor.

In this era of informal politics based on personal connections, Sakhon protected himself and effectively legitimated his land ownership by making contacts with the army generals who ran the national government. His main protector was General Narong Kittikachorn, one of the triumvirate in power from 1963 to 1973. Over time, Sakhon converted all his lands into legal ownership with title deeds.

He became one of the largest planters of sugar, cassava, and rubber in the region. He became headman of his village in 1968, then *kamnan* in the 1970s, and president of the Rayong association of sugarcane planters. In the late 1970s, he received an award from the Interior Ministry for being an outstanding *kamnan*, and was elected chairman of the provincial association of village officers. This phase of primitive accumulation through pioneer occupation of forest land underwritten by force and protected by the military regime of the era came to an end in the 1980s. There was little forest left to grab. New laws and new environmental concerns made grabbing less simple. Narong's military clique was driven from power in 1973, and military influence in local affairs dwindled over the next decade. At the same time, a new phase of urbanization began with new roads and the Eastern Seaboard project in the 1980s, while a new network of local government bodies began to replace the informal influence of local strong men. This transition coincided with a change of generations in Kamnan Sakhon's family as his sons came of age. These sons switched from guns to politics and from agriculture to construction.

Election and construction

In 1985, Kamnan Sakhon sent his eldest son Piya to contest successfully for a position on the PAO. In 1992, two of the established MPs from the province persuaded Piya to run for election as an MP. He failed the first time, but succeeded on the second in 1995. The youngest son, Sathit, qualified as a lawyer, contested successfully for a seat on the PAO, and later contested the general election in 2001.

Politics helped to bridge wider connections with the local power elite of the region. In particular, the Pitudecha family began to associate closely with Kamnan Po, who dominated the local and electoral politics of neighboring Chonburi. In the local argot, Kamnan Po was referred to as *ban yai*, the Big House. Kamnan Po offered a model that the Pitudecha family could imitate, as well as an ally with whom they could exchange business and political connections for mutual benefit.

Around the same time that Piya went onto the PAO, the family began to develop sand and gravel quarries to supply the booming local construction industry. From there they extended into construction contracting, manufacture of concrete products, property development, and supply of other construction materials. By the time of the 1997 crisis, they had become the largest construction business in the province. Under the *kongsi* system, as each son came of age and got married, the patriarch placed him in charge of one part of the business. Piya looked after the quarries and construction contracting, while the two next siblings managed housing developments, and supply of concrete and other construction materials, respectively. The family still operated like a holding company, and the patriarch Sakhon remained in overall control of the whole enterprise.

Political influence was crucial to the family's success in construction and property development. Quarries for sand and gravel were often located on public land. Prime sites were sometimes in areas where blasting was technically illegal. The most lucrative construction contracts came from government bodies. Government was also a crucial part of profiting from land speculation. In 2001, government paid 110 million baht to the family to acquire over a thousand rai of their land to build a public water reservoir. In such ways the assets accumulated in the earlier phase of primitive accumulation were converted into the capital required for success in the emerging urban economy.

As an MP, Piya could find ways to manufacture lucrative public construction projects within the area of their influence. He would suggest the project to local people and get a base of support. Then he would talk to the appropriate government agencies to propose the project for approval under a government budget. As Piya said (interview, 2 May 2004), "I asked local people what they wanted, and once I had their agreement I could mould the project proposal with my own hands." Once the government agency put the contract up for bid, the family would use its local influence to ensure that it was won by one of their own companies or an associate. As a general rule, the Pitudecha group specialized in contracts valued over a 100 million baht apiece. Smaller contracts were shared out to associates, thus winning friends and political supporters. The Pitudecha family also helped to finance associates to win positions in local government in order to strengthen their own network.

Political power was also crucial for managing the disputes that were inevitably generated by this profitable business. The use of violence, which had been critical in the earlier informal era, had not totally disappeared. Political influence was crucial for ensuring that such violence could still be used without incurring any consequences in an era when law and regulation was supposed to have more effect.

Early in their career in construction, the Pitudecha family got into a dispute with an influential *kamnan* who also had a quarry business. Both families wanted to control a particular quarry location. According to local folklore, the *kamnan* decided to settle the matter by the old methods, and went off to borrow a gun from an associate lawyer. Later the *kamnan* and three other were found shot dead. No culprits were ever identified, but local people believe the deaths were related to the quarry dispute.

In 1990, a lawyer who headed the PAO took up the case of villagers who objected to the Pitudecha family dredging sand from a local river in a way that caused the river to change course and the banks to collapse, threatening the villagers' houses. The lawyer openly confronted the family and asked them to stop. When the family refused, the lawyer used his legal expertise to help the villagers make a formal protest to the authorities with good legal backing. In the middle of the dispute, the lawyer was shot dead. Again no culprit was found, and again local people drew their own conclusions.

In the early 1990s, government planned to build a facility to process the growing volume of industrial waste in the province. The project was allocated to a private company, Genco. The location was sited in the territory considered the fief of the Pitudecha family so they expected to benefit from the land preparation, construction, and supply of labor. But local villagers objected strongly to the Genco project, highlighting concerns that leakage or run-off would affect the water supply for agriculture. The initial location had to be abandoned, and an alternative was found, still within the Pitudecha area of influence. But protests restarted, and became so fierce that the construction was halted. In 1996, a prominent leader of the protests was shot dead. The police believed the death was linked to his activity against the Genco project. A scapegoat was caught and put on trial but the case failed (Chaiyon 2002).

Another incident revolved around a quarry located in a reserve forest. Although the location was off-limits for quarrying under the Forestry Law of 1992, a company was able to gain a ten-year concession. Local people believed this unusual concession resulted from the influence of Piya over local officialdom. A local conservationist campaigned against the project on grounds that the location was not only technically illegal but a valuable archaeological site. The conservationist was threatened with the words, "you will not die of old age," and shortly after in 2000 was found dead.

By the eve of the crisis, the Pitudecha family had converted their assets from the old pioneer agrarian economy into the new urban and industrial economy, and had taken a strong position in local politics. Their influence in the politics of the province had been crucial in gaining access to profitable opportunities, building linkages with other local businessmen and with regional heavyweights, and protecting themselves from effective scrutiny of some of their business methods.

KLAENG

From social capital to political business

The father of Sermsak Karun was a skilled practitioner of herbal medicine who moved to Klaeng and gained a reputation as a social activist. He took a leading role in building a *wat* and a private school. He became an associate of Sawet Piempongsan, who was the leading political figure in the province from the 1930s to the 1970s. Sawet was a member of the local aristocracy who enhanced his local reputation by becoming a prominent figure in the new constitutional politics of the nation. He won the local seat in seven parliamentary elections held between the 1930s and 1970s, moved in the circles of generals who dominated politics in this era, and served as a minister seven times between 1948 and 1976.[4] Sermsak's father became part of Sawet's local network in Klaeng. Sawet rewarded him by helping to secure an agency to distribute cigarettes from the government tobacco monopoly in part of the province.

Sermsak followed his father in practicing medicine. He also continued the family tradition of social activism by training as a lawyer and helping local people on legal matters. When the PAO was first established in 1975, Sermsak was elected a member for two consecutive terms. His political base was a strong network of local leaders, monks, and teachers. At parliamentary elections in 1979, Sawet was defeated for the first time in his political career. His rival was a rising local businessman (Sin Kumpha) and this victory symbolized the transition from the era of military politics to a new era of business dominance. At the next election, Sawet's group decided to run Sermsak as a candidate because of his prominence

---

4. Minister under Phibun, 1948–1949; deputy finance minister under Phibun, 1949–1951; deputy finance minister under Phibun, 1957; minister under Thanom, 1958; deputy prime minister and finance minister under Seni three times, 1975, 1976, 1976.

and popularity as a social activist. Sermsak had few resources of his own for electioneering and claimed to have spent only 100,000 baht of his own money. He received financial help from a local businessman who traded in logs imported from Cambodia. Sermsak was elected MP under the Chat Thai party in 1983, and went on to be reelected as MP at successive elections from that time onwards. He became an important figure in the parliament by sheer force of personality, rather than through organizing a faction, and served as a deputy minister for two brief periods.[5]

The family was not significantly wealthy before entering politics. Its prominence came from a tradition of social activism, and association with a leading political figure in the past. In this case, politics was the means for capital accumulation. After Sermsak became an MP, his wife became a prominent entrepreneur in the urban boom that began in the 1980s with the Eastern Seaboard project. She speculated in land and made high profits from rising land values. In two cases, she bought land on sites designated for dam construction, and later sold them to government for a high profit. She also collected commission fees on the construction projects which her MP husband was able to generate in their area of influence. She used some of her capital to invest in a loan shark business which charged high interest rates, while her husband invested in share speculation in a consortium with other MPs.

While the family thus became rich, the social capital accumulated from social activism and from association with Sawet was gradually eroded.

ON CRISIS EVE

By the 1990s, the Ban Phe, Ban Khai, and Klaeng families were perceived within the province as the major centers of wealth and political influence. The foundations of their original prominence were very different. One had accumulated prominence in the fishing industry, another on the agrarian frontier, and the third by association with the old elite of status.

---

5. As deputy minister of labor under Chuan, 1993–1994; as deputy minister of finance under Banharn, 1996.

All three had then risen to the front rank of the province's new elite of wealth and influence by exploiting the opportunities made possible by a booming new urban economy and the extension of electoral politics. All three made super-profits by using political influence to make money from rising land prices and the booming construction business.

The three families had distinct spheres of influence in the southwest, north, and east of the province. The Ban Phe and Ban Khai families had strong a family network in local government on their home patch. The Klaeng family acted as part of a more diverse and often divided network of local businessmen.

As the three families expanded, their interests inevitably clashed at the margins of their respective fiefs. They were often rivals for the same budget at the provincial level. These rivalries converged over the election of MPs. Prior to the 1997 constitution, Rayong province acted as a single constituency at the general elections, returning two candidates. From the early 1980s, these two seats were usually shared between the Klaeng and Ban Phe families. But in 1992, the Ban Khai family also entered the fray, starting a pattern of three-cornered conflict. At the 1992 poll, the Ban Phe and Ban Khai families made an electoral pact, but it was not enough to secure both seats. The candidates put up by the Klaeng and Ban Khai families secured the most votes, and a member of the Ban Phe family was ignominiously defeated. A three-cornered battle over the two seats was repeated at the elections in 1995 and 1996. The Ban Khai group was especially aggressive at extending its network of family and associates into local government in areas that the Ban Phe family considered part of their fief. The Ban Khai and Klaeng families also had reasons for conflict. Sermsak of Klaeng was a friend of both the environmental campaigners who were killed over disputes in the Ban Khai fief.

THE BUSINESS IMPACT OF THE 1997 CRISIS

The provincial business elite was not affected by the crisis in the same way as the national conglomerates. For the most part, they had not borrowed in dollars and so were not bankrupted by the depreciation of the baht.

But they were strongly affected in secondary ways. The property boom collapsed, and the price of land fell nationwide. The overall consumption level dropped by a fifth, especially hitting discretionary spending on items such as tourism and entertainment. Government revenues fell, and a large slab of the expenditure budget had to be diverted to the bailout, resulting in a steep fall in the funding for construction. The depreciation of the currency raised the price of imported items including oil.

All three of the Rayong groups were badly hit.

Ban Phe

For the Ban Phe group, costs in the fishing industry rose steeply, mainly because of the rising price of oil. They tried to increase returns from their fishmeal factory, but this also proved difficult because costs of imported inputs rose while the selling price weakened because of falling consumption demand. Tourism in Ban Phe also slumped, and the supply of construction contracts dried up. The group had to borrow 60 million baht from the banks to support their fishing operation, and in total went into debt to the tune of 300 million baht.

In response, the group sought help through its political contacts, particularly with Kamnan Po. In 2001, three of Kamnan Po's sons entered Parliament, and Bo enjoyed some influence in the ruling Thai Rak Thai (TRT) Party of Thaksin Shinawatra. One of Bo's sons became a minister, and from October 2002 onwards was in charge of the tourism portfolio. Through this route, Kim Haw got some assistance, but still had to fall back on selling off some of the family assets, including several fishing boats and tracts of land. Such sales represented not only a decline in their assets, but a great loss of face in the locality.

Klaeng

The Klaeng group was hit principally by the collapse of the property market. Before the crisis, Sermsak's main income had come from property speculation, and this source totally dried up. His wife's loan sharking business became riskier, and incurred large bad debts. The family was forced to rely more on the commission income generated by the distribution of government contracts, but this source was also reduced. They raised the commission rate up to 40 percent, but this was considered excessive in the locality, and their popularity suffered. The family was able to generate some other income from their political contacts. Under the patronage of the prime minister's sister, they were allocated a share in the local operation of the "above-ground" lottery.[6] When the stock market revived from 2001 onwards, Sermsak joined with other MPs in share speculation.

In effect, the crisis completed the transition of the Klaeng family from local social activism to politics-as-a-business. They were increasingly perceived as not only living off politics, but also as being unable to generate a large enough income to distribute to others in ways that showed their generosity. They were more parasites than patrons and were increasingly distanced from the networks of monks, teachers, local leaders, and other former followers of Sawet Piempongsan, which had earlier been the bases of their local support.

Ban Khai

Before the crisis, the Ban Khai group had drawn its main income from construction through the family's many political positions. As the flow of construction contracts declined, the family reacted by grabbing a larger share. Formerly the family's practice had been to bid only on contracts worth at least 100 million baht, and to allow its associates to enjoy the smaller projects. After the crisis, it abandoned this practice and bid on smaller projects too, turning local allies into enemies.

The Ban Khai family also turned to new ventures in entertainment and exporting. First, they invested in a pub and microbrewery in the provincial capital. Because the baht depreciation boosted exports, the Eastern Seaboard prospered through the crisis with the location of yet more factories owned by multinational firms producing for export. Rayong city continued to grow as a residential and entertainment center for both expatriates

---

6. To counter the widespread "underground lottery" which was often run by local "influential figures," the Thaksin government launched a legitimate equivalent.

and locals working in these industries. The Ban Khai family entered into these new ventures jointly with the mayor of the town.

A second venture drew on the family's past experience in agriculture. Rayong had become a center of pineapple growing. The province's only canning factory, owned by a foreign company, was seized by a bank for non-payment of loans. The family bought the factory. Despite the crisis, their credit was good enough to borrow 600 million baht to supplement their own capital.

They were able to use their political influence to assist this new venture in several ways. They could speed up the various bureaucratic procedures involved in getting permissions and licenses. They made arrangements for the government's agricultural bank to extend loans to pineapple growers with the family acting as co-guarantor. Local government budget was spent on building a new road to the factory.

With the depreciation of the baht, the export of canned pineapple increased. This new venture increased the family's prominence as a local patron because the factory employed six hundred workers, and pineapple growers had an outlet for their produce.

In response to the crisis, the Ban Khai family had used their political influence to shift their economic base further towards the economy of globalization. Although this family had been the closest to the "godfather" style, it reacted to the crisis by modernizing its economic base. Compared to its two rivals, the Ban Khai family emerged stronger. This strength was reflected in a more aggressive stance in provincial politics.

FROM BUSINESS PRESSURE TO POLITICAL CONFLICT

The pressures of the crisis exacerbated the political conflict among the three groups. For all the groups, retaining political influence was necessary to maintain their economic position. Indeed, as economic opportunities shrank, the utility of political influence as a way to make money increased. The triangular conflicts that had been brewing in the 1990s took on added intensity. However, these conflicts were complicated by changes in the distribution of political goods brought about by the 1997 constitution, 1999 Decentralization Act, and the rise of Thaksin. The influence attached to becoming an MP was significantly weakened. MPs no longer had direct control over a budget for spending in their constituency. Under the 1997 constitution, Thaksin was able to increase executive control over the budget, and diminish the ability of MPs to influence the budget allocation through parliamentary committees. Under the Decentralization Act of 1999, more of the national budget was shifted from the center to local government bodies. The chairmanship of the Provincial Administrative Organizations (PAO) became a directly elected post for the first time.[7] New elective Tambon Administrative Organizations (TAO) were established across the country by 2002. In sum, an MP now had less access to budget for local construction and services, while the heads of the PAO and TAO councils had much more.

The Ban Khai group reacted quickest to these changes by concentrating on getting kin and associates elected to the new TAO. But in the beginning the national elections had not lost their importance by any means. An MP still had vital access to the center of power. A strong political base in the province now required a network that spanned from the Parliament to the PAO and TAOs.

The 2001 election

The conflict between the three groups reached a new stage at general elections in 2001.

Under the 1997 constitution, the electoral system was changed. Provinces were broken down into several single-member constituencies. The number of seats from Rayong increased from two to three. An additional hundred seats were elected on a national vote by party, known as the party-list system.

---

7. PAOs were first formed under an act of 1955, but until 1997 the provincial governor was the ex-officio chairman. Although the decentralization under the 1997 constitution and 1999 act intended to make the TAOs the most important level of local government, the PAO still had considerable power in allocating budget to the TAOs (Achakorn 2006).

With three constituencies, each containing the headquarters of one of the big families, the election should have presented no problem. But the Pitudecha family had come through the crisis better than its two rivals and bid to translate this commercial advantage into political advantage as well.

In the northern constituency, the Pitudecha family safely won the seat. In the eastern constituency including Klaeng, there was also no problem. Through his long experience in parliamentary politics, Sermsak was given the thirty-ninth position on the party list slate of the Thai Rak Thai Party, and duly elected. An associated local businessman, Sin Kumpha was elected for the constituency seat.

The southwestern constituency was in the area traditionally dominated by the Ban Phe family. The family fielded Kim Haw's brother Yongyot who had been an MP under the old system. But the Ban Khai family announced its new aggression by fielding a second, younger sibling Sathit in this seat. As part of their campaign, the Pitudecha group attacked Kim Haw over the irregularities about public land on the Ban Phe coast. At the poll, Sathit won convincingly by 39,184 votes to 22,312. This victory perhaps reflected the Pitudecha family's comparatively stronger financial position in the aftermath of the crisis, as well as its entrepreneurial move into the provincial capital in partnership with the mayor. The Ban Phe group had invested heavily in the election, and the loss added to their financial weakness. They considered the candidature of Sathit was a betrayal of cooperation between the two families in the past. Kim Haw commented, "Before, Piya [Pitudecha] always called me mother, but now he is contemptuous of me as a poorly educated old woman."

Provincial elections, 2004

These rivalries intensified over the following years. The Klaeng camp concentrated on defending its local fief. But the Pitudecha family of Ban Khai was intent on translating its comparative economic strength into political domination at the provincial level. That brought direct conflict with the Ban Phe camp. At elections for the PAO in 2004, the two sides invested heavily to secure access to a large local budget, but also to win the status as the preeminent political family of the province.

The Pitudecha group was nervous about running a candidate from the family because of growing local resentment of the group's dominance. Instead they initially supported a former policeman. He had a personal base of support from his popularity as a local radio broadcaster, good relations with monks through his assistance to several *wat*, and popularity with vendors and other female groups through his social activities. He had run in two previous MP elections but lost because he lacked money and because he was not of local origin and easily deprecated as a "stray dog." His personal assets combined with the Pitudecha family's funding and network were a powerful combination. The Ban Phe group countered by running Kim Haw's brother, the incumbent head of the PAO, who had the advantage of the PAO's patronage. The Ban Phe group also made a deal with the Klaeng camp, promising to support the Klaeng candidate in the coming general election as long as Klaeng gave assistance to the Ban Phe candidate for headship of the PAO.

In March 2004, after a vituperative mud-slinging contest, the Pitudecha candidate won election as head of the PAO by the narrow margin of 2,000 votes. But the Ban Phe camp successfully petitioned the Election Commission that the Pitudecha candidate had broken the election law.[8] The result was overturned, the policeman candidate was banned from politics for five years and dunned for the cost of a replacement election. For the re-poll, the Pitudecha camp found another nominee candidate among local politicians. This Pitudecha nominee topped the polls, but the election was again overturned on a technicality (the candidate's publicity materials claimed he had a Ph.D. when in reality he was still studying).

The Pitudecha camp had invested heavily to gain these two Pyrrhic victories. At the third polling, it offered no candidate, and the Ban Phe nominee appeared to win easily. However, it emerged subsequently that the Pitudecha camp had simply changed tactics. To guarantee his

---

8. He had organized a ceremony for offering alms to the monks of a *wat* within the period of the election.

victory, the candidate fielded by the Ban Phe camp had secretly made a deal with the Pitudecha. Once installed in office as the new chairman of the PAO, he used his power to favor the Pitudecha group. Kim Haw was furious, and the chairman was obliged to surround himself with police protection.

General election, 2005

The general election of 2005 took place within this heightened atmosphere of conflict. As the population of the province had expanded with industrialization, the number of constituencies was expanded from three to four. The competition between the three groups again spilled across the former boundaries of their separate fiefs. Each group put up a strong candidate in its own backyard, but also backed candidates in their rivals' backyards. The new fourth constituency was another site of competition.

The results were decided by the interplay of local rivalries, but also by influences from national politics. In their own backyards, each of the groups put up their strong candidate under the TRT Party. This was partly because the TRT Party leader, Thaksin, and his policies of cheap health care and local development funds were highly popular with the electorate. But it was also partly due to the role of Kamnan Po. For twenty years Kamnan Po had dominated the business and politics of neighboring Chonburi province, and had appeared immune to attempts to constrain his power by police, judiciary, and political opponents. But over 2003–2004, he was convicted twice—first, for corruption in the sale of a plot of land to Pattaya municipality, and second, for masterminding the murder of a local opponent.[9] While these cases awaited

---

9. The first conviction carried a jail term of five years, the second of twelve. In the land case, 150 rai of land in a forest reserve had been bought for 7.5 million in 1992, and then sold for 93 million a year later to the Pattaya municipality to use as landfill. The murder case concerned Prayun Sitthichot, a construction contractor from Rayong, who was assassinated gangland-style at a wedding in Chonburi on 9 March 2003. A team of gunmen gave evidence that Kamnan Po had tried to hire them for the job. The Appeals Court confirmed both convictions. The Supreme Court confirmed the conviction in the land case, but Kamnan Po disappeared before the Supreme Court ruling over the murder.

appeal, Kamnan Po hoped to gain leverage with the prime minister by becoming an indispensable source of political support, not just in Chonburi but across the eastern region. He moved his faction of MPs out of the Chat Thai Party and into TRT. He took a larger role in the election campaigns throughout the eastern region. He used his influence to ensure the three power groups in Rayong all fielded their strong candidates under TRT. He appeared personally at TRT campaign events in the province. According to local folklore, in the last few days of the campaign a "torrent" of money put the result beyond any shadow of doubt.[10]

Many other candidates stood with backing from non-TRT parties, including a very popular doctor with a record of working for the poor and support from the Democrat Party, but none made any impression on the combination of the TRT name, the power of a local network, and Kamnan Po's intervention. As local people summed up, "They were boxing in a different weight division. Defeat was inevitable, whatever they did."

The Pitudecha patriarch ran one son under the TRT banner in his own backyard, but in the new fourth constituency, he tried another tactic, running a son under the Chat Thai party. Kamnan Po was reportedly angry and offered large inducements, all in vain. Possibly the Pitudecha were both politically and financially indebted to the leader of the Chat Thai party. Possibly they were calculating that Chat Thai would become a junior partner in a coalition government, and their man would have a better chance to acquire a ministership through this route, rather than being submerged in the TRT ocean. But Thaksin publicly rejected any possibility of a coalition with Chat Thai at the same time the "torrent" was released, and the Pitudecha candidate lost heavily.

Ultimately, however, the election confirmed the rising star of the Pitudecha group.[11] Despite the son's loss in the fourth constituency, a

---

10. According to this folklore, sums as high as three to four thousand baht were paid to voters, while officials in control of the ballot boxes were also suborned.

11. Constituency 1: Yongyot (TRT) 34,283, Sathit Pitudecha (DP) 33,153; constituency 2: Krisda Karun (TRT) 30,656, Banyat Jetanajan (DP) 30,417; constituency 3: Thara Pitudecha (TRT) 43,622, Manop Satihenket (DP) 23,126; constituency 4: Pramot Wiraphan (TRT) 37,652, Direk Sila (DP) 17,737, Surachai Pitudecha (CT) 10,013.

second-string candidate won with their support in the new fourth constituency under the TRT banner. In their backyard, another son won with ease. In the southwest, the Pitudecha again stood against Kim Haw's son and almost repeated the 2001 success—eventually losing by the narrow margin of 1,100 votes.

The Senate election in the following year went the same way. Although the election was run without party labels and the three camps invested less money and political capital in the contest, one seat went to a nominee of the Pitudecha group, and the other to the ex-policeman who had figured in the PAO contest, this time running independently.

Although the sweep by TRT candidates in Rayong was a victory for Kamnan Po, the consequences did not turn out as hoped. His eldest son was rewarded with an advisory post rather than a meatier ministership. Kamnan Po's convictions were upheld on appeal, but he was mysteriously allowed to jump bail and disappear before being consigned to jail.

CONCLUSION

In 1960, Rayong was still considered a remote province, largely covered with forest, and poorly connected by roads to the outside world. Over the next generation, the province first became a frontier for the exploitation of its untapped natural resources, and then the site of the country's major concentration of export-oriented industry. Three families rose to prominence. Two were frontier entrepreneurs who rose by primitive accumulation—exploitation of natural resources, hard work, and informal political protection. The third rose under the patronage of the old noble elite. All three became involved in politics as a means to promote and protect their wealth. All three deployed political influence to make the transition to the new phase of urban growth which came with the Eastern Seaboard project in the 1980s. Business and politics were closely intertwined.

All three families were hit hard by the crisis, particularly because of the collapse of the property market and the declining revenue from construction contracting. Their difficulties stimulated their mutual rivalry for political prominence, and for control over the rents that went with it. The Klaeng family had the weakest commercial base, being almost totally dependent on income from its political position. It struggled to retain dominance in its own backyard (scraping through the 2005 election by a majority of just 149 votes), and took little part in a wider provincial contest for dominance. The Pitudecha clan from Ban Khai emerged strongest from the crisis. Perhaps because it had been the most godfather-like of the families, it had the resources to shift away from the old mode of primitive accumulation and into a new economy of manufacture, exporting, and urban services. With a stronger commercial base, it expanded its influence across the province through the new network of national and local politics, often at the expense of the other two families.

Although Rayong is only one of Thailand's seventy-six provinces, there is some evidence that the themes in this story were replicated elsewhere. Certainly, the involvement of prominent local families for construction contracting was a nationwide trend in the pre-crisis era.[12] Certainly too, many prominent local families whose economic base still rested on resource extraction and informal power were rattled by the crisis. In several provinces, the post-crisis era saw the rise of new families with a firmer base in the modern, urban economy.

By mid-2006, however, Piya Pitudecha had failed to make profits from his pineapple factory or his entertainment ventures in Rayong. He owed 40 million baht to the pineapple farmers. The potential income from politics now became even more important. He decided to stand for election as head of the PAO. He forced the incumbent to step down,

---

12. Nopphanun (2006) found that among the MPs, ministers, and their secretaries and advisers during the first Thaksin government, there were seventy-five whose families had a construction business registered with the Department of Public Works or the Office of Town Planning (such registration is a condition for bidding on government contracts). Of these seventy-five, thirty-six were in the Thai Rak Thai Party, five in New Aspiration (absorbed into TRT), three in Seritham (ditto), thirteen in Chat Thai, and thirteen in the Democrats. At least eleven of these families had a member serving in the Cabinet over 2001–2005. In addition, there were many other construction contractors who were closely linked to current politicians in ways other than kinship.

and invested heavily in the contest. But with the fall of Thaksin, the end of the influence of Kamnan Po, and the declining fortunes of the Pitudecha clan, local political alignments changed like a kaleidoscope. The former MP from Klaeng, Sin Kumpha, stood against Piya Pitudecha with backing from Ban Phe. According to insiders he spent 60 million baht on the campaign in November 2006. He won, but the election was subsequently voided on grounds of malpractice, and a new poll was called for July 2007. For Piya the stakes were now very high. Ban Phe and Ban Khai now went head-to-head, with fragments of the Klaeng campaign aligned with each side. Piya's father, Kamnan Sakhon, the pioneer patriarch, stepped in to try and persuade Sin Kumpha to stand for deputy head of the PAO on a joint ticket, but Sin refused. The saga continues...

8

CHIANG MAI: FAMILY BUSINESS, TOURISM, AND POLITICS

Viengrat Nethipo

CHIANG Mai is one of the few Thai provincial centers where the economy depends not so much on the resources of its hinterland but on its functions as an urban place. Chiang Mai has long been a trading center on routes between southern China and the Chaophraya basin. For at least seven centuries it was a political capital until the principality of Lanna was absorbed by Bangkok over the nineteenth century, and it remains the semi-official first city of northern Thailand. Like other cities that were capitals in the past but not the present, its cultural heritage has not been completely overwhelmed by modern development and so it is attractive for tourism. Chiang Mai's commercial life is shaped by the city's role as a center of trade, power, and culture.

The business history of Chiang Mai is best viewed through the fortunes of its prominent families. A handful of families that emerged at the turn of the twentieth century formed an old commercial and social elite that was still identifiable a century later. Rapid changes that began in the development era around 1970 allowed several other families to rise, in some cases from meager origins to the front rank of the city's business in the space of two decades.[1]

In the 1997 crisis, the major impact on the city's economy was not a debt crunch but the collapse of a property boom. The old business families, which had come to rely heavily on income from property development, were badly hit. Meanwhile, the fall in the currency boosted tourism, which was a major contributor to the Chiang Mai economy.

---

1. Gen Endo (1996, 2000) divides the business development of Chiang Mai into four periods: 1. prior to the completion of the railway in 1921; 2. from 1921 to 1932; 3. from 1932 to the eve of the first development plan; 4. from the first plan (1961–1966) onwards.

The rise to power of Thaksin Shinawatra, whose family hailed from Chiang Mai, also brought extra government patronage.

This chapter sketches the origins and commercial foundations of these two elite groups, the families of old and new wealth, and then examines how they fared in the crisis of 1997.

OLD FAMILIES, TRADE, AND LAND

Through the nineteenth century, Chiang Mai was a sparsely populated backwater. A handful of Chinese migrants who settled around the turn of the twentieth century formed the core of a new commercial and social elite (Vatikiotis 1984: 87–89).

The old families

In the last quarter of the nineteenth century, Bangkok absorbed the Lanna principality. It sent bureaucrats north to establish a new administration, invested in a new grid of roads to modernize the city center on the west bank of the Ping River, and began building a railway to Bangkok which was completed in 1921.

In this era, merchants migrated north to act as tax farmers for the new administration, to sell goods to members of the new bureaucracy, and to trade between Chiang Mai and Bangkok. A handful of these merchants who arrived before the completion of the railway established commercial dynasties that dominated the commercial, political, and social life of the city for almost a century (Plai-Or 1987: 29).

Nai Toi Sae Chua migrated to Siam from Swatow and became a tax farmer in Lamphun. He moved to Chiang Mai in 1883 and married Nang Khamthiang. Their son, Nai Sun Hi, became a wealthy trader, moneylender, tax farmer, and founder of the Chutima family, while their daughter married Nai Ki who was the founder of the Nimmanahaeminda clan (Prani 1980: 140).[2]

---

2. The Laohavad and Nimmanahaeminda-Chutima clans also come from the same stock.

To encourage settlement and make the city prosper, the Chiang Mai ruling family gave these early merchant families grants of land, which formed the foundations of their prosperity for three generations. Initially they built markets on this land, traded to Bangkok, and lent money to later Chinese settlers and to the declining old aristocracy. The Chutima-Nimmanahaeminda clan developed the Anusan, Warorot, Khamthiang, and Ton Lamyai markets in the old city center. As the city expanded over later generations, the clan was borne up by the rising value of their early land acquisitions. Kraisi Nimmanahaeminda, the grandson of the family founder, took an M.A. from Harvard, modernized the family business, and also became a famous local intellectual. Another relative, Bavorn, became the agent for a Bangkok bank and trading company, built the Rincome Hotel in 1969, and the Chiang Mai Cultural Center, a handicraft emporium, in 1971. He also established a vocational school, and was active as a property developer (Anu, 8 November 2000: 5).

Nai Jaran, founder of the Kitibutr family, was another Siam-born Chinese who settled in Chiang Mai in this pre-railway era, and became related in marriage to a prominent noble family.[3] The family's early businesses were rice-milling and trade between the city and Bangkok. They also acquired land in the old city center, and prospered over two future generations by developing these assets. They owned the sites of the fresh market at Chiang Mai Gate, the Chiang Inn Hotel, and the Lanna Polytechnic School. From 1967, they developed some major retail complexes such as Chiang In Plaza and Chiang In shopping center, as well as educational institutions and rental apartments (Samit n.d.: 100).

The railway era

After the completion of the railway in 1921, many other migrants came and founded families that formed a secondary stratum of this old elite. Nai Chiang, founder of the Shinawatra clan, had arrived before the

---

3. Phra Thippayamonthon was a Chiang Mai man who was recruited into Bangkok's new administrative system, and won fame and high rank through his role in suppressing the Phaya Phap revolt in 1902, and helping to suppress robbery in Hangdong (Samit n.d.).

railway, but came to prominence in the post-railway era as a manufacturer of silk popular with the growing bureaucratic elite in Chiang
Mai and in Bangkok (Prani 1980: 187–203; Plai-Or 1987: 53–54). Nai
Phanasit, founder of the Chantaraviroj clan, came from Moulmein in
Burma, and secured a logging concession through his association with
the colonial firm, East Asiatic. His family became the biggest logging
and timber firm in the north with concessions in Chiang Mai, Chiang
Rai, and Mae Hong Son. They continued to expand their logging interests after the colonial logging firms withdrew in the Second World
War. In the third generation, Udornphan Chantaraviroj expanded into
mining, construction contracting, wooden furniture, tobacco, entertainment, and a shopping complex in Bangkok (interview, Udornphan
Chantaraviroj, 4 March 1999). The Wongwan family also rose from a
logging concession in Phrae.

The Sakdatorn family was founded by Nai Iewhok Sae Eng, a Taechiu
who emigrated from China before the construction of the railway. He
married a Lamphun woman, Nang Sai (1876–1957), who took the leading role in their business of trading gems from Burma by elephant caravan,
and trading to Bangkok by riverboat (Narong 2000).

This handful of old families formed a distinctive elite. They married
among one another, and occasionally joined in business partnerships.
They were regularly elected to the head of the local chamber of commerce, and appointed by the governor as chairman of the municipality
(Rüland and Bhansoon 1993: 83). Although they had difficulties during
the periods of nationalist posturing against the Chinese by the Bangkok
government, these periods were short and did not disturb their local
dominance, based principally on the rising value of their landholdings
in the old city center.

THE DEVELOPMENT ERA: AUTOMOBILES, EDUCATION, AND TOURISM

The city entered a new era around 1970. Four new aspects to its economic
life opened up a new range of commercial opportunities, on which a
new business elite arose to rival the old families (Watchara n.d.).

First, Chiang Mai was connected by road to Bangkok on new highways completed in 1970. New opportunities opened up in trade, in bus transport, in auto dealerships, and in construction contracting for roads and bridges. Increased availability of a wide range of new goods also spurred the retail trade.

Second, with the foundation of Chiang Mai University in 1964, and several other institutions of higher education in subsequent years, the city became an education center, drawing in an additional population of students.

Third, the city was targeted as a regional center in the development plans of the era, especially from the late 1970s onwards. More government money was invested in infrastructure. The ranks of local bureaucrats increased. In 1985, Chiang Mai was named as a growth pole, and a new industrial estate in nearby Lampang became popular among Japanese electronics manufacturers which migrated to Thailand in this era.[4]

Fourth, from around 1970, government promoted Chiang Mai as a center of tourism. At first, the city appealed mainly to adventurous foreign backpackers. By 1980, it had begun to attract the Bangkok middle class as a vacation spot, site for a second home, or vacation retreat. In the mid-1980s, government began to invest heavily in attracting international tourists, and Chiang Mai became one of the designated major locations. The Chiang Mai airport was declared an international airport in 1971, and underwent a major expansion to receive tourists in the mid-1980s.[5]

Old families in the development era

Some of the families who prospered on the new opportunities thrown up by these changes came from the ranks of the old elite families who had arrived in Chiang Mai in the railway era.

---

4. There were sixty-two Japanese factories in 1995.

5. The airport was built as a military airstrip in 1921, expanded by the US in the 1960s, used for commercial flights from 1969, separated from the military in 1977, and came under the national Airport Authority of Thailand in 1984.

The Sakdatorn clan had settled in Chiang Mai along with the old families in the pre-railway era. However, its fortunes were based more on trade than land, and it flourished in the conditions of the development era. Riw, the eldest son of the second generation, worked as a manager of the Singer company, and then became a manufacturer of umbrellas, soap, and candles when imports ceased during the Second World War. In 1949, he formed a retailing company, Niyom Panich, which sold radios, TVs, cars, motorcycles, and sewing machines on hire purchase, using his experience from Singer. In the third generation, Narong Sakdatorn expanded and diversified the store as the city's population expanded with its development. He became a leader in the sale of cars and motorcycles in the era of motorization as an agent of Toyota, Yamaha, Honda, and Suzuki (Siri 2000: 12). As the population expanded, especially with more students, tourists, and middle-class families demanding new products and new forms of retailing, Niyom Panich expanded from a single branch in Chiang Mai to a total of 120 outlets spread all over the north, with three thousand employees (Siam nakkhao thurakit 1993: 22–23). Narong hired professional consultants to streamline the management system for this expanded scale (interview, Panupong Sakdatorn, 13 February 2004).

The Tantranont family dates back to Nai Nguan Chun, a China-born Taechiu who figured among the ranks of pioneer traders who came just after the railway was built in 1921. He worked for the Borneo Company importing canned food and other specialties for members of the local aristocracy, who subsequently helped him to set up his own business. He established a large store selling imported goods that were popular among bureaucrats and elite families. His business prospered, and he moved closely with members of this old elite. He also founded a Chinese school and was appointed to posts in local government. In 1942, the family took the surname Tantranont, and renamed their store as Tantraphan (Jeerawat 1996: 98–100).

In the late 1930s Nai Nguan Chun, together with other Chinese merchants in Chiang Mai, collected money to send back to China to fight the Japanese. Because of this he was exiled to China by Phibun for a time but returned to die in Chiang Mai in 1950 (Anu 14 November 2003: 5).

In 1951 his sixth son, Thawat established Tantraphan Department Store, a much larger store in Tha Phae selling consumer goods, including imports at fixed prices. For the next three decades, Tantraphan was the city's largest store, and its growing revenues made the Tantranont into one of the most prominent families of the development era (Tantraphan Department Store 1992).

New families in the development era

Several other families of this era arose out of the ranks of smaller shopkeepers and market traders.

The Tananuwat family hailed from a Chinese migrant who began in the post-railway era as a vendor in the Warorot market specializing in the sale of paint and ironware. His son, Aphisit, started a consumer goods wholesaling business in Warorot market in 1955, but later turned to selling furniture as demand grew with the rising population and prosperity of the city. Initially he acted as a middleman, then imported directly from Bangkok, and finally set up his own factory in 1960. Seven years later, he built a larger factory in Hangdong,[6] and began to bid on large-scale contracts to furnish government offices and company premises. His son, Narong, studied accountancy and computing at Chulalongkorn University, and upgraded the systems of the family business. After Japanese firms started to move to Lampang, the Tananuwat firm was successful at winning contracts in this new market. They built a much larger factory as well as expanding its import of other furniture from Bangkok. In the great boom of the 1980s, the firm expanded again on the new demand from housing developments (interview, Narong Tananuwat, 11 May 2005).

The Suvitsakdanon family also originated from a vendor in Warorot market but rose to prominence only in the 1970s. Nai Bakjua Sae Lim migrated to Siam in 1932 and initially worked as a laborer in the market before opening a small shop selling dried fish, fish sauce, and shrimp paste. Shortly after his death in 1965, the shop was destroyed

---

6. A town six kilometers south of the city that became a center of manufacture for sale to tourists.

in a major fire at the market in 1968. The eldest son, U-that, left school and became a market laborer as his father had once been, ferrying goods by tricycle. He progressed from the tricycle to a truck, and gradually expanded until he was the largest transport contractor in the city with a fleet of three hundred vehicles, some owned and others leased. U-That also rode the motorization era by setting up Nimseeseng Leasing to provide credit for car buyers. He specialized in giving small loans to buyers of second-hand cars at a high rate of interest (18–20 percent) (Apiradi 1992: 128). The business expanded to thirty-eight branches in Chiang Mai, and a total of two hundred branches around the northern region (Arunotai 2002: 21–23).[7]

The most prominent of these families that started from the Warorot market is the Buranupakorn. Nai Chai was a Taechiu born in Thailand who opened a small shop in the market in 1921. He had eleven children, and the family remained poor through until the development era. Their turning point came in the 1970s when the family diversified into selling souvenirs to tourists. Boonlert Buranupakorn invested the proceeds in manufacturing furniture for sale to tourists, and the business boomed. He said, "The profits turned out to be huge. I remember that tourists came in busloads and bought so much of my goods that I couldn't push the dollars into the drawers fast enough" (Anon. 2002b: 89).

The business grew with rising tourist numbers through the 1980s. In 1993, the Buranupakorn bought out their largest competitor in the tourist furniture business, Chiang Mai Sudaluck, which had a factory triple their size. They added factories making other tourist goods such as umbrellas, wood-carving, jewelry, and brassware. Besides selling locally, they exported their furniture to Japan and Germany, and took a part share in twenty restaurants in Europe. In 1995, the family invested half a billion baht in the Empress, a five-star hotel, as well as two other hotels in the four- and three-star category (interview, Boonlert Buranupakorn, 14 May 2003).

Their expansion was possible because there were seventeen siblings in this generation of the family. They ran the business as a *kongsi*, and shared out the responsibilities of management. Beginning in the 1990s,

7. http://www.nimseeseng.com, accessed April–May 2005.

several members of the family became prominent in local government. They invested in buying prime road along major roads, and developing housing estates (interview, Praphan Buranupakorn, 12 May 2003).

The new elite

Beginning around 1970, Chiang Mai grew rapidly as a center of government, education, industry, and tourism. Many families of the old (pre-railway) elite prospered through this era from the steadily rising value of their city-center land, embellished with a few projects to tap the new tourist income through hotels and retailing. Some of the other older families, especially the Sakdatorn and Tantranont, more fully grasped the opportunities that came with motorization, rising incomes, and tourism (Thanet 1992: 21–24).[8] More strikingly, the rapid growth and change of this era allowed some families to rise from very modest origins in Warorot market to the forefront of the city's business. Most spectacular of all was the rise of the Buranupakorn family within two decades. They began in a modest way by selling souvenirs but then expanded across a range of businesses designed to relieve tourists of their funds.

Although they originated from very different strata of the city's society, the families that rode this boom shared one thing in common: they were local, and they faced little competition from outsiders. At the height of the great boom, however, that began to change. For the business families

---

8. One of the few families based from the beginning on industry rather than trade was the Luangchairat. They began making leather products under the Season brand, and expanded by setting up a factory in Bangkok in the 1950s.

Other families that rose on motorization include the Chaisaowong clan, who started a city bus service and later expanded to other provinces, as well as becoming agents for Hino vehicles.

Viraphan was another family that rose as a pioneer in the tourist industry. Rachan Viraphan began as a tour guide and later established a tour company.

In this era, a few families prospered from agribusiness. The Akkrashinoret started with rice milling and liquor distilling, and later got a concession to mine iron. Wibun Wangwiwat had a rice milling business that succeeded in developing export of Basmati rice, as well as tobacco curing, and the production of tea (Cha Raming). Banthun Jirawatthanakun was the most successful of several orchard farmers, but faced allegations about manipulation of land titles and exploitation of illegal immigrant labor.

of Chiang Mai, the boom and bust of the 1990s had an added element besides globalization, namely the intrusion of Bangkok capital.

BOOM, BUST, AND BANGKOK

Dollar-based loans, the deceptive poison of financial liberalization, came to Chiang Mai in the 1990s. Government encouraged banks and finance companies to expand their branches in the provincial areas as one of the strategies to counter the tendency for business and wealth to concentrate around the capital.

Real estate buy-outs

As elsewhere, much of this credit was invested in real estate development, inflating the real growth of demand from a prospering population into a speculative bubble. The holding of the Southeast Asian Games in Chiang Mai in 1995 added to the enthusiasm for building condominiums to the west of the city, and housing estates on the outskirts. In 1994 alone, sixty-six condominium projects were started. Most of the big commercial families were already involved in real estate, but many other local investors joined in this final phase. Some estimated that the supply of estate housing outstripped demand by ten times at the peak of the boom (*Angkaew*, 10 July 1997: 4). As in the capital, the collapse of this market in 1997, coupled with the exchange impact on dollar-denominated loans, crippled the accounts of many of Chiang Mai's business families.

In the retail property market, there was an added factor—investments from Bangkok and beyond. Swept up by the boom, the Tantranont family had invested a billion baht in the massive Airport Plaza retail complex in 1992. But shortly before the Plaza opened, the Bangkok-based Central group of the Chirathivat family opened a store in the new Kat Suan Kaeo complex built by local entrepreneur Suchai Kengkarnkha. In addition, Makro opened a branch in 1993, while Lotus, Carrefour, and Au Chan (a French discount store, later taken over by Big C) all arrived in Chiang Mai in 1997.

The Tantranont family was vastly over-stretched by its Airport Plaza investment. It sold its older Tantraphan department store to Cathay Trust to raise funds, and it invited the Central group to open an outlet of its second-string Robinson department stores in the Airport Plaza. But ultimately the group was forced to close down the remaining Tantraphan stores, and sell the Airport Plaza to the Central group in 1996 (*Prachachat thurakit*, 25–28 January 1996: 56). The Tantranont family continued to operate supermarkets and convenience stores, but lost leadership in the city's retail market, which the family had enjoyed over the prior generation (Pantop 2002: 78).

Many other Chiang Mai properties were sold by their cash-strapped owners to Charoen Sirivadhanabhakdi, who was almost uniquely cash-rich at the height of the crisis because of the sustained cash flow of his liquor business (see chapter 4). A shopping center built by a local hotel-owner, Thawi Sukchiradet, was sold to Charoen in 2000 and converted into a replica of Charoen's Panthip Plaza electronics mart in Bangkok. Charoen also bought the Kalae shopping center, the Chiang In Plaza belonging to the old Kitibutr family, and the Anusan market, one of the earliest market developments by the Chutima-Nimmanahaeminda clan, sold for 675 million baht. Both the latter properties were bought from prominent old families. Chumphon Chutima sold Charoen a prime plot of land along the Ping River which the family would not have ceded unless under dire pressure (Chalit 2005: 19). Charoen's TCC group also bought up the Suriwong Hotel, and all the hotels that had formerly belonged to the Imperial group.

Some of the families that had risen on motorization and retailing over the past generation now faced increasing competition from the outside. The multinational automotive firms that bought out their local partners in auto assembly after the crisis (see chapter 3) also took direct charge of their dealerships, and displaced their old local agents. Some electrical firms such as Sony adopted the same strategy. The Sakdatorn family's Niyom Panich company lost several such dealerships, while its formerly successful hire-purchase system crumbled in competition with the price-cutting strategies of the new hypermarkets such as Carrefour and Lotus. After 1997, Niyom Panich downsized and shed a third of its workforce (interview, Panupong Sakdatorn, 13 February 2004).

The furniture business of the Tananuwat family was hit by the slump in real estate and the advent of new forms of competition. But the family's finances were sound as their debts were modest and none denominated in dollars. The family responded by taking up a franchise of the Index home retail chain, and bringing in more professional staff to supplement the family's management resources. As the real estate slump bottomed out, the family returned to developing more commercial space (interview, Narong Tananuwat, 11 May 2005).

Similarly the Suvitsakdanon family's Nimseeseng trucking business was only slightly damaged, as the family's debts were modest. After the crisis it expanded into more long-distance trucking, a DHL-like express delivery service, and cold storage (Arunothai 2002: 34–35).

Tourism to the rescue...

The 1997 crisis brought both disasters and opportunities in Chiang Mai. While the property market crashed, tourism boomed as a result of the cheaper baht. Between 1997 and 2002, value added in the hotel and restaurant business in the province grew by 72 percent.[9]

Most of the investment in hotels to cater to this expansion came from outside the city. The Mandarin Oriental was built by a consortium of business groups from southern Thailand; the Shangri-La by the Mitrphol Sugar group from Bangkok; the Conrad by a Phuket entrepreneur; the Le Meridien Chiang Mai by Charoen Sirivadhanabhakdi; the Chedi Hotel by the Bangkok-based Natural Park group of the Samalapa family; and the Four Seasons Mae Rim by Bill Heinecke, a Bangkok-based entrepreneur.[10]

While some of this added revenue was captured by outside entrepreneurs investing in luxury hotels, the positive impact was also felt by local entrepreneurs. Boonlert Buranupakorn invested 700 million

---

9. Figures from the Gross Provincial Product tables published by the National Statistical Office.

10. The Four Seasons had been built several years earlier and previously managed by the Regent chain. Heinecke had been raised in Bangkok, and made a business career in hotels and food franchises.

baht in the Meritus Chiang Mai Riverside and Spa Hotel which opened in 2004 (*Phuchatkan rai sapda*, 30 September 2005[11]). Several other local entrepreneurs invested in more modest hotels, restaurants, craft souvenirs, and retailing.

Others continued to do well from the generally buoyant economy of the city. Paradorn Bricks is an example of a small company that survived the crisis with help from the government. Som Cherdchutrakuntong was a wage laborer engaged in transporting bricks. His son, Wichien, got a B.A. in business administration and M.A. in economics from Chiang Mai University, and set up a small brick kiln with a 30,000 baht investment in 1980. He gradually expanded to a larger site in Hangdong in 1984, and a second factory with gas-fired kilns in 1990. In the 1990s, he became involved in the real estate market, but also expanded the brick business with exports to Europe and Japan. After the crisis, he got assistance from the Ministry of Industry to hire consultants to improve his productions systems, reduce costs, and standardize quality. He received a quality certification from the ministry, which helped him to sell to government and to high-end customers. In 2001, he streamlined the company by splitting the marketing and production divisions, and was able to expand his market by selling hand-made bricks manufactured in the villages as well as his own product. He also became an agent for modern machinery (Paradorn Bricks 2005).

... and politics

In the past, political positions such as the chairmanship of the municipality were valued more as a token of social recognition than a business resource. But that changed around 2000 as a result of decentralization, the crisis, and the rise of Thaksin.

Until 1995, the chairman of the municipality was appointed by the governor. The position tended to circulate among members of the old families, and even continued to do so for a time after the post became elective. Worakon Tantranont served two terms from 1985 to 1995, and

11. http://www.manager.co.th/mgrWeekly/ViewNews.aspx?NewsID=9480000134255

his Ananthaphum grouping dominated local politics over this decade (Viengrat 2000: 206–207).

In November 1995, a group of the newer businessmen defeated the Tantranont-led party at the municipal elections, and took charge of the municipality. Praphan and Pakorn Buranupakorn were among those elected, and three years later Pakorn was elected to the chairmanship.[12] At the next election in November 1999, this group was again successful, and Pakorn Buranupakorn became the municipal chairman until he resigned in 2000 to stand for election to parliament. Boonlert then took the position for the next two terms.[13]

The Buranupakorn family had links to Thaksin Shinawatra, who formed the Thai Rak Thai Party in 1998 and was elected prime minister in 2001. Boonlert Buranupakorn had been a classmate of Phayap Shinawatra, Thaksin's younger brother, at Chiang Mai's premier secondary school, Montfort College (interview, Boonlert Buranupakorn, 14 May 2003). With the decentralization reforms implemented in the late 1990s, local government bodies gained higher budgets and wider powers. The revenues of the Chiang Mai municipality expanded from 700 million baht in 1997 to over a billion baht in 2002.[14] These local bodies became more attractive for local politicians. This in turn increased the linkages between local and national politics. A firm base in local government gave patronage, contacts, and local prominence, which could help to win elections at the national level. National parties were keen to recruit local politicians who had such foundations. Local politicians could gain from the aura of being associated with a prominent national party. The organization, resources, and techniques for winning elections were the same, whether at the local or national

---

12. The 1995 grouping, known as Naowarat Phatthana, split after a killing in the tourist Night Bazaar brought to light protection rackets preying on the market's vendors. The breakaway was known as Chiang Mai Khunnatham.

13. In 2004, the chairman was chosen directly by the electorate for the first time. Prior to that, the chairman was elected by the municipal councilors from among themselves.

14. The figure is from the municipality's annual income, from 631 million baht in 1997 to 1,162 million baht in 2002. This figure does not include subsidies from the central government and loans, which increased dramatically in Thaksin's period.

level. Throughout Thailand in these few years, these decentralization reforms led to the rise of local networks that contested elections at both the local and national level. In Chiang Mai, the dominant network coalesced around the wealth and influence of the Buranupakorn family and their links to Thaksin.[15]

In 2000 Pakorn Buranupakorn vacated the municipal chairmanship in favor of his brother, and stood successfully for election as an MP under the TRT Party in 2001. The local election campaigns of the Buranupakorn group became more lavish, and more explicitly identified with the TRT Party. Campaigns began six months ahead of polling day and used the same wide range of techniques deployed at general elections. At the municipal polls in 2004, a group led by the scion of one of the old families[16] challenged the Buranupakorn group but family standing and old-style patron-client ties were no match for the new electoral techniques (Phengkamon 2004). Boonlert Buranupakorn returned for a second term as municipal chairman. In 2005, Pakorn retained the city's MP seat, defeating a descendent of the city's old princely family, while Phayap Shinawatra won the constituency on the city's outskirts. In 2000, Praphan Buranupakorn won election to the Senate, but the result was invalidated by the Election Commission on grounds of malpractice. He ran again successfully in 2006.

The headship of the Provincial Administrative Organization (PAO, *obojo*) was also opened up to direct election for the first time in 2004. The TRT became involved in these elections all over the country. In Chiang Mai, it discretely gave support to more than one of the competing groupings. Praphan Buranupakorn was part of the winning TRT team and became a deputy chairman of the PAO (as did Udom Suvitsakdanon). Another Buranupakorn sibling, Thasani, was elected mayor of Changphuek, a tambon municipality adjacent to Chiang Mai.

---

15. It should be pointed out that the links between the Shinawatra and the Buranupakorn clans were not especially close prior to this time. They came together around 2000 for mutual advantage. The Buranupakorn gave Thaksin a local base in the city he preferred to claim as his home. Thaksin gave the Buranupakon the patronage and prestige of access to the center of power.

16. Chumphon Chutima supported a grouping led by Surachai Liewsawatipong, member of another old family (Liew).

This alliance between the Buranupakorn family and Thaksin's TRT was mutually advantageous. The Buranupakorn local network ensured that Chiang Mai was a strong base for TRT, and that Thaksin could claim the mantle of the city's favorite son even though he had moved away since teenage years and built his business career in Bangkok. The Thaksin government steered many large projects to Chiang Mai, including upgrading the airport; building a Night Safari park, Conference and Exhibition Center, a center for SME products, and a regional center for agricultural products; dredging the Ping River, upgrading the Mae Sa watershed, and preventing flooding in the Si River; constructing a cable car on Doi Chiang Dao; building a craft center, new government offices, upgraded road, and room honoring Thaksin in his birthplace of Sankamphaeng; making Chiang Mai an "e-province" (meaning, many government websites); and constructing or upgrading several roads to promote tourism. With Thaksin's encouragement, Boonlert diverted municipal budget to dredging the city's moat, and burying electric and telephone cabling underground. Significantly, most of these projects were designed to boost Chiang Mai as a center of tourism, the sector in which the Buranupakorn family were the leading local entrepreneurs. Many projects also generated large construction budgets that became patronage to boost the fortunes of certain rising businessmen and tie them to the Buranupakorn–TRT network.[17]

In May 2007, Boonlert Buranupakorn was defeated in the municipal council over an emergency budget for flood relief. He resigned and stood for reelection, presumably hoping to strengthen his position. But on 24 June 2007 he lost to Dueantemduang na Chiang Mai by the big margin of 24,985 votes to 18,051. Dueantemduang belongs to an old Chiang Mai family with long involvement in politics. At the 2005 general election, she lost to Pakorn Buranupakorn as a Democrat Party candidate. Her victory, and Boonlert's loss, may have many causes. She appealed to the middle class and students who felt they got little from Boonlert. The Democrat Party assisted with her campaign. The Buranupakorn dominance had generated resentment. A former deputy fell out with Boonlert over the division of municipal patronage, criticized Boonlert in public,

---

17. For example, Bunsong Teriyaphirom.

stood against him in the mayoral election, and came in third, splitting the vote. Some leaders of poor communities, which were Boonlert's main vote base, seem to have defected in protest at unfair distribution of benefits. Dueantemduang, a former military officer, may have been able to use military influence to block vote-buying. Perhaps sensing a turn in the tide, the Buranupakorn camp had tried to disqualify Dueantemduang's candidature on a technicality (failure to affix a tax stamp to one document), but the ruling was overturned by the Administrative Court just two days before the poll, generating a strong sympathy vote for Dueantemduang. The shift in power at the locality may also reflect the fall of Boonlert's ally, Thaksin, at the national level, and the possibility that the military will try to engineer a Democrat-led coalition in the near future.

CONCLUSION

The century prior to the 1997 crisis had thrown up two main commercial elites. The first was founded on land holdings in the city center acquired in the pre-railway era. The second rose on the back of the city's rapid expansion in the development era, especially by exploiting opportunities thrown up by motorization, retailing to the growing population, and tourism.

Families from both the new and old elite were caught up in the property bubble that burst in 1997. Several of the old families, which had long relied heavily on the rising value of their landholdings and which had launched little new enterprise in recent generations, were obliged to sell-off valuable plots. The crisis was a sharp step down in a longer process of gentle decline.

For Chiang Mai business families, the impact of the crisis was intertwined with the intrusion of capital from Bangkok and beyond. Local retail business faced new competition from the Bangkok-based Central group, and from the transnational hypermarkets. The Tantranont family, an old family that had become the single most prominent business group in the development era, misjudged its investment strategy at the peak of the boom and was virtually wiped off the map. Charoen

Sirivadhanabhakdi, the cash-rich liquor king, became a major owner of Chiang Mai commercial properties within the space of a few years. Auto and electrical dealers were pushed aside by Japanese multinationals establishing their own networks. The highly successful Niyom Panich was tripped up by the arrival of the hypermarkets.

The recovery from the crisis was helped by tourism and by government investments. Tourism boomed on the cheaper baht. Again, the cream of this boom was skimmed by new investors arriving from elsewhere in Thailand and overseas, yet some of the benefits trickled down to Chiang Mai's business families.

Politics was perhaps even more important than tourism. Decentralization made local government bodies much more important as sources of power and patronage that could affect business fortunes. Decentralization also strengthened the linkages between local and national politics. The alliance between the currently dominant Buranupakorn family and Thaksin's TRT Party brought large government investments into the city, especially to boost tourism on which the Buranupakorn family fortune was built.

INTERVIEWS

Boonlert Buranupakorn, 14 May 2003.
Chumphon Chutima, 11 February 2004.
Panupong Sakdatorn, 13 February 2004.
Praphan Buranupakorn, 12 May 2003.
Narong Tananuwat, 11 May 2005.
Noppadon Anontawilat, 6 May 2005.
Udom Suvitsakdanon, 17 January 2005.
Udornphan Chantarawiroj, 4 March 1999.
Worawat Tantranont, 6 May 2005.
Praphan Buranupakorn, 12 May 2003.

The author would like to thank Anurat Phuntungpoom and Warangkana Mutumol for their assistance in the research.

PROSPECTS

9

FINDING SOME SPACE IN THE WORLD:
THAI FIRMS OVERSEAS

Pavida Pananond

As Thailand's economy becomes more globalized, it is ever more important for Thai firms to be able to compete at a global level.

Until the great boom of 1987–1996, overseas investment by Thai firms was negligible. Over the boom, however, the outward flow increased rapidly. The pioneers included several of the largest Thai conglomerates. They were followed by many medium-sized firms extending their activities in Thailand across the borders into neighboring countries in Asia. Telecom firms, hoteliers, property developers, restaurant chains, construction companies, agribusinesses, mining companies and several others replicated their Thai ventures in nearby countries with similar climate, culture, consumption patterns, and political environment. A handful of larger firms were more adventurous. They had ventured overseas in a small way in earlier years, but over the great boom began to perceive these outward ventures as something more integral to their corporate strategy. For Thai entrepreneurs, who were virtually all of Chinese origin to some extent, the opening of China, and China's subsequent breakneck growth, were an added incentive to look outward.

What happened to this trend in the crisis? This chapter briefly reviews the pattern and scale of Thai outward investment in the pre-crisis era, and then looks at the trends, policies, statistics, and company strategies since 1997. It concludes by suggesting that Thai firms must look outwards in order to grow, and that the government needs to rethink how it can help.

THAI OUTWARD INVESTMENT IN THE PRE-CRISIS ERA

Prior to 1986, virtually no firms ventured overseas. A small trickle of outward investment was created by banks and trading companies setting up overseas branches, mainly in the US and other advanced countries.

After 1986, however, the outward flow increased gradually up to a peak in the mid-1990s of around 20 billion baht a year, equivalent to 0.45 percent of GDP, or a third of the inflow of foreign investment (see figure 9.1).[1] Financial liberalization, especially the lifting of exchange controls in 1990, significantly eased the financial difficulties for Thai firms venturing broad.

FIGURE 9.1 Thai overseas investment, 1978–2006

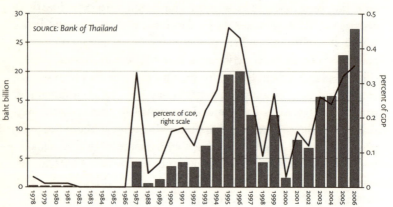

The pioneers of Thai outward investment included several of the largest Thai conglomerates. The prime example was Charoen Pokphand (CP).

Beginning in the early 1960s, CP began to replicate its core integrated poultry business and other agri-processing lines in several countries,

---

1. Note that these figures underestimate the real flow as they include only cash transfers through commercial banks and thus exclude overseas loans, overseas savings, parent companies' loans to overseas subsidiaries, and so on. However, these figures published by the Bank of Thailand are the only data available.

most fully in Indonesia, but also in India, China, Taiwan, Malaysia, Philippines, Burma, Cambodia, Vietnam, and the US. It also established a trading network for distributing its food and other agri-processing products on a much broader scale. More strikingly, from the late 1980s, CP invested strongly in China as the country's economy opened up. Dhanin Chearavanont, the patriarch of CP and a second-generation Chinese immigrant, established strong political contacts in both Beijing and Shanghai. CP's ventures in China ranged across its core agri-processing expertise, replication of some of its new boom-era ventures in Thailand including petrochemicals, telecoms, and retailing, but also a vast range of other ventures such as brewing beer, refining oil, assembling cars and motorcycles, building power plants, and developing shopping malls.

In short, CP primarily relied on its skills in agribusiness to expand to neighboring countries. In some other sectors, however, CP leveraged its general business skills and its strong political contacts to venture into many areas where it had no special expertise but where there were attractive opportunities in the special conditions of China's early economic liberalization. For a time, CP was the largest single overseas investor in China. In 1997, it opened a US$100 million headquarters in Shanghai. By that year, CP had over two hundred subsidiaries operating in twenty countries, listed on seven stock markets, and employing over one hundred thousand people. In 1994, Dhanin said, "We are really going to go global in the future" (*The Nation*, 29 July 1994).

The Siam Cement Group (SCG) was the second largest overseas investor. It had first ventured overseas in the early 1990s with a project in the US. Soon after, SCG had taken a strategic decision to concentrate its expansion in Asia, and had launched twenty-seven projects over 1993–1997 in China, Indonesia, and the Philippines in cement, ceramics, other construction products, paper, petrochemicals, and machinery (Pavida 2001b). By 1998 the group had 130 subsidiaries with thirty-five thousand employees.

Another major overseas investor was the leading Thai-owned hotel chain, Dusit Thani. Beginning in the 1980s, the group built hotels in other countries of Southeast Asia under its two established brand names, Dusit and Princess. In the early 1990s, the group purchased the German-owned Kempinski hotel chain, and other hotel properties in Europe and the US, in the first step of a planned larger global expansion. By 1997, the group operated sixty-four ventures in seventeen countries.

In the boom decade, and especially after financial liberalization, these larger firms were joined by many other ventures, mostly in neighboring countries. Outward investment from Thailand showed no particular focus. The destinations were scattered, and the projects ranged across finance, mining, construction, property development, industry and services (see figure 9.2). Many of the Thai telecom firms took up projects to replicate the same services they supplied in Thailand in other countries of South and Southeast Asia. Several firms specializing in labor-intensive industries relocated some of their production facilities to neighboring countries, especially after labor costs in Thailand began to rise steeply from the late 1980s onwards. Some firms with expertise in food processing, or manufacture of parts for the automotive or electrical industries, also ventured overseas, mostly into neighboring countries in ASEAN. Real estate developers, construction firms, and hoteliers followed the same pattern. In short, several enterprises of the sort that flourished in Thailand during the great boom used some of their increased profits to dabble in similar ventures overseas, usually in the rapidly expanding neighboring region.

Motivation and competitive advantage

In some of these ventures, the Thai companies had ventured overseas in order to gain access to resources or to cheap labor. Most, however, had crossed the borders in order to extend their market. In general, their ability to operate and compete in overseas locations was not entirely based on a superior technological capability or brand property. Rather, their expertise often lay in management and organization, proven ability to operate in their specific industry, and skill in adapting technology and processes to new local situations (cf., Malerba 1992; Grieve 2004).

The Thai overseas entrepreneurs also generally fortified their own skills by networking with various partners (Pavida 2001a, 2001b, 2002). They tended to work closely with a bank or banks. They often entered into joint ventures or licensing arrangements with an overseas government,

FIGURE 9.2 Shares of Thai overseas investment, 1987–2006

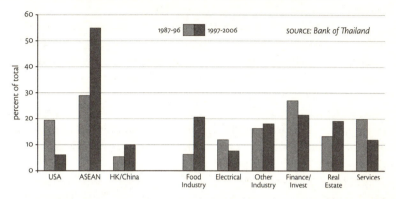

or local companies with strong political ties to a host-country government. They paid close attention to political connections, as in the case of CP in China. On many occasions they worked jointly with a multi-national partner whom they already worked with in Thailand, and who could provide technology. On some occasions they ventured overseas in partnership with other Thai firms allied by marriage, ethnic sub-group links, or established business partnerships. In a few cases, they leveraged family linkages within the Chinese diaspora. In sum, these expansive firms relied heavily on their ability to network with a whole range of partners to compensate for their weak industry-specific technological skills. Their major overseas ventures, other than trading networks and rep offices, tended to be concentrated in neighboring countries where the similarity of culture, climate, and business practice allowed them to get maximum advantage from their management experience and networking skills. Besides, in these neighboring areas opportunities were rapidly expanding, thanks to the regional economic growth in the early 1990s.

AFTER THE 1997 CRISIS

In the immediate aftermath of the crisis, many of the small- and medium-scale overseas ventures were sold off or abandoned. Several firms now looked on their overseas ventures as assets that could be liquidated to help preserve their main business in Thailand.

The Jasmine telecom group provides a typical example. In the 1990s, it had invested in a mobile phone project in India, paging in the Philippines, and a planned region-wide mobile service (ACes), and was in the course of developing projects in Laos, Vietnam, and Nepal. The crisis left the group with huge liabilities that it struggled to restructure over the next five years (see chapter 4). It sold its Philippine venture in 1998, slashed its stake in the regional project in 1999, sold its stake in India to a local partner in 2000, and put the holding company for these projects into bankruptcy in 2002 (Pavida 2004).

Similarly, the Sahapat group sold off stakes in three noodle-making projects and a garment manufacturing enterprise in China. The Dusit group sold off the Kempinski chain and its US hotels, as well as withdrawing from some projects in Asia.

In some cases where operations were up and running successfully, selling off was not worthwhile. But as a whole, Thai entrepreneurs withdrew from a slew of telecom ventures, property developments, construction projects, and other schemes in neighboring countries.

Survivors

Among the bigger investors, the pattern was similar but with some important variation. Groups like CP and SCG underwent major restructuring exercises at home. Both conglomerates defined a restricted range of core businesses for themselves, and slated peripheral ventures for divestment (see chapter 1). Both resumed their overseas expansion after only a short interlude, but made important changes to their outward strategy.

CP decided to streamline its vast activities by focusing on two core areas: production and processing of agribusiness and food industry; and services, including telecommunications, logistics, and retailing. Within these selected areas, the group concentrated on adding value to their products through brand-building activities and producing more value-added products. It also placed a stronger emphasis on downstream activities of retailing and distribution, including creating its own outlet, CP Fresh Mart, to carry a broad range of the group's food products (*Phuchatkan Rai Duen*, March 2005)

However, its strategy for divestment overseas seemed based more on a regional than a sectoral rationale. In the US, it sold off its agribusiness and telecom ventures. In China, it disposed of several peripheral ventures including its brewery, but it remained involved in the automotive industry and petrochemicals. In short, it retained a much broader span of businesses in China than in any other country, even in its Thai home base. CP expanded its retail operations in China, extended its agribusiness more into finished and branded products rather than less value-added ones, and strengthened its operations in other meat industries on top of poultry. Nonetheless, CP did not entirely shake off its pre-crisis ways. From around 2000 onwards, CP returned to its old China pattern of plunging into opportunistic projects that had little or no relation to its avowed corporate mission. It expanded its real estate investments in China, and even became involved in a wine-making venture in Sichuan. Moreover, it replicated the same behavior elsewhere in Asia, investing in a fast-food franchise in Malaysia (Pavida 2004).

Around the Asian region the group retained its agribusiness interests, and set out to enhance its overall efficiency through integration of the group's overseas production bases. Rather than focusing on producing separately for each domestic market, CP started to create more specialized units. For example, Thailand was designated as a production center for cooked and processed meats, while China served as a base for poultry production for export to Japan, and Turkey was developed as a base for export to the European Union.

The CP group made efforts to build formal cooperation with host-country governments. In July 2004, the group signed a Memorandum of Understanding with the provincial government of Queensland, Australia, to promote R&D cooperation in agribusiness technology as well as to expand markets for CP products in Australia. Later in October, a more extensive memorandum was signed with the State of California to promote cooperation in agribusiness, retailing, education services, and entertainment (CP Group Annual Report 2004).

SCG also underwent a major restructuring exercise that included defining the group's core businesses as cement, construction goods, paper, and petrochemicals (see chapter 6). Most of its existing overseas ventures fell within this scope. SCG reduced its involvement in ceramics and machinery, which fell outside that scope, and it generally rationalized its portfolio by disposing of less profitable or less strategic ventures. The group also resolved to focus more on profitability than growth, especially through product innovations.

Prior to 1997, Siam Cement had responded to investment opportunities that became available in various markets, without any coordinated strategy (Pavida 2001b). After the crisis, it focused more on the contribution of any new venture to the overall profitability of its network. SCG continued with investments to create an integrated network of petrochemical plants within Southeast Asia. In 2005, it added to the upstream end of its petrochem business by investing in a high-density polyethylene plant in Iran in joint venture with the Iranian government and a Japanese partner. SCG also added to the upstream end of its paper business by expanding its holding in United Pulp and Paper in the Philippines from 43 to 99 percent in 2003. It continued to work with strategic partners for technology, including Dow Chemical for a venture in the US, and Japanese Itochu in the Iranian project.

The main significance of both these cases is that these big business groups continued to see overseas expansion as a major strategy, with CP focused even more firmly on China, and SCG on Southeast Asia. In addition, both groups' post-crisis international expansion reflected an increased focus on efficiency for their overall operations. Although the search for new markets remained a key objective, they also gave greater prominence to upstream or downstream expansions that increased overall efficiency. Although these attempts may not have clearly borne fruit, the shift in emphasis showed a marked difference from their pre-crisis pattern of international expansion. Similarly, the two firms' post-crisis focus on network relationships differed in nature rather than in kind. In the pre-crisis period, they focused on links with financial institutions and foreign technology partners. In the post-crisis period, their emphasis was more on cultivating links with foreign partners who could strengthen their industry-specific competitive advantage. Both groups played down the aspect of political and social networks and stressed formal links with host country authorities instead.

Other Thai groups changed their outward strategies after the crisis. The Dusit group became less interested in expansion by investing in hotel properties, but more focused on marketing itself as a hotel management company, leveraging the Thai reputation for service delivery as a competitive asset. The Banpu mining group, which before the crisis had only one overseas venture, invested in five projects in Indonesia and China to meet a growing level of world demand for coal, and innovated by selling its coal under the "Banpu" brand name, successfully raising its share in European and Japanese markets. By 2005, 90 percent of the group's income came from overseas investments.

Thai Union Foods (TUF), a large fish canning firm that had not ventured overseas prior to the crisis but had been little damaged by the crisis due to conservative management, ventured aggressively outwards in the aftermath. In 1997, TUF bought a stake in Van Camp, the third largest seafood canning firm in the US, and acquired full control in 2000. Three years later, TUF acquired Empress International, a leading importer and distributor of seafood products in the US. TUF also established a trading company in Shanghai to prospect for entry into the China market, and began prospecting in Vietnam (Pavida 2004). Over the post-crisis decade, the company quadrupled its revenues, with 45 percent derived from the US market (*Bangkok Post 2007 Mid-year Review*: 25).

Scale and destination

The outward flow of investment experienced only a brief lull in the years immediately following the crisis. By 2003, outward investment expanded strongly, and by the mid-2000s had returned to the same absolute level (over 20 billion baht a year) and almost the same proportion of GDP as before the crisis (see figure 9.1). The pattern remained the same as the earlier era: while most of the volume was contributed by major players such as SCG and CP, there were also a large number of modest ventures by medium-scale corporations. Between 1999 and 2003, almost a fifth of all Thai listed firms had some kind of overseas venture, particularly those involved in consumer goods, manufacturing, or agro-industry. Seventy percent of these ventures involved an investment below 100 million baht, and only a sixth were over half a billion.[2]

The geographical distribution of outward investment shifted to focus much more within Asia, especially ASEAN and China. The proportion of outward investment flowing to the US or European Union was reduced from 25 percent of the total in the boom decade to only 8 percent in the post-crisis decade. By contrast, the proportion flowing to ASEAN neighbors expanded from 29 to 55 percent, and that to Hong Kong and China from 5 to 10 percent. The type of projects was still scattered, with projects ranging from industrial estates in Vietnam to shipping in Singapore and retailing in China. But a larger proportion of the outward investment was in industry, up from 34 to 47 percent, with food industries as the leading sub-sector.

While much of the post-crisis outward investment was primarily in search of markets, there was significantly more investment aimed at securing resources and increasing the overall efficiency of business groups. The emergence of a more region-wide market within Southeast Asia under the impact of the AFTA tariff-reduction scheme, and the spectacular rise of China, created opportunities for Thai firms to enlarge their market reach as well as to increase the overall efficiency of their operations through closer integration. Thai firms in primary sectors went outward to overcome the limitations on the supply of resources at home.

Policy

The Thai government had flirted with plans to promote outward investment since the mid-1990s without any concrete result. Finally in 2003, the Board of Investment (BOI) launched a scheme that targeted three types of industries: those in which Thailand might become a regional center, including petrochemicals, auto parts, and agribusiness; those

---

2. For more detail on this point, please see the Thai version of this chapter.

where local firms needed to move outwards because of poor prospects for expansion at home, such as garments, fisheries, and jewelry; and those where Thailand might have global potential including animal feeds, sugar, leather products, and tourist-related services. The BOI gave priority to projects in Laos, Burma, Vietnam, Cambodia, China, and India, with a secondary target elsewhere in Asia including Central Asia.

Nonetheless, the existing policy regime toward outward investment could be called reactive at best and futile at worst. The Thai government considers overseas investment simply as a response to the increased competition in the global economy rather than as a key part of a broader strategy to develop Thai firms' competitive advantage. At present government policies encourage Thai firms to expand abroad in order to seek lower-cost resources or to find new markets for their existing products and services without a thorough understanding of where Thai firms stand in global value chains. Instead of giving incentives for firms to invest overseas, policies should become more proactive and should concentrate on building firms' capacity and capability, without worrying whether that capacity and capability is applied in the domestic economy or overseas.

CONCLUSION

Although the scale of outward investment is still modest, Thai firms are highly disposed to expanding investment beyond the national boundaries. Although the crisis forced considerable divestment of overseas ventures, the momentum to expand transnationally was not seriously damaged. Calculated as a fraction of GDP, the outward flow in the post-crisis decade was only marginally below the level in the boom decade—0.22 versus 0.27 percent.

In venturing overseas, Thai firms compensate for their lack of any proprietary technology by deploying skills in management and by networking with a range of partners including banks, governments, multinational partners, and allied Thai firms. The Thai business groups that survived the crisis have been strengthened by restructuring, streamlining their operations, and becoming more focused on their business efficiency. While the pre-crisis phase of outward investment was scattered both sectorally and geographically, there is now a clearer focus on Asia, on industrial projects, and especially on food industries. While outward-investing firms still rely heavily on their ability to draw strengths from network partners, they are also investing in adding more value from innate advantages including branding and images of national origin. The larger firms like CP and SCG are now more likely to evaluate any overseas project's contribution to the overall efficiency of the group.

Recently the government has become aware that outward investment needs to be a part of national economic strategy. The Thaksin government was very active in leading delegations of potential Thai investors to Asian destinations, particularly China and, to a lesser extent, India. Since 2003, the BOI has a strategy and a framework for promoting outward investment. However, at present these support efforts are sporadic, often inept, and poorly thought through. Yet the role of the government could and should be important. The Chinese government has played an important role in helping major Chinese firms to enter the world market. Zhang (2003) argues that such political backing can compensate for other economic factors.

The principal constraint on the expansion of overseas investment may be the limited number of Thai corporate groups with the scale to venture overseas on the pattern of CP and SCG. Perhaps, however, the differential impact of the crisis which has tended to sift winners from losers and result in greater concentration of ownership in several sectors may eventually result in more outward investment. The example of the liquor industry is one possibility (see chapter 5). Now that Charoen Sirivadhanabhakdi has a near monopoly in both the mainstream liquor and beer markets within Thailand, his prospects for further expansion within this sector in Thailand are limited. Now that he has floated his firms on the stock market, pressure for expansion will be unavoidable. For these reasons, he has begun to acquire assets overseas (distilleries in Scotland), prospect for ventures in neighboring countries, and make preparations to create a global brand (by putting Beer Chang on the shirts of Everton footballers).[3]

There are a variety of challenges facing Thai multinationals in their future growth. Among the most important ones are the need to develop capacity and capabilities to compete at the regional and global levels. The continuous increase in global FDI flows in recent years come not only from established multinationals based in developed economies, but also from rising new players based in developing economies. The depth of players is a sign that global competition is becoming more intense and approaching closer to home. With this level of competition from multinationals on the doorstep, Thai firms in general and Thai multinationals in particular can no longer be complacent in their comfortable domestic status quo. International expansion is no longer one of several options for growth but perhaps a key strategy for survival. It should not be considered simply as relocation to lower-cost countries, but as an integrated part of the firm's overall strategy.

To successfully implement an internationalization strategy, Thai firms need to seriously consider where their competitive strengths lie. The competitive advantages of Thai multinationals change as these firms evolve. In the early stage of international expansion, Thai multinationals relied on the strengths they could draw from network partners. Now they are faced with challenges to sustain their competitive advantages in the long run, and that will require more technological capabilities.

---

3. Over the past decade, Thailand has been the base for a new global brand, but in a very curious way. In 1962, Chalieo Yoovidhya began marketing *Kratingdaeng*, a copycat competitor of a Japanese energy drink, Lipovitan-D. In Thailand, these cheap caffeine-and-sugar drinks are popular with truck drivers, laborers, and students. Dietrich Maeschitz, an Austrian toothpaste marketing executive, adapted the drink by reducing the sugar and adding carbonation, and launched in Europe under the brandname Red Bull using youth-focused marketing, association with extreme sports, and sponsorship of motor racing. The drink acquired cult status, especially as a mixer for vodka in dance clubs. By 2006, sales amounted to 3 billion cans in 130 countries, generating a revenue of US$2.5 billion. Chalieo and Maeschitz, each of whom owns 49 percent of the company (the other 2 percent belongs to Chalieo's son), ranked 292 and 317 on the 2006 Forbes list with fortunes of US$2.5 and 2.4 billion, respectively. Although Red Bull was born from Thailand, the global product is very different, and most international consumers have no idea of the Thai origin.

10

RENTS AND RENT-SEEKING IN THE THAKSIN ERA

Thanee Chaiwat and Pasuk Phongpaichit

ONE of the recurrent themes of several chapters of this book has been the role of political processes in determining business profit and business success. The pre-crisis conglomerates grew in part by their access to generals and politicians. The banking cartel survived by investing in political protection. The massive profits in liquor and mobile phones were generated by political decisions. The entry of big retail was possible because of passive political acceptance at the national level. Businessmen in Chiang Mai and Rayong have grasped the opportunities created by decentralization of local government to use political power as business strategy.

In the eye of the crisis, neoliberal critics attributed the disaster in part to "cronyist" ties, and hoped that market liberalization reforms would reduce their importance. There is little sign that this has come about. Indeed, several of the above chapters show that in and after the crisis businessmen reverted *even more* to political means to achieve business goals.

This chapter presents a general framework for understanding the impact of the crisis on the relationship between business and politics at the national level. The analysis draws on the study of rents and rent-seeking, and on some game theory.

The first section of the chapter summarizes several earlier studies on the relationship of business and politics in the pre-crisis era. After sketching a model of business-political relations in the second section, the third examines how the crisis, coupled with broader changes in the political and business environment, prompted an ambitious attempt to restructure the relationships between entrepreneurs, bureaucrats, and politicians under the Thaksin government (2001–2006).

CONTROLLED OLIGOPOLY PRE-CRISIS

The dominant character of the political economy of Thai business in the era before the crisis was competitive clientelism (Doner and Ramsay 2000) or what may be called "controlled oligopoly."

All firms try to make unusually high profits, a concept which economists call a rent.[1] These can be earned by many methods: by innovation; by building powerful brand properties; by mergers and acquisitions to remove competitors; or by government protection such as tariff barriers, tax breaks, or monopoly concessions. These rents do not come from nowhere, but usually out of the pockets of consumers or competitors. In an extreme version of ideal economics, such rents are pictured as always bad. But in fact most capital accumulation is fuelled by rents. Particularly at an early stage of capitalist development, capital is often accumulated from the high profits of illegal business carried out under political protection.[2] Whether rents have a good or bad effect on economic growth and equity depends partly on how large these rents are, and partly on how they are used. If rents are invested effectively they will add to overall growth. If they are hoarded for indulgent consumption, they may injure growth and increase inequity. If they are spent on politics in order to sustain the flow of rents then they may be detrimental both to the economy and to the functioning of the political system (Khan and Jomo 2000: 5; Khan 2000a: 40–63; Pasuk and Nualnoi 2003).

In the pre-crisis era, Thai firms were able to earn rents by gaining privileged, oligopolistic positions in the market, but the level of those rents was limited by a degree of competition within the system. The success of firms in this era came from three principal sources. First, they needed good political connections, especially in the early stages of urban growth when commercial opportunities were allocated by authoritarian centralized governments. Second, they needed access to the capital

---

1. "The term 'rent' is used to describe (not always precisely) incomes which are above normal in some sense. But what is a 'normal' return? Often the benchmark used in the income which an individual or a firm would have received in a *competitive* market" (Jomo and Khan, 2000: 5).

2. Imperial Britain's opium traders are one example; Thailand's provincial godfathers are another.

accumulated in the major commercial banks. Third, they were often aided by strategic alliances with multinational firms to gain technology. In all three of these aspects there was a degree of competition. In most major sectors, several multinationals were interested in doing business in Thailand. There was a handful of commercial banks. The military was highly factionalized and soon gave way to a parliamentary system with competitive parties and a high turnover of cabinets. Within this system, certain entrepreneurial families and family groups were able to establish monopolistic and oligopolistic market positions that delivered high levels of rent. The prime example was the banking system, which was dominated by six or seven families. But at the same time, there were relatively few absolute monopolies, and most firms had to invest both in innovation and in the maintenance of their political and commercial ties in order not to cede their position to competitors. The result was an overall high level of investment, sustained over several decades, which in turn drove a high level of growth in the urban economy.

Mushtaq Khan sketched the flows between patrons and clients in Thailand from the 1970s to the 1990s (see figure 10.1). Capitalists (c) bankrolled other capitalists or politicians (p) who redistributed some of the funds to Non-Capitalists (n, meaning anybody else) in order to secure election. Once in power, they might influence Bureaucrats (b) to provide subsidies, licenses, or other favors which allowed

FIGURE 10.1 Resource flows in patron-client networks, pre-crisis era

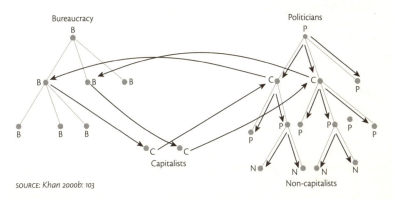

SOURCE: Khan 2000b: 103

their businesses to earn rents. The system was competitive because politicians as a group accepted funding from many different capitalists, because politicians had to compete to gain power, and because the bureaucracy was riven with overlapping jurisdictions. Although a large part of the rent was dissipated in political investment (and yet more on luxurious consumption), there was still enough to fuel the expansion of the major family corporations and to drive the growth in the urban economy.

Towards monopoly in business

This system had begun to disintegrate in the 1990s. Financial liberalization and the rise of the stock market displaced the banks from their crucial central role. The great boom brought in new corporate players, increasing the level of competition. Governments became less stable, and the rate of turnover of prime ministers and cabinets increased. Consumer advocates, international bodies, and technocrats argued that the dissipation of rents in political competition imposed costs that prevented Thailand from emulating the growth performance of East Asian states. The example of the Anand governments of 1991–1992 encouraged a view that more powerful and stable governments would be able to reduce oligopoly, and transfer rents from political investment to productive investment.[3] These ideas helped to shape the 1997 Constitution, which explicitly aimed to produce stronger and more stable governments (Rangsan 2003: 1, 178).

The 1997 crisis completed the destruction of the old pattern of rent-seeking, but not in the way that the reform lobbies of the 1990s had imagined. While the crisis evoked a wave of support for market liberalization reforms to undermine protected monopolies and crony relationships, the outcome of the crisis within many sectors was to

---

3. The Anand governments, which were installed by a coup junta rather than election, were able to carry out several reforms to liberalize markets. It began the liberalization of the auto market described in chapter 2, and planned the liberalization of the liquor market described in chapter 4. It also thwarted some flagrant attempts at rent-seeking, especially over a contract to install telephone lines (Sakkarin 2000).

increase the levels or monopoly or concentration. Mostly this came about because there were many losers but few winners. In several sectors such as steel and petrochemicals, forced mergers reduced the number of key players. In others such as big retail, the acquisitions and expansion policies of powerful multinationals created a totally new level of market concentration. Even in banking, while capital ownership became more diversified, management control became even more concentrated under a few families. In the case of the liquor industry, Charoen Sirivadhanabhakdi not only tightened his monopoly control over the liquor market in the teeth of a formal market liberalization, but also annexed a virtual monopoly in beer from its long-standing owner, Boonrawd.

The decline of competitive clientelism was also a function of politics. To understand this point, we will first examine the relationship of business and politics through a rather formal model.

A BUSINESS MODEL FOR ENTRY INTO POLITICS

Business groups can relate to politics in three main ways: clientage, agency, or direct participation.

Clientage, agency, or participation

Under clientage, business groups do not enter politics directly, but rely on political figures to provide protection and to influence policy on their behalf. It is a rather remote and discontinuous relationship, and hence somewhat unreliable and risky. In particular, such a relationship may not be efficient in dealing with the overlapping jurisdictions within the bureaucracy. For example, in the early 1990s, one government department granted an exclusive concession for one company to operate a mobile telephone service for a period of time. The firm had reason to believe that the concession amounted to a monopoly. However, only shortly after, another department issued concessions to a second company, subjecting the original concessionaire to competition.

Under agency, business groups dispatch their representatives to work on their behalf in politics by serving as MPs or as officers of a political party. Such agents have the opportunity to occupy ministerships that have authority over the sector in which the business groups operate. This method requires more skill and insight into the working of politics. The business groups have to make decisions on which party or parties have the opportunity to form a government, and need some influence to ensure their agent occupies an appropriate ministry. There is also a problem of controlling such agents once they are in place. For example, during the Chavalit government in 1996–1997, one telecommunications company successfully inserted its representative in the appropriate ministry. However, the declaration of assets made after the cabinet left office revealed that the agent had accumulated more wealth than the business owner over that time, and the agent subsequently switched to working with another party associated with the business owner's rival. The owner launched legal proceedings that ultimately forced the agent to withdraw from politics and disassociate himself from the rival company (*Khao hun*, 17 January 2000).

Under the third option, businessmen involve themselves directly in politics. This method eliminates the uncertainties and problems of control inherent in the two earlier methods, but has its own problems. It exposes the businessman to criticism over conflict of interest. It reduces the flexibility to deal with multiple parties, which may become a risk in a system with high turnover of cabinets.

In the pre-crisis period, most major business groups adopted the clientage or agency methods. Under military dictatorship, clientage was really the only option. As the parliamentary system became better established in the 1980s, many big firms still tried to develop clientage relationships, often by bankrolling several rival parties in order to ensure their political access. Also over this time, some firms began to cultivate their own political agents, and some political figures enthusiastically provided agency services to a roster of firms. In this era rather few businessmen chose to involve themselves directly in party politics. One exception to this rule was the telecommunications sub-sector.

As the profits in this sector were heavily dependent on concession arrangements granted by political fiat, several of the leading players began to take an active political role in the mid 1990s in order to exert closer control over these political decisions.

The relationship of business and politics changed dramatically in the late 1990s. Business was shocked by the severity of the economic slump, and by the refusal of the Democrat Party government (1997–2001) to assume any responsibility for defending domestic capital against its impact. Businessmen had stronger motivation to take a direct role in politics. At the same time, the 1997 Constitution introduced the party list system, which provided an opportunity for businessmen to enter politics without electioneering. In addition, the crisis discredited old politicians and old parties, creating an opportunity for new parties and new leaders to rise.

More businessmen took advantage of the party list to enter politics themselves, or to insert closely related agents (wives, sons-in-law, cousins, etc.). Besides, several changes in the business environment created motivations for businessmen not just to enter politics but to form their own party and bid to become prime minister. Some of these changes are as follows.

First, as more firms had made use of the stock market, the returns to the business owner depended not only on the firm's performance but also on the level of the stock market as a whole. This level was a function of the performance of the overall economy, and the degree of investors' confidence in its future prospects. In the case of Thailand, the stockmarket level is greatly affected by the allocation decisions of international investment bodies, which depend a great deal on cross-country comparisons and predictions about market sentiment. An ordinary MP or minister would have very little opportunity to affect the overall performance of the economy or investor sentiment. But a prime minister might be able to boost overall economic performance *and* improve investor sentiment by talking up the prospects at every opportunity. In such a case, there would be a possibility for the stock market index to multiply as much as five times, and for the prime minister's family wealth to rise by that much or more.

Second, with business becoming more globalized, overseas expansion presented opportunities to expand markets and reduce average costs. In certain sectors (such as telecommunications), overseas expansion depended heavily on government-to-government negotiation and on availability of financing from international finance bodies. Overseas profitability was now also greatly affected by changes in international trade arrangements, such as those negotiated under FTAs. Again these are all matters which could be not influenced by a mere MP, only by a prime minister.

The aura of being a prime minister may convey some special advantage in transnational business negotiations, especially when having to deal with counterparts, such as military juntas, which also combine political authority and business interests. It may be especially useful in the event the owner wishes to sell the family concern to a equivalent politico-business family in a neighboring state.

Third, successful Thai firms had often grown by extending laterally into new businesses, which might be remote from their core concern but present high potential because of a changing business environment. For example, a family firm established to make a percentage on peddling computers might be attracted to enter fields as diverse as mobile phones, satellites, budget air travel, shark loans, property development, television, advertising, and health care. An ordinary politician would not be in a position to secure special privileges for the family firm over such a wide swathe of business sectors. An ordinary politician would certainly not be in a position to launch national policies which boost the profitability in so many sectors by such measures as liberalizing the regulation of credit, declaring open-skies policy, promoting health care for export, increasing officials' allowances for mobile phone usage, reducing taxes on property transactions, and so on.

In sum, the 1997 crisis increased the motivation for businessmen to participate directly in politics, and the 1997 constitution facilitated their entry, while the growing role of the stock market as a generator of wealth and the increased globalization of business raised the potential returns from holding the office of prime minister.

Computing the costs

The decision for a businessman to enter politics under the party list or to take the more ambitious step of forming a party also involved different sets of costs.

For a businessman hoping to enter politics via the party list, the first decision was on the choice of party able to amass enough votes to secure a large number of party list places, and be in a position to participate in the government. Under Thailand's old system of fragmented parties and high turnover, there was some flexibility in building coalitions from a selection of parties. However the 1997 constitution was designed to produce a two-party system, imposing on the businessman a very high-risk initial decision. Next, the businessman might have to bid for a good ranking on the party list. Political parties offered high-ranking positions on the list to public figures that added something to the party image, but few businessmen would qualify for this treatment. More likely the businessmen would have to make a blind bid in the hope of securing a good ranking. Judging what bid level would achieve what ranking on the party list could be tricky. Moreover, this bid would be a recurring expenditure. After the government fell or completed its term and a new election was called, the bidding would have to be repeated.

The alternative to forming a new party involved very high upfront costs to attract other politicians, to establish a public image for the party, and to achieve success in elections. The party leader might be able to raise some funds from businessmen keen to enter through the party list system, but these initial costs would be largely borne by the leader himself. Once the party was established, however, these costs could be minimized in several ways. The costs of attracting other politicians, which are very high in the first instance, should subsequently decline and may in some cases even be reversed; some party expenses may be subcontracted to leaders of the parties' constituent factions; some could be raised by the usual percentage methods on major infrastructure projects such as a new airport.

Clearly, entering politics on the party list was the low-risk low-return option, while forming a party to aim for the premiership was more high-risk high-return. The choice between these two options is probably not simply a cost-benefit exercise. Certain types of businessmen thrive on risk-taking.

MONOPOLISTIC POLITICS

What emerged from the 1997 crisis and the new constitution was an attempt to create a new monopolistic politics in place of the old competitive clientelism. This attempt had three parts. First, many more businessmen entered politics through clientage, agency, and direct participation. Thaksin Shinawatra formed a party that attracted the support and participation of many of the major family corporations that had survived the crisis. Second, this party was able to recruit to its banner enough of the old provincial politicians (outside the south) to win a convincing election victory in January 2001, and then mopped up most of the remaining MPs through merger and acquisition of other parties and factions. Third, Thaksin centralized power under the prime minister by taking advantage of new constitutional provisions designed to achieve "stability," by making important changes in cabinet practice, by a major overhaul of the budget procedure, and by building high popular support for his leadership.

FIGURE 10.2 Resource flows in patron-client networks, Thaksin era

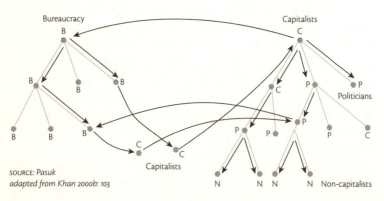

SOURCE: Pasuk
adapted from Khan 2000b: 103

As a result, the balance of power and the flows of rent changed from the old pattern (see figure 10.2).

The business groups that had formerly served as clients of the politicians now had a dominant position. The strength and independence of the bureaucrats declined dramatically. To participate in the distribution of rents, bureaucrats had to become clients of individual politicians or of the dominant party. The position of non-business politicians also declined. Being a constituency MP was no longer a route towards a ministership. The cabinet was recruited from the party list or from non-MPs. After the 2005 election, the overwhelming majority of Thaksin's choices for the cabinet were from outside the parliament altogether. MPs also had much less opportunity to influence the budget process to ensure flows to their constituencies. The MPs fund, which guaranteed each MP a development budget for local spending, had been cancelled. The budget process was firmly under the prime minister's control. MPs were obliged to petition the prime minister or other ministers to gain funds. Many MPs were still able to reap rents by operating as construction contractors, which were granted public-sector contracts, but even this opportunity declined because of the low level of capital expenditure by the Thaksin governments. Several local politicians gave up the parliament in favor of positions in local government, especially the Provincial Administrative Organizations, where they had access to budgets under the 1998–1999 decentralization laws. Other MPs worked closely through local political machines to gain access to these local budgets (see chapters 7 and 8).

Under this new pattern, the decision-making power over the allocation of rents rested with the business politicians (C) and with the bureaucrats (B) working under their clientage. Rents were distributed through political groups (P) and other businessmen allied to the ruling party, and then further redistributed to others through such devices as populist policies.

The nature of rents also changed. Gatekeeping rents collected by bureaucrats and ordinary politicians decreased. Rents accruing to businessmen-politicians through profits inflated by policy corruption increased.

The corruption indices published by Transparency International and the Political and Economic Risk Consultancy both showed a

FIGURE 10.3 Corruption indices, 2000–2006

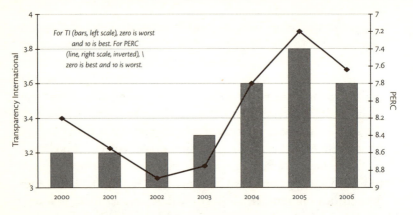

distinct trend of improvement over the Thaksin government (see figure 10.3). These indices are constructed from the perceptions of foreign businessmen, and thus tend to measure the gatekeeping style of corruption operated by bureaucrats and politicians. The trend in these indices confirms the changed pattern of rent allocation in which bureaucrats and local politicians had less influence and less opportunity to command gatekeeping rents. In addition, the government was motivated to reduce rents from gatekeeping as these irritate the ordinary people and businessmen (local and foreign), which were the government's two major support constituencies.

Business politicians collected rents through increased profits engineered by the abuse of executive power. Three main methods were available: first, by changing government regulations concerning the promotion, protection, or regulation of a business sector; second, by allocating public resources to a business sector; and third, by using executive power to give benefits to a specific firm (Ammar et al. 2002). These rents were invested in politics, creating interlocking flows of power and money (see figure 10.4).

Over the initial years of the first Thaksin government, this new pattern appeared to be very successful. The distribution of rents through populist policies to win support raised the popularity of the ruling

FIGURE 10.4 Resource flows among government and clients

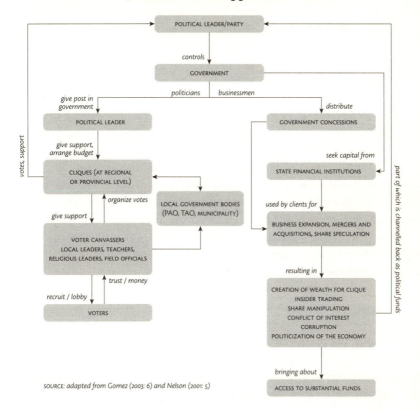

SOURCE: *adapted from Gomez (2003: 6) and Nelson (2001: 5)*

party, and contributed to an even more convincing electoral victory in 2005. The distribution of rents to the business allies in the party also appeared to be successful. The families[4] of eight leading figures in the government had controlling interest in twenty-three listed firms which collectively accounted for one seventh of market capitalization. The annual returns (dividend plus capital gain) was significantly higher than the market average. The ratio between their market value and

---

4. Shinawatra, Photharamik, Maleenont, Chearavanont, Thepkanchana, Mahagitsiri, Charn-virakul, and Srivikorn.

book value was 54 percent higher than for other firms. These results were not related to the firms' financial performance but were purely a result of their political "premium" (Pramuan and Yupana 2005; see also Somkiat 2004).

Risks and costs

However, rent seeking is not a simple matter. The new pattern of control and distribution established by the Thaksin government generated a new set of costs and risks that had to be managed.

The allocation of rents was heavily concentrated among the companies that were closely tied to Thaksin and his party. The scale and concentration of these benefits provoked a scramble by other companies to be included in the distribution, and fomented resentment among companies that were excluded. The larger the number of competitors for such rents, the higher the costs and risks of negotiating the distribution.

Some disgruntlement spread among the non-business politicians. In part this can be attributed to a difference of time perspective. The businessmen were engaged in politics in order to effect a long-term change in the control and distribution of rents. By contrast, the politicians were involved in a succession of short-term exercises to ensure they had access to power by winning election, choosing the right party, and having access to the leader. The businessmen were focused on a continuous game with no end in sight, while the politicians were focused on the next short-term game.

The politicians were also disgruntled over the shrinkage of their rent allocation, and hence increased competition over the pot that remained. The party became increasingly fractured into cliques (*mung*) that competed to influence the decisions that affected the allocation of rents.

Thaksin hoped to counter this disgruntlement by using the stock market to achieve a wider distribution of rents. Many other businessmen had listed companies that would benefit from an overall rise in the index. Politicians were also enthusiastic investors, often in consortiums. In 2005, there was a proposal to install a real-time stockmarket display in the Parliament building. Thaksin put heavy focus on boosting GDP growth, besides talking up the stock market at every opportunity, and occasionally offering stockmarket tips on his weekly radio address. He pursued privatization of state enterprises through stockmarket listing as a way to boost the overall market capitalization and increase its attraction to foreign investors. Thaksin's party spokesman pointed out to critics that "With a high tide, all boats rise" (Crispin 2003).

However, the reliance on the stock market as a mechanism for distributing rents had some risks. When the state petroleum agency, PTT, was partly privatized by listing and became one of the largest stocks on the exchange, large share allocations mysteriously fell into the hands of businessmen closely associated with the government, provoking further discontent over the monopolization of opportunities. In 2004, a state enterprise union opposed the privatization of the state electricity generating arm (EGAT), and an NGO successfully challenged the legality of the privatization in the Administrative Court. Thaksin's reaction to this opposition was instructive. He did not rail against union power or rehearse the theoretical benefits of privatization, but let loose his fears that this opposition would cause the stock index to fall. "If I back down, I can tell you the economy and stock market will crash... The SET index would nosedive" (*Bangkok Post*, 29 February 2004). In fact the post-crisis revival of the stockmarket index had already run out of steam in late 2003. After a peak in December of that year, the index meandered, and the market no longer aided Thaksin as a means to distribute rents through rising stock values (see figure 7).

Several strategies were used to economize on the costs involved in rent seeking. The independent bodies established to monitor the abuse of power were undermined or hamstrung by various methods. Public criticism was stifled in an attempt to limit its detrimental impact on the image of the party and leader that might prejudice their future hold on power. The leader also attempted to devolve more of the management costs of the party onto its other members but appears to have faced considerable resistance. Party members acted as free riders, enjoying the benefits of rent seeking without contributing to the costs. As a result, there seem to have been attempts to unload more of the costs of party management onto the public by financing the party through old-fashioned forms of corruption.

Most of the criticism against Thaksin that emerged from 2004 onwards can be related to the difficulties and failures in the attempt to establish a new pattern of control and distribution of rents. The monopolization of the business benefits within a small circle gave rise to criticism about conflict of interest. The partial or complete exclusion of groups that had benefited under the old system gave rise to criticism of populist policies for diverting such a large share of rents. The attempts to minimize costs gave rise to criticism of authoritarianism, abuse of power, and old-style corruption.

CONCLUSION

The political crisis of 2006–2007, the fall of Thaksin, and scrapping of the 2007 constitution suggest that the businessmen's attempt to form a more monopolistic political system and to rejig the control and distribution of rents has been a failure. The new constitution explicitly sets out to engineer a return to a more competitive, dispersed pattern of power. The interim government has promised legal reforms to impose more controls on monopolies, to limit the abuse of power, to outlaw the conflict of interest, and to isolate politics more from business. Arguably, Thaksin's arrogance and political clumsiness has set back the political cause of Thai capitalism with a vengeance.

But this setback for the business sector may not be permanent or overwhelming. There is a high degree of monopolistic control in the economy, and this has increased under the impact of the 1997 crisis and its aftermath. In many sectors there is now a higher concentration of control, whether under domestic or multinational firms. The majority of firms are still controlled by families or by a very small number of dominant shareholders. A couple of handfuls of families dominate domestic holding on the Thai stock exchange. According to one estimate, 150 families dominate Thai domestic capital, with a very high concentration among the top twenty or thirty (Brooker Group 2001).

It is also significant that Thaksin's project was halted only by an extremely primitive political maneuver—a coup performed by trundling tanks through the capital, the first such successful coup in half a century—which only commanded the support of a small minority at the beginning, and rapidly forfeited much of that narrow support by its own ineptness.

Besides, Thai domestic capital has strong motivation to look to the state for support. Entrepreneurs in a latecomer country on the periphery of world capitalism have limited chances to compete in increasingly globalized markets where rules are being set to favor the expansion of multinational firms from the world's advanced economies. They may find temporary advantages from mobilization of underutilized and underpriced reserves of land, labor, and other resources, but such positional advantages are soon exhausted. It is dreamy to imagine that large investment in technology and research would really create the ability to compete against the leading centers of the world economy. The history, culture, and context are not there. Large economies such as China and India still have opportunities because of the scale of their internal markets, their higher bargaining power against the advanced economies, and the residual mechanisms of their former command-style economies. Thailand has none of these advantages and is increasingly squeezed between the advanced economies on one side and the new rising mega-economies on the other.

Thai domestic capital has reacted against the onslaught of global competition by a mix of strategies. Many firms have attempted to modify their structure and management practice while retaining the family basis, which is their key strength. Many have retreated to areas of the economy that still provide some legal or institutional protection against transnational competition. Some have drawn on cultural capital. Many have hoped to mobilize the very special powers of the state to their own advantage.

But these strategies are difficult to sustain within an economy that has become so integrated with the world economy that its major dynamism comes from outside. Consider the history of Thaksin. It is now often forgotten that he initially entered politics with a promise to protect Thai business from globalization. The innovative part of his "dual-track" economy policy was a promise to energize the domestic economy in order to counterbalance the trend towards greater outward exposure. Ultimately, however, he presided over a further opening of the economy to outside influence. He explicitly abandoned the attempt to defend domestic capital from competition (over the issue of big retail, see chapter 3) precisely because it would antagonize multinational companies and foreign investors. In the dying months of his premiership, he launched the "Partnership for Development" or "Kingdom of Thailand Modernization Framework," a scheme to vastly increase the level of foreign investment in Thailand in both the private and public sectors, and justified the need for such a scheme on grounds that Thai capital and entrepreneurship was inadequate.[5] In the very same month, his family sold off Shin Corp, one of the largest Thai corporations, to a foreign buyer. One reason he was so fiercely rejected was that he had become a public symbol of the failure of his own original political mission to save Thai capitalism.

Thaksin hoped to redistribute economic rents in order to accelerate the growth of Thai capital. Although his political project has failed, the growing level of monopoly and concentration of capital almost certainly means that rents are high and possibly getting higher. This may be damaging to the economy if the rents are badly used, and damaging to the polity if it encourages efforts to increase, defend, and capture those rents through corruption of the political process. But equally, rents can have a positive effect if they are invested in growth or distributed in ways that increase equity. Understanding how rents are created and used, and what part politicians and interest groups play in these processes, are a necessary foundation for maximizing their benefits and minimize their effects.

---

5. Part of the brief invited foreign investors to bid on projects to "to instill a sense of belonging and pride in Thais as well as to incorporate its invaluable legacy, "Thainess", into Thailand's economic and social development" (NESDB 2006).

CONCLUSION

THE 1997 crisis was a major turning point for the Thai economy. Significant parts of several major sectors were shifted under foreign ownership. The ranks of Thai entrepreneurial families were severely winnowed, with many losers and a few spectacular winners. The roles of capital became rather clearly divided, with multinational capital dominating export-oriented industry, and domestic capital clustered mainly in service sectors where it still enjoys forms of implicit and explicit protection. The commercial banks have lost their core role as the engines of capital accumulation and the exemplars of a wider process of family-based conglomeratization. Possibly, Thailand's capitalism has lost its dynamism, though whether that is a temporary or permanent condition is not yet clear.

FROM DEVELOPMENT TO GLOBALIZATION

Behind the idea of "development" in the post–Second World War era was an assumption that backward countries could replicate the growth of more advanced nations rather as infants grow to adulthood following their forebears in past generations.

By the last quarter of the twentieth century, Thailand was frequently celebrated as a success story of the development era. It had entered that era at a low level—as an overwhelmingly agrarian economy under a state which had only recently exited from an *ancien regime*. Its urban economy had very little inheritance of infrastructure, institutions, or business culture. The distance that Thailand traveled over the development era, at least as measured by GDP growth, was unparalleled among countries of similar size.

Government contributed to this success by building infrastructure and keeping the economy stable, but did much less than the developmental states of Korea and Taiwan. The success was attributed to the country's natural resource base (especially abundant land in relation to population until well into the late 1970s), the dynamism of its entrepreneurs, the country's relative openness to the outside world, and its muddled politics, which fostered a "competitive clientelism" avoiding the dead hand of total monopoly.

This era was a golden age for a small number of family businesses. They gained access to limited supplies of capital from banks, technology from overseas partners, and political favors from those in power. Some grew into conglomerates by riding the rapid trends of change in the economy and successfully multiplying the management resources within the family. In the provincial areas, many other families prospered from primitive accumulation on a resource-rich frontier, and gradually moved into property development, construction contracting, and provision of local services as an urban economy emerged. A few prospered well enough to transfer from the locality into the city.

In this era, domestic capital groups were largely shielded from foreign competition. The transaction costs of overseas business were still high. Thailand ranked low on the scales of international attraction. It was a small market in a risky part of the world, and had no former colonial patron with vested interests. Government further protected domestic capital by placing restrictions on foreign equity, and corralling certain sectors with licenses and concessions. In this situation, successful family firms were able to reap large rents.

The development era came to an end around 1980. With the passing of the cold war, Western governments lost their interest in cultivating local capitalisms throughout the world. Multinational capital demanded the right to roam the world without restriction. Technological changes decimated the transaction costs of transnational business. Neoliberalism celebrated the virtue of free markets on a global scale.

At first this change brought huge benefits to Thailand's domestic capital. The great boom of 1987–1996 was founded on growing world trade, the relocation of industry, and access to cheap sources of finance. Thailand's family firms earned unprecedented profits in this boom as partners of the multinationals, investors in new businesses rising on growing prosperity, and owners of assets with escalating values.

But the boom made Thailand attractive to international capital, and thus removed one of the last shields protecting domestic firms from competition. In the 1997 crisis, transnational capital teamed up with international institutions and neoliberal theorists to demand removal of the laws, licenses, and concessions that were the last lines of defense. It all happened very quickly.

LOSERS

In the 1997 crisis, around a quarter of Thailand's major business families were badly damaged. Some disappeared almost completely, while others were reduced to a small fraction of their former scale, and deprived of their dynamism. The losers included several of the great dynastic surnames of the postwar business community. Two factors seem to have fated them—sector and structure. Several had prospered as joint venture partners of multinational firms in the export-oriented sectors of manufacturing, and were now discarded. Some were in other sectors targeted by foreign capital such as finance. The most vulnerable were families that had expanded into conglomerates without modifying the *kongsi* structure of family management. These families were even more at risk if they were simultaneously negotiating the difficult transition from the second to third generation, and had either failed to multiply the family's managerial resources, or had fallen into internal conflict.

In the decade after the crisis, three times as much foreign capital entered Thailand as over the boom decade. Thailand was confirmed as a host for multinational manufacturing. In the aftermath, most of the dynamism in the economy came from exports, spearheaded by the automotive, electrical, electronic, and other technology-based sectors now dominated by multinational capital. In the automotive industry, where domestic capital had been nurtured by industrial policies over three decades, multinational capital now controlled not only assembly but also the first tier of parts making, and penetrated down to the second tier of components and service industries. This reflected a process of concentration on a global scale. Thailand became a world-ranked center for manufacture of pickup trucks, and a major hub of Asian networks for producing passenger cars. Domestic capital in manufacturing industry was now, for the most part, confined to agribusiness and some other sub-sectors based on local resources or cheap labor.

Over the crisis there was a silent policy decision to permit transnationalization of manufacturing, but to reserve much of the service sector for domestic capital. This division was written into the Alien Business Law adjusted in 1999, and supported by other laws and concession arrangements. Many of the domestic firms that survived the crisis were in sectors that still enjoyed some government protection such as real estate, entertainment, media, liquor, healthcare, telecoms, and some segments of tourism. In the aftermath, these were the areas that attracted new domestic investment.

But in practice, the attempt to liberate industry while defending services made no sense. Multinational manufacturers wanted to buy services from their global providers in the same way that the automakers wanted to buy parts from their global suppliers.[1] In addition, government was not prepared to police this division, especially when neglect suited the interests of domestic capital groups desperate for money. Thousands of companies were allowed to evade the Alien Business Law by a simple work-around.

These included some big retail companies that entered Thailand in a rush, building 130 hypermarkets in a decade, to take advantage of low land prices and the lack of regulation. Their success was not solely or even largely due to their technological advantages, as they failed in other Asian markets with exactly the same assets. Rather, the institutional environment in Thailand was welcoming. Government had no tradition of defending small-scale local capital. Big domestic

---

1. In 2006, government proposed to amend the Alien Business Law to prevent the conventional work-around. In the draft amendment, the percentage of voting rights rather than of share ownership would determine whether a company counted as Thai or foreign. This would prevent the conventional work-around using preference shares. Although Japanese manufacturing firms were not directly affected by this amendment, they joined the protest against it, precisely because it would affect service companies that acted as their suppliers.

business groups chose to profit by cooperation. Consumers had been educated in the superiority of foreign brands. Opposition to big retail was confined to some provincial areas where business leaders united to mobilize localist sensibilities.

The case of the mobile phone market offers a variation on this story. The market was reserved for domestic capital by a concession system, and by a telecoms law that outlawed majority foreign ownership. Under this structure, the mobile phone proved to be a pot of gold, delivering some of the biggest family fortunes over the great boom and the bust. The concessionaires invested heavily in retaining the political influence to defend themselves, even to the extent of forming a political party and securing election as prime minister. But, as in the auto industry, this heroic defense had to face up to the logic of competition and concentration on a global scale. The Thai telecom firms had to accept the challenge of competing on a global stage, or sell out to firms that would. Over 2005–2006, the two leading Thai firms both took the sale option.[2]

WINNERS

Yet Thai domestic enterprise is far from dead. Three-quarters of firms survived the crisis in some form. The model of the family firm was not dismantled. After all, such firms predominate everywhere in the world outside the Anglo-American business culture. Indeed, the crisis ultimately strengthened many of the family firms that had already embraced modernization by streamlining their structure, adding professional management, and becoming more transparent, without losing family control. The crisis forced them to streamline further, to rationalize their scope of business, and perhaps to become even more transparent. The crisis also cleared away many of their competitors, opening up more space to grow. Among the hundreds of Thai auto parts firms that existed prior to the

---

2. The Thaksin government conveniently eased the law restricting foreign ownership in the telecoms segment to make this possible.

crisis, only a handful of groups survived as first-tier suppliers, but they were able to recommence expansion by the early 2000s. Despite all the changes in the banking industry, the handful of top banks retained their dominance and led the way in the development of consumer banking and specialized banking services.

In the more remote corners of the Thai business world, there are suggestive instances of firms changing for the better over the crisis. In Rayong, the Ban Khai family moved on from older forms of primitive accumulation to become a manufacturer and exporter, thus rising head-and-shoulders above its local rivals. In Chiang Mai, Paradon Brick began to develop from a craft business into a more expansive manufacturing and trading enterprise.

Charoen Sirivadhanabhakdi, the liquor king, did not just survive the crisis but became the country's richest man in the process. Several factors contributed to this extraordinary result. First, his business was very unsophisticated. He sold a commodity to the low end of the market, and made most transactions in cash. He suffered much less damage than colleagues who operated in more glamorous markets using more sophisticated methods. Second, he commanded an enormous cash flow delivered by an old-fashioned state-protected monopoly. Third, he turned the crisis into an opportunity by leveraging his cash and applying his unparalleled skill in managing such monopolies. He was able to defeat the aims of liberalizing the liquor market in part because the post-crisis environment discouraged competition. He stole the beer market by competing on price at a time when this strategy had great appeal. And he used his uniquely healthy cashflow to buy up property and other assets on a massive scale.

The success of the Crown Property Bureau through the crisis was also due to extraordinary reserves of cash that were the product of a politically created rent. When around three-quarters of its income disappeared, the CPB was able to borrow a vast amount, possibly on the surety of its reserves of land, possibly through the prestige of the institution it represented. Over the five years before its banking and industrial investments returned to profit, the CPB restored its income by raising the returns from this massive stock of land. The major CPB companies were in a position to restructure and restart expansion ahead of their rivals. They revived faster, and were able to profit from their rivals' greater difficulties. Although the crisis was initially a great shock, the CPB emerged with a significantly increased income.

POLITICS AND RENT

The crisis emphasized the importance of politically generated rents. The extraordinary success of Khun Charoen and the CPB were based on this factor. The Shinawatra mobile phone empire, which was based on a politically granted concession and defended by Thaksin's expanding political role, was able to reap massive rents through the crisis period. In both Rayong and Chiang Mai, the decentralization of local government in the late 1990s opened up positions of local power and patronage whose importance was immediately recognized by local business families. While neoliberals imagined that the crisis would result in liberalizations and regulatory reforms that would reduce the importance of politically contrived rents, the crisis has perhaps taught businessmen just how important such rents are.

Thaksin's political project, launched in the immediate aftermath of the crisis, was an ambitious attempt to create a single rent-gathering coalition that included many of the big business families, and that attached the local networks extending out to Rayong, Chiang Mai, and elsewhere. His strategy was strikingly similar to Charoen's method of managing the old liquor cartel, by accommodating everybody profitably within the cartel in order to prevent competition that would reduce the level of rent.

In the short term, this grand coalition was a great success. The big families that clustered around the Thai Rak Thai party benefited from various gifts and favors. Local business families that went with Thai Rak Thai, such as the Buranupakorn in Chiang Mai and the Ban Khai camp in Rayong, profited from their connections in an atmosphere of increased business competition. Ultimately, however, this project created internal tensions and external distrust which brought about its downfall.

THE FUTURE

Now that the Thai economy has been further integrated into the global economy, the future of domestic capital depends on its ability to live with the realities of this environment. Thai firms will have to compete.

One problem they will face is scale. Size matters. With only a handful of exceptions, Thai firms are small by global standards. Even among firms that have modernized, the family format often remains a constraint. Family businesses may have been launched on the stock market, but the families retains tight control through pyramid structures and cross-holdings. As a general pattern, some ten persons or institutions hold around 60 percent of the shares. This structure discourages outside investors, and thus limits their ability to raise funds for expansion.

Moreover, the stock exchange itself remains problematic. As a small exchange on the periphery of global financial markets, it is tossed around by international money flows, which are not dictated by the prospects of individual companies or the general health of the Thai economy but by international capital's gambles on currency and interest rate movements around the world. Locally also, the exchange is repeatedly subject to manipulation that appears to go unchecked and unpunished because of political connections. These factors make the exchange unreliable, and impose invisible risks on participating firms. For these reasons, the attempts to attract more firms to list since the crisis have had only very modest results. Thailand needs to develop long-term debt and equity markets that suit the needs of its family firms. Now that the banks have learnt to live with a new regulatory environment and apply professional tools for assessing risk, perhaps they will return to merchant banking with more enthusiasm. There are some signs this is happening.

Being able to compete in the globalized environment also means going global. As more transnational capital comes in, more Thai capital needs to venture out. Thai firms have ventured overseas in significant numbers since the great boom, but generally in a rather ragged and non-strategic fashion. The crisis seems to have caused only temporary withdrawal, and has resulted in some rationalization. The rise of China is a powerful lure. Firms like SCG and CP have a clear vision of their future as regional or global firms. Recognizing the limitations of the domestic market, Khun Charoen is also plumbing for overseas opportunities on both a regional and global scale.

Government has to contribute to these changes. The laws, institutions, and thinking behind government policy still carry the traces of the old era of "development," which has passed into history. Policy has to come to terms with Thailand's new role as a host for the multinationals, with the increased importance of foreign capital in the economy, and with the realities facing domestic capital. What then should be the roles of government in this new era?

First, to make a success out of the economy's de facto role as a host for multinational firms. Principally that must mean investing in infrastructure and human capabilities. In the decade since the crisis, these two areas have been badly neglected, creating a deficit that will take some time to overcome. Public investment in infrastructure slumped after the crisis because budget was diverted elsewhere. The Thaksin government focused on other priorities for four years, and began drawing up ambitious investment plans only shortly in advance of its overthrow. The political interregnum of 2006–2007 has extended this delay. The Thaksin government also abandoned the broad-based plans for reform in education drawn up in the late 1990s, probably because it would not be able to reap any credit for them. These two areas need to be brought back to the top of the government agenda.

In addition, it is time to abandon the idea of protecting certain sectors for domestic capital. Thaksin came to power in 2001 promising to pursue such an agenda, but quickly abandoned it. Yet this idea explicitly underlies part of the Alien Business Law (list 3). This law is widely circumvented by a simple legal device for the very reason that the prohibition is hopelessly unrealistic. The current situation allows the state the hypocrisy of claiming to act as the defender of domestic capital on paper, while conniving in the circumvention of the law for the sake of economic growth. Reducing the number of protected sectors and then enforcing the law would deprive law firms of lots of fees, but would create a more honest and transparent environment.

Instead of trying to police the nationality of capital, government should concentrate on regulating what capital gets up to. One critical area is monopoly and competition. The existing legislation on fair competition has proved a total failure. The crisis has resulted in increased concentration of ownership in many sectors, and hence both consumers and business competitors are now more vulnerable to monopolistic practices. In advanced economies, fair-competition laws have been highly significant in creating opportunities for small and medium enterprises.

The second role for government must be to assist companies to enhance their capabilities and competitiveness.

There is still a role for government in providing a supportive environment for small and medium enterprises, especially via human resource development, supply of market information, and assistance for improving technical capability. This is especially important where small domestic entrepreneurs face imperfect financial markets and asymmetries of information.

Government also needs to promote Thai firms going outward (as exporters or investors), rather than protecting those that stay at home. Government is in a position to reduce the transaction costs and information costs of going overseas. Japanese capital's venture into the outside world was supported by a wide array of government agencies. Over the last decade, Singapore has had great success in directing its entrepreneurs to look outwards. Thaksin tried to batter the bureaucracy into becoming more business-friendly, but his aggressive stance may have been counterproductive. He dabbled with joint business-government overseas delegations, but in a rather haphazard way. He promoted greater regional cooperation but subordinate to a personal agenda. He pushed for free trade agreements but without enlisting business input or social support. In all these cases, his objectives were right but the methods clumsy or inadequate. Perhaps the support of Thai outward investment needs a new institutional approach rather than disconnected political campaigns.

Thai firms face the new reality that they must share the domestic market with global players, and that they cannot avoid going global, or else they will be wiped away from the domestic market too.

A third role for government must be in social provision appropriate to the nature of society. Over the last generation, the society has relied heavily on the rural economy and community to provide a cushion for the strains of the transition to urbanization. The village has provided a refuge in time of crisis, a counterweight to unemployment, and a retreat in old age. Over time, this works less and less effectively. As more people are bound primarily to an urban economy, the demand for appropriate social provisions grows. The popularity of the Thaksin government's populist schemes was clear evidence. Meeting this demand is a challenge that no government can now avoid.

There are compelling political reasons too. The political disorder of Thailand in the mid-2000s is founded deep-down on the wide income gap between top and bottom in Thai society. Populism has grown in its appeal because of the massive demand for fairer treatment. The elite has reacted fiercely against this populism precisely because it has so much privilege to lose. There is a danger that the increasing internationalization of the Thai economy will tend to widen rather than narrow the gap. This trend has been seen in other societies with similar economies. Rather few people benefit directly from the multinational-owned export industries that now underlie economic growth. Trickledown does not work so efficiently. Government must play a part in redistribution (through social services) or this political tension will remain.

Finally, domestic capital needs to be weaned away from its dependence on political power to make profits. This dependence remains because it works, and it works because the society allows it to. Parliaments and elective local governments are dominated by business owners, who are only a small minority in the population. The courts rarely serve as a means to challenge business power. The solution has to be more democracy, and more continuous democracy over the long term.

REFERENCES

Achakorn Wongpreedee. 2006. "Decentralization in Thailand 1992–2006: Its Effects on Local Politics and Administration." Ph.D. diss., University of Kyoto.

Agency for Real Estate Affairs. 2006. *Prime Development Locations in Bangkok 2007: The Survey of Land Prices at 200 Locations, 1994–2007.* Bangkok: Agency for Real Estate Affairs.

Ammar Siamwalla et al. 2002. *Khrongkan wichai kan tit tam lae pramoenphon bangkap chai ratthathammanun* [Project to Evaluate the Constitution]. Bangkok: King Prajadhipok Institute.

Anon. 1971. "The Biggest Estate. The Crown Property Bureau, a Major Investor." *Investor,* February, 124–125.

Anon. 2002a. "Doktoe Chirayu Isarangkun na Ayutthaya poet yutthasat mai so no ngo sapsin" [Dr. Chirayu Isarangkun na Ayuthaya Introduces New Strategies for the Crown Property Bureau]. *Kan ngoen thanakhan* [Money and Banking], March, 54–57.

Anon. 2002b. "Chiwit phunam" [Lives of Leaders]. *Phunam thongthin* [Local Leaders] 3 (25), December, 83–95.

Anon. 2003a. "Samnak ngan sapsin suan phra mahakasat khong wai kaen thae" [The Crown Property Bureau Keeps Its Core]. *Corporate Thailand,* December, 32–42.

Anon. 2003b. "Thawikon khong sapsin suan phra mahakasat thun ladawan wang sinsap" [The Two Investment Arms of the Crown Property Bureau: CPB Equity and CPB Land]. *Corporate Thailand,* December, 46–48.

Anu Noenhat. "Sapha rueang kao" [Collection of Old Stories]. *Thainews,* 16 February 1999; 8 November 2000; 12 April 2002; 14 November 2003.

Apiradi Khantaket. 1002. "Nimsiseng khonsong mareo haeng mueang Chiangmai" [Nimseeseng Transportation: The Mounted Scout of Chiang Mai City]. *Khukaeng* [Competitor], November, 124–126.

Arunothai Suvitsakdanon. 2002. "Phawa kan damnoen ngan thurakit khonsong sinkha sueksa korani borisat nimsiseng khonsong 1988 chamkat" [Perfomance

Analysis of Transportation Business: A Case Study of Nimseeseng (1988) Company Limited]. Master of Accounting diss., Chiang Mai University.

Athiwat Sapphaithun. 2002. *Sut yot 4 chomyut Charoen Siriwatthanaphakdi Piya Phiromphakdi Surat Osathukhro Chalieo Yuwitthaya* [Four Giants: Charoen Siriwatthanaphakdi, Piya Bhirom Bhakdi, Surat Osathanukhro, Chalieo Yoovidhya]. Bangkok: Wannasan Press.

———. 2003. *Trakhun Chinnawat* [The Shinawatra family]. Bangkok: Wannasat.

Backman, M. 1999. *Asian Eclipse: Exposing the Dark Side of Business in Asia.* Singapore: John Wiley & Sons.

Batson, B. A. 1984. *The End of the Absolute Monarchy in Siam.* Oxford and New York: Oxford University Press.

Brooker Group. 2001. *Thai Business Groups. A Unique Guide to Who Owns What.* Bangkok: Brooker Group.

———. 2002. *Thailand's Automotive Industry.* Bangkok: Brooker Group.

Brown, I. 1988. *The Elite and the Economy in Siam c.1890–1920.* Singapore: Oxford University Press.

Bunchai Jaiyen. 2002. *Burut thi ruai thi sut nai prathet Thai Charoen Siriwatthanaphakdi* [The Richest Man in Thailand, Charoen Siriwatthanaphakdi]. Bangkok: Dokya Group.

———. 2005. *Chiwit mahasetthi thai mahasetthi lok che sua Charoen Siriwatthanaphakdi* [The Life of the Mega Millionaire, the World Millionaire, Charoen Siriwatthanaphakdi]. Bangkok: Than bandit.

Chaiyon Praditsil. 2002. "Khwam khatyaeng nai kan chatkan panha kakphit utsahakam nai khrongkan phatthana chaifang ta-le tawan-ok: Sueksa korani chenko" [Conflict over Industrial Waste Management in the Eastern Seaboard: A Case Study of Genco]. A research report in the project on Good Governance and People's Participation in the Management of the Environment, supported by the Thailand Research Fund.

Chaiyuth Punyasavatsut and Nipon Poapongsakorn. 2003. "Thailand Strategy for Industrial Upgrading." In ASEAN-*Japan Competitive Strategy*, edited by Ippei Yamazawa and Daisuke Hiratsuka. Chiba: Institute of Developing Economies, JETRO.

Chalit Kittiyamsab. 2005. "Thueng khao thueng khon" [To News to People]. *Krungthep thurakit*, 21 January, 19.

Chang, Ha-Joon. 1998. "South Korea: The Misunderstood Crisis." In *Tigers in Trouble: Financial Governance, Liberalisation and Crises in East Asia*, edited by K. S. Jomo. London: Zed Books.

———. 2000. "An Institutionalist Perspective on the Role of the State: Towards an Institutionalist Political Economy." In *Institutions and the Role of the State*, edited by Castro Burlamaqui and Ha-Joon Chang. Cheltenham: Edward Elgar.

———. 2003. *Globalization, Economic Development and the Role of the State*. London: Zed Press.

Chang, Li Dong and Brenda Sternquist. 1993. "Taiwanese Department Store Industry: An Overview." *International Journal of Retail and Distribution Management* 21 (1).

Chanthra Thanawattanawong. 2002. "Kanmueang rueang lao: Korani sueksa khruea khai lao phuean ban haeng prathet thai" [Politics of Liquor: Case Study of Local Informal Producers]. M.A. diss., Faculty of Political Science, Thammasat University.

Chirawat Rochanawan. 2004. *Kolayut lae khletlap Charoen Siriwatthanaphakdi* [Strategy and Secrets of Charoen Siriwatthanaphakdi]. Bangkok: Wannasan Press.

Choi, Sang Chul. 2003. "Moves into the Korean Market by Global Retailers and the Response of Local Retailers: Lessons for the Japanese Retailing Sector?" In *The Internationalisation of Retailing in Asia*, edited by John Dawson et al. London: RoutledgeCurzon.

Chollada Wattanasiri. 1986. " Phra khlang khang thi kap kan longthun thurakit nai prathet pho so 2433–2475" [The Privy Purse and Business Investment, 1890–1932]. M.A. diss., Silapakorn University.

Chodechai Suwannaphon, Nawaphon Sutthachip, Thammarit Khunhiran and Manun Phutthawong. 2005. "Naeothang kan phatthana thurakit sathaban kanngoen thi mai chai thanakhan (Non-Bank)" [Directions for the Development of Non-Bank Financial Institutions]. A working paper for the seminar under the same name at the Fiscal Policy Office, Ministry of Finance.

Chung, Henry. 2001. "An Analysis of Taiwan's Distribution System." *International Journal of Retail and Distribution Management* 29 (2).

Coe, Neil M. and Lee Yong-Sook. 2006. "The Strategic Localization of Transnational Retailers: The Case of Samsung-Tesco in South Korea." *Economic Geography* 82 (1), January.

Crispin, Shawn W. 2003. "Thailand: Prime Minister Mixes Business and Politics." *Far Eastern Economic Review*, 11 December.

Crown Property Bureau. 2006a. *Samnak ngan sapsin suan phra mahakasat yangyuen duai khwam phophiang* [The Crown Property Bureau on the Path of Sustainability]. Bangkok: Crown Property Bureau.

———. 2006b. "Kho naenam kiao kap rang phon ngan wichai 'Samnak- ngan sapsin suan phra mahakasat kap botbat kan longthun thang thurakit' khong ro so do ro Pophan Uyanon" [Comments on the draft research report on "The Crown Property Bureau and Business Investment" by Asst. Prof. Porphant Ouyyanont]. 30 August. This document was prepared by Dr. Chirayu Isarangkun na Ayutthaya and given to the author.

Dawson, John, and Roy Larke. 2004. "Japanese Retailing through the 1990s: Retailer Performance in a Decade of Slow Growth." *British Journal of Management* 15 (1): 73–94.

Deunden Nikomborirak, Saowalak Chiwasitthiyanon, and Rajitkanok Chitmanchaitham. 2002. "Pruttikam kan chamkat kan khaengkhan nai phak kan phalit thai" [Barrier to Entry in Thai Industry]. Paper prepared for the workshop on 3–4 June. Bangkok: TDRI.

Deunden Nikomborirak and Suneeporn Thawannakul. 2006. "Foreign Business Operation in Thailand." Paper presented at the seminar on Towards Clarity in Corporate Governance: Issues Relating the Sale of Shin Corporation, organized by the Faculty of Economics, Thammasat University and TDRI, 25 August.

Deunden Nikomborirak et al. 2006. "Khrongkan botbat khong borisat chamkat nai prathet thai: Rai-ngan khwam kaona khrang thi 1" [Project on the role of transnational companies in Thailand: First progress report]. Bangkok: TRF.

———. 2007. "Khrongkan botbat khong borisat chamkat nai prathet thai: Rai-ngan khwam kaona khrang thi 2" [Project on the role of multinational companies in Thailand: Second progress report]. Bangkok: Thailand Research Fund.

Doner, Richard F. 1991. *Driving a Bargain: Automobile Industrialization and Japanese Firms in Southeast Asia*. Berkeley: University of California Press.

———. 1992. "Politics and the Growth of Local Capital in Southeast Asia: Auto Industries in the Philippines and Thailand." In *Southeast Asian Capitalists*, edited by Ruth T. McVey. Ithaca: Cornell University Press.

Doner, Richard F., and Ansil Ramsay. 2000. "Rent-Seeking and Economic Development in Thailand." In *Rents, Rent-Seeking and Economic Development: Theory and Evidence in Asia*, edited by Mushtaq Khan and Jomo Kwame Sundaram. Cambridge: Cambridge University Press.

———. 2003 "The Challenges of Economic Upgrading in Liberalising Thailand." In *States in the Global Economy: Bringing Domestic Institutions Back In*, edited by Linda Weiss. Cambridge: Cambridge University Press.

Doner, Richard F., Gregory W. Noble, and John Ravenhill. 2005. "Production networks in East Asia's Automobile Parts Industry." In *Global Production Networking and Technological Change in East Asia*, edited by Shahid Yusuf, M. Anjum Altaf, and Kaoru Nabeshima. Oxford: Oxford University Press/World Bank.

EEPC (Engineering Export Promotion Council). 2000. *Report on Thailand Automotive and Parts Market*. Singapore: EEPC.

Ellis, E. 2003. "Royal Rehab: Thailand's Crown Property Bureau Gets a Corporate Makeover." *Fortune*, 10 July, at http://www.ericellis.com/cpb.htm (downloaded 30 April 2007).

Endo, Gen. 1996. "Tai ni Chihojitsugyoka no Jigyohatten: Chianmai o Jireitoshite" [The Business Development of Thai Local Entrepreneurs: Chiang Mai as a Case Study]. *Ajia Keizai* [Asian Economics] 37 (937): 54–82. (In Japanese.)

———. 2000. "Tai ni okeru chihoushobaizaibatsu no keisei to tenkai: Tantorapan gurupu no jirei" [The Origins and Development of Local Retail Business Groups in Thailand: Tantranont as a Case Study]. *Keieishigaku* 36 (1): 28–59. (In Japanese.)

Gomez, Edmund Terence. 2003. *The State, Governance and Corruption in Malaysia*. Kuala Lumpur: University of Malaya.

Greene, S. L. W. 1999. *Absolute Dreams: Thai Government Under Rama VI, 1910–1925*. Bangkok: White Lotus.

Grieve, R. H. 2004. "Appropriate Technology in a Globalising World." *International Journal of Technology Management and Sustainable Development* 3 (3): 173–187.

Higashi, Shigeki. 2002. "Institutional Reform and Corporate Restructuring in Thailand: From Crisis to Recovery." In *Development Strategies Toward the 21st Century: The Experiences and Perspectives of Developing Economies and Globalization*, edited by Ippei Yamazawa and Naoko Amakawa, Chiba: Institute of Developing Economies, JETRO.

Hitoshi, Tsuchiya. 2003. "The Development of Foreign Retailing in Taiwan: The Impacts of Carrefour." In *The Internationalisation of Retailing in Asia*, edited by John Dawson et al. London: RoutledgeCurzon.

Hollingsworth, Roger. 2000. "Doing Institutional Analysis: Implications for the Study of Innovations" ICE Working Paper Series, at: www.iwe.oeaw. ac.at/workingpapers/ Hollingsworth-WP9.pdf.

Horn, R. 1999. "The Banker Who Saved the King." *Time* (Asia edition) 154 (22), 6 December 1999, at www.time.com/time.asia/magazine 99/1206/ thai3.moneyman.html index.htm (downloaded 30 April 2007).

Inoguchi, Takashi, Miguel Basanez, Akihiko Miguel, and Timur Dadavaev. 2005. *Values and Life Styles in Urban Asia: A Cross-Cultural Analysis and Sourcebook Based on the AsiaBarometer Survey of 2003*. Mexico City: Siglo XXI.

Iwasa, Y. 2000. "Case Study: Impact of the Crisis on the Automobile Industry in ASEAN and Outlook for the Future." In *Restoring East Asia's Dynamism*, edited by Seiichi Masuyama, Donna Vandenbrink, and Chia Siaw Yue. Singapore: ISEAS and Nomura Research Institute.

Japan Automobile Manufacturers Association (JAMA). 2004. *Hand-in-Hand: Partnership in Auto Industry*. Bangkok: JAMA.

Japan External Trade Organization (JETRO). 2004. "JETRO Market Reports: Retail Business." At www.jetro.go.jp/en/jetro/.

Jeerawat Yansopon. 1997. "Wattanatham ongkan khong thurakit khropkhrua nai changwat Chiang Mai: Sueksa korani chapho trakhun Chutima-Nimmanhaemin, Sakdathon lae Tantranon." [Corporate Culture of Chiang Mai Family Business Firms: Case Study of Chutima-Nimmanahaeminda, Sakdatorn, and Tantranont Families]. M.B.A. diss., Payap University.

Jirapar Tosomboon. 2003. "The Impact of World Class Distributors on the Retail Industry in Thailand." In *The Internationalisation of Retailing in Asia*, edited by John Dawson et al. London: RoutledgeCurzon.

Jomo, K. S., ed. 1988. *Tigers in Trouble: Financial Governance, Liberalisation and Crises in East Asia*. London: Zed Books.

Jun Kanchanalak. 1987. *Funeral Conmemeration Volume*. Wat Thepsirin, Bangkok, 22 November.

Khan, Mushtaq H. 2000a. "Rents, Efficiency and Growth." In *Rents, Rent-Seeking and Economic Development: Theory and Evidence in Asia*, edited by Mushtaq Khan and Jomo Kwame Sundaram. Cambridge: Cambridge University Press.

———. 2000b. "Rent-seeking as Process." In *Rents, Rent-Seeking and Economic Development: Theory and Evidence in Asia*, edited by Mushtaq Khan and Jomo Kwame Sundaram. Cambridge: Cambridge University Press.

Khan, Mushtaq H., and Jomo, Kwame Sundaram. 2000. *Rents, Rent-Seeking and Economic Development: Theory and Evidence in Asia*. Cambridge: Cambridge University Press.

Kriengkrai Techakanont and Yoshi Takahashi. 2004. *Globalization Strategies of Automobile Assemblers in Thailand and Adaptation of Local Parts Suppliers*. Bangkok.

Krirkkiat Phiphatseritham. 1982. *Wikhro laksana kan pen chao khong thurahkit khanat yai nai prathet thai* [Analysis of Large-Scale Business Ownership in Thailand]. Bangkok: Thammasat University Press.

Lecler, Yveline. 2001. "The Cluster Role in the Development of Thai Car Industry: Some Evidence from Case Studies." Paper presented at Gerpisa/Cokeas Workshop on The Changing Geography of the Automotive Systems, Bordeaux, 30–31 March.

Ma Nok and Dek Nok Krop. 2006. *25 kham tham bueang lang dil tekowoe Shincorp* [25 Questions behind the Shin Corp Takeover Deal]. Bangkok: Open Books.

Malerba, F. 1992. "Learning by Firms and Incremental Change." *Economic Journal* 102: 845–859.

Masuyama, Seiichi. 2000. "The Role of Japan's Direct Investment in Restoring East Asia's Dynamism Focus on ASEAN." In *Restoring East Asia's Dynamism*, edited by Seiichi Masuyama, Donna Vandenbrink, and Chia Siaw Yue. Singapore: ISEAS and Nomura Research Institute.

McVey, Ruth, ed. 2000. *Money and Power in Provincial Thailand*. Singapore: ISEAS; Chiang Mai: Silkworm Books.

Mori, Minako. 2002. "The New Strategies of Vehicle Assemblers in Thailand and the Response of Parts Manufacturers." *Pacific Business and Industries* 2 (4) (Tokyo: Center for Pacific Business Studies, Japan Research Institute).

Muramatsu, Yoshiaki. 1997. "Automotive Industry Developments in Thailand During the Last Decade." Paper presented to the Asia Business Forum on Asian Automotive 1997 Conference, Royal Cliff Beach Hotel, 8 September, Pattaya.

Narong Sakdatorn. 2000. *Cremation Volume*, 27 August, Sankulek Crematorium, Amphoe Muang, Chiang Mai.

Natenapha Wailerdsak. 2005. *Managerial Careers in Thailand and Japan*. Chiang Mai: Silkworm Books

———. 2006. *Klum thun—thurakit khropkhrua thai kon lae lang wikrit 2540* [Business Groups and Family Business Before and After the 1997 Crisis]. Bangkok: BrandAge Books. (T).

———. 2007. "Family Business in Thailand: Ownership Structures and Stock Market." In *A Compendium on the Family Business Models Around the World*, edited by V. Gupta et al. 10 vols. Hyderabad: ICFAI University Press.

Nayok Thaksin khui kap prachachon lem 2 [Prime Minister Thaksin's Speaks with the People, vol. 2]. Bangkok: Public Relations Department, n.d.

Nelson, Michael H. 2001. "Bangkok Political Games Confront Provincial Election Realities." KPI *Newsletter* 2 (1): 9–15.

NESDB. 2006. *Thailand: Partnership for Development*, distributed January 2006. At: www.mfa.nl/contents/pages/11028/thailandpartnershipfordevelopment.pdf.

Ninnart Chaithirapinyo. 2004. "Could Thailand Really Become Another Detroit?" In *Automotive Handbook and Directory 2003–2004*. Bangkok: Society of Automotive Engineers of Thailand.

Nipon Puapongsakorn and Wangdee Chayanit. 2000. "The Impact of Technological Change and Corporate Reorganization in the ASEAN Automotive Industry." Pacific Economic Cooperation Council, Project on the ASEAN Auto Industry.

Nipon Puapongsakorn et al. 2002. *Kan kha plik khong thai: Phon krathop khong kan khaengkhan chak phu prakopkan kha plik khanat yai chak tang prathet* [Thai Retailing Business: The Impact from Competition of Foreign Large Retailers]. Bangkok: Thailand Development Research Institute.

Nithi Eoseewong. 2006. *Mahawitthayalai thiang khuen* [Midnight University]. Bangkok: Matichon.

Nopphanun Wannathepsakun. 2006. "Kosang kanmueang kanmueang kosang" [Constructing Politics, Politics of Construction] in *Kan tosu khong thun thai: Kanmueang watthanatham puea khwam yurot* [*The Struggle of Thai Capital. Volume 2: Politics and Culture for Survival*], edited by Pasuk Phongpaichit. Bangkok: Matichon Publishing.

Nopphon Wasuthepragsan. 1999. "Kan sueksa khrongsang talat lae kolayut kan khaengkhan nai utsahakam bia khong thai" [Study of the Market Structure and Competitive Strategies in the Thai Beer Industry]. M.A. diss., Faculty of Economics, Thammasat University.

Ockey, James. 1999. "God Mothers, Good Mothers, Good Lovers, Godmothers: Gender Images in Thailand." *Journal of Asian Studies* 58 (4), November, 1033–58.

Orathip Tessiri. 1981. "Kan thue khrong thi din nai prathet that pho so 2444–2475 sueksa chapho monthon krungthep" [Land Holding in Thailand from 1901 to 1932: A Case Study of Monthon Krungthep]. M.A. diss., Chulalongkorn University.

Our Correspondent. 2007. "Thailand's Royal Wealth," *Asia Sentinel*, dated 2 March, at http://www.asiasentinel.com/index2.php?option=com_content&task=view&id=402&pop=1.

Paisal Sricharatchanya. 1985. "For King, Country and Profit: Siam Cement in the Fast Lane." *Far Eastern Economic Review* 128 (25), 27 June.

———. 1988. "Thailand's Crown Property Bureau Mixes Business with Social Concern: The Jewels of the Crown." *Far Eastern Economic Review* 140 (26), 30 June.

Pantop Tangsriwong. 2002. "Yisip pi Chiang Mai: Kan tosu khong thurakit doem" [Twenty Years of Chiang Mai: The Struggle of Old Business]. *Phuchatkan raiduean* (Manager Monthly), February.

Paradorn Bricks. 2005. Company Profile and Profile of Mr. Wichien Cherdchutrakuntong, document provided by Paradorn Bricks Company.

Pasuk Phongpaichit and Chris Baker. 2000. *Thailand's Crisis.* Chiang Mai: Silkworm Books.

———. 2004. *Thaksin: The Business of Politics in Thailand.* Chiang Mai: Silkworm Books.

Pasuk Phongpaichit and Nualnoi Treerat. 2003. "Korrupchan khachao lae phatthanakan setthakit" [Corruption, Rent, and Economic Development].

Setthasat Thammasat [Thammasat Economic Journal] 21 (4), December, 1–28.

Pavida Pananond and C. P. Zeithaml. 1998. "The International Expansion Process of MNEs from Developing Countries: A Case study of Thailand's CP group." *Asia Pacific Journal of Management* 15 (2): 163–84.

Pavida Pananond. 2001a. "The Making of Thai Multinationals: The Internationalisation Process of Thai Firms." Ph.D. diss., University of Reading.

———. 2001b. "The Making of Thai Multinationals: A Comparative Study of Thailand's CP and Siam Cement Groups." *Journal of Asian Business* 17 (3): 41–70.

———. 2002. "The International Expansion of Thailand's Jasmine Group: Built on Shaky Ground?" In *Asean Business in Crisis*, edited by M. Bhopal and M. Hitchcock. London: Frank Cass.

———. 2004. "Thai Multinationals after the Crisis: Trends and Prospects." ASEAN *Economic Bulletin* 21 (1): 106–126.

———. 2006. "Foreign Direct Investment and the Development of Thai Firms: A Case Study of Electronics Industry." Proceeding of the Annual Seminar of the Faculty of Economics, Thammasat University, entitled Thai Economy in the Changing Global Economy and Society. Bangkok.

Phatchari Sirorot. 1997. *Rat thai lae thurakit nai utsahakam yanyon 2545–2549* [The State and the Automotive Industry, 2002–2007]. Bangkok: Thammasat University Press.

Phengkamon Marnarath. 2004. "Kanmueang rueang kan lueakthang: Sueksa korani kan ronnarong hasiang lueakthang nayok tessamontri tesaban nakhon Chiangmai pi pho so 2547" [Politics of Elections: A Case Study of the Chiang Mai Mayoral Election Campaign 2004]. Masters of Political Science diss., Chulalongkorn University.

Phra Paisarn Visalo. 1994. *Prawatisat kan boriphok sura nai prathet thai* [History of Liquor Consumption in Thailand]. Bangkok: Desire.

Piyawan Suksri. 2001. "Kan wikhro setthakit kan phalit sura phuean ban korani phalit lao khao changwat Chiang Rai lae Phrae" [Economic Analysis of Local Liquor Production in Chiang Rai and Phrae]. M.A. diss., Faculty of Economics, Chulalongkorn University.

Plai-Or Chananon. 1987. *Naithun phokha kap kan kotua lae khayai tua khong rabop thunniyom nai phak nuea khong Thai pho so 2464–2523* [Traders in the

Origin and Development of Capitalism in Northern Thailand, 1921–1980].
Bangkok: Social Research Institute, Chulalongkorn University.

Porphant Ouyyanont. 1994. "Bangkok and Thai Economic Development:
Aspects of Change, 1820–1970." Ph.D. diss., University of New England.

Pramuan Bunkanwanicha and Yupana Wiwattanakantang. 2005. "Tycoons
Turned Leaders: Market Valuation of Political Connections." Available at
SSRN: http://ssrn.com/abstract=676763.

Prani Sirithon na Phatthalung. 1980. *Phu bukboek haeng Chiang Mai* [Pio-
neers of Chiang Mai]. Bangkok: Ruangsin.

Praphad Phodhivorakhun. 2002. "Perspective of Thai Private Sector on Investment Incentives and Opportunities in Automobile Industries." Paper presented at the Thai Board of Investment seminar, Tokyo, 26 August.

PricewaterhouseCoopers. 2005. "From Beijing to Budapest: New Retail &
Consumer Growth Dynamics in Transitional Economies." At www.pwchk.
com/home/eng/retail_bj_budapest_ 2005.html.

Rangsan Thanaphornphan. 2003. *Setthasat ratthathammanun : Bot wikhro
ratthathammanun haeng ratcha-anajak thai pho so 2540* [Constitutional
Economics: Analysis of the Thai Constitution of 1997]. 3 vols. Bangkok:
Matichon Printing.

Renu Ruenklin. 1999. *Khwam pen ma khong nayobai sura seri* [The Roots of
the Liquor Liberalization]. Bangkok: Excise Department Press.

Ruenai Wiriyatrakunchai. 1998. "Kan wikhro khrongsang utsahakam bia
thai kap kan phuk khat thurakit korani sueksa kan bangkhap khai sura
phuang bia" [Analysis of Monopoly in the Thai Beer Industry: The Case
of Bundling Beer with Liquor]. M.A. diss., Faculty of Economic Development, NIDA.

Rüland, Jürgen and M.L. Bhansoon Ladavalya. 1993. *Local Associations and Municipal Governnment in Thailand*. Berlin: Arnold-Bergstraesser-Institut.

Sahat mahakhun anuson. 1961. [Memorial Volume for Sahat Mahakhun]. 22
November.

Sakkarin Niyomsilpa. 2000. *The Political Economy of Telecommunications
Reforms in Thailand*. London and New York: Pinter.

Sakuna Thewaratmaneekul. 2000. "Kan chatkan sapsin suan phra mahakasat"
[Administration of the Crown Property Bureau]. M.A. diss., Faculty of Law,
Thammasat University.

Samart Chiasakul. 2004. "Production Networks, Trade and Investment Pol-icies, and Regional Cooperation in Asia: A Case Study of Automotive Industry in Thailand." Paper presented at the 6th ADRF General Meeting, 7–8 June, Bangkok.

Samit Thippayamonthon. n.d. "Setthakit nakhon Chiang Mai kap trakhun kitibutr-thippayamonthon" [Chiang Mai's Economy and the Kitibutr-Thippayamonthon Family]. In *Sethakit nakhon Chiang Mai chak adit su anakhot* [Chiang Mai Economy from Past to Future). n.p.

Seksan Prasertkul. 2005. *Kanmueang phak prachachon nai rabop prachathip-patai thai* [People's Politics under Thai Democracy]. Bangkok: Amarin Printing.

Siam nakkhao thurakit. 1993. "Niyom phanich yak yai khrueangchai faifa rotyon nai phak nuea" [Niyom Panich: Giant of Electrical and Automo-bile Business of the North]. *Chalongchai khunsu pi thi 5 borisat Siam nak-khao thurakit chamkat* [Celebration entering the 5th Year of Siam Nakkhao Thurakit Limited]. Bangkok: Siam Nakkhao Thurakit.

Siri Intarin. 2000. "Chaosua Narong Sakdathon tamnan thi yang khong yu khu mueang" [Tycoon Narong Sakdatorn: A Legend of the City]. *Chiang Mai News,* 24 August.

Siriporn Sukosol. 1996. "Kan chat ongkan: Korani sueksa samnakngan sapsin suan phra mahakasat" [Organizational Structure: A Case Study of the Crown Property Bureau]. M.A. mini-thesis, Faculty of Political Science, Thammasat University.

Somboon Siriprachai. 1993. "Prasopkan 30 pi khong utsahakam rotyon: Fan thi mai pen ching" [30 Years Experience of the Auto Industry: Dreams That Did Not Come True]. In *Phasi rotyon lae utsahakam rotyon* [Auto Taxes and the Auto Industry], edited by Rangsan Thanaphornphan, study paper 501 of the Parliament and Policy Study Institute, Bangkok.

Sombun Rujikhajon. 1998a. "Sing patha chang patibat kan lai la rong lao seri" [Singha attacks Chang over Liquor Liberalization]. *Thurakit kaona* 11 (124), November.

———. 1998b. "Poet seri kan phalit lae chamnai sura: Tit tang lae naeo nom kan khaengkhan" [Liberalization of Production and Sale of Liquor: Com-petitive Trends]. *Prasa sang* 16 (10), October, 14–28.

———. 1999. "Bot sarup pramoen rong lao Charoen Siriwatthanaphakdi yangrai ko chana" [Summary on Liquor Bidding: How Charoen Won]. *Thurakit Kaona* 2 (136), November, 89–94.

———. 2001a. "Kan rung ik kao khong Charoen Siriwatthanaphakdi" [Another Aggressive Step Forward by Charoen Siriwatthanaphakdi]. *Phuchatkan raiduean*, October.

———. 2002a. "Sing-chang Rise&Fall" [Singha and Chang Rise and Fall]. *BrandAge* 3 (12), December.

———. 2002b. *Thai grocer*. Bangkok: Tipping Point.

Somkiat Tangkitvanit. 2003. "Phon krathop khong kan plaeng kha sampathan pen phasi sanphasamit" [Effect of Converting Concession Fees into Excise Tax]. Unpublished paper.

———. 2004. "Sai samphan thang kanmueang kap phon top thaen nai talat hun thai" [Political connections and returns in the Thai stock market]. Unpublished paper.

Somsak Jiamteerasakul. 2006. "Samnakngan sapsin suan phra mahakasat kue a-rai" [What is the Crown Property Bureau?]. *Fa Diao Kan* 4 (1), January–March, 67–93.

Songkiat Chatwatthananon. 2002. "Yuk ni khue yuk khong Charoen Siriwatthanaphakdi" [This is the Age of Charoen Siriwatthanaphakdi]. *Dok bia* 21 (151), May, 26–39.

———. 2004. " Kot keng Chirayu Itsarangkun na Ayutthaya yuet es si bi khuen chak khlang" [Dr. Chirayu Isarangkun na Ayuthaya Cleverly Buys SCB Stake Back from the Ministry of Finance]. *Dok bia*, May, 34–45.

Sonthi Limthongkul. 2002. *Chao pho*. [Godfathers]. Bangkok: Phuchatkan Publishers.

Sorakon Adulyanon. 1993. *Thaksin Chinnawat asawin khloen luk thi sam* [Thaksin Shinawatra, Knight of the Third Wave]. Bangkok: Matichon.

———. 1994. *Chomyut nam mao Charoen Siriwatthanaphakdi phu han kratuk nuat sing* [Liquor King Charoen Siriwatthanapakdi: The Man Who Dares to Pull the Lion's Moustache]. Bangkok: Matichon Press.

Sternquist, Brenda, and Jin, Byoungho. 1998. "South Korean Retail Industry: Government's Role in Retail Liberalization." *International Journal of Retail and Distribution Management* 26 (9).

Suehiro, Akira, and Natenapha Wailerdsak. 2004. "Family Business in Thailand:

Its Management, Governance, and Future Challenges." ASEAN *Economic Bulletin* 21, 1 April.

Suehiro, Akira. 1989. *Capital Accumulation in Thailand 1855–1985*. Tokyo: UNESCO and Centre for East Asian Cultural Studies.

———. 2001. "Family Business Gone Wrong? Ownership Patterns and Corporate Performance in Thailand." ADB Institute Working Paper 19. Tokyo: ADB Institute.

———. 2003. "Big Business Groups, Family Business and Multinational Corporations in Thailand 1979, 1997 and 2000 Surveys." Paper Presented at Medhi Wichai Awuso Project, 8 January 2003, Faculty of Economics, Chulalongkorn University.

———. 2003. "Big Business Groups, Family Business, and Multinational Corporations in Thailand: 1979, 1997, and 2000 surveys." Paper Presented to the Medhi Wijai Awuso project, Chulalongkorn University, 8 January.

Sungsidh Piriyarangsan. 1983. *Thai Bureaucratic Capitalism, 1932–1960*. Bangkok: CUSRI.

Suntharee Asavai. 1990. *Wikrit kan setthakit lang songkhram lok khrang thi nueng* [The Economic Crisis after the First World War]. Bangkok: Thammasat University Press.

Suphot Jangrew. 2002. "Khadi yuet sap phrabatsomdet phra pokklao" [The Case of King Prajadhiphok's Seized Property]. *Sinlapa Wattanatham*, June, 63–80.

Suprani Khongniransuk. 1992. "Poet daen sonthaya so no ngo sapsin" [Shedding light on the Crown Property Bureau]. *Phuchatkan raiduean,* November, 191–212.

Tantraphan Department Store. 1992. *Nangsue thi raluek khroprop hasip pi* [50th Anniversary of Tantraphan Department Store]. Chiang Mai: Tantraphan Department Store.

Terry, Edith. 2002. *How Asia Got Rich: Japan, China and the Asian Miracle*. New York and London: M. E. Sharpe.

Thai Beverage. 2006. "Nangsue chi chuan borisat thai beweretchet chamkat mahachon" [Document Introducing Thai Beverage Plc]. 30 June.

Thailand Automotive Institute. 2002. *Khrongkan chatham phaen maebot utsahakamyanyon 2545–2549* [Project to Create an Automotive Masterplan, 2002–2007]. Bangkok: Office for Industrial Economics.

———. 2006. *Rang phaen maebot utsahakam yanyon thai, 2549–2553* [Masterplan for the Thai Automotive Industry, 2006–2010]. Bangkok.

Thanet Charoenmuang. 1992. *Rabop setthakit kap nak thurakit chan nam nai phak nuea tonbon* [The Economy and the Business Elite in the Upper Northern Region]. Chiang Mai: Faculty of Social Science, Chiang Mai University.

Ukrist Pathmanand. 2005. "Thaksin and the Politics of Telecommunications." In *The Thaksinization of Thailand*, edited by Duncan McCargo and Ukrist Pathmanand. Copenhagen: NIAS Press.

Vallop Tiasiri. 2002. "Can Thailand Maintain its Competitive Edge?" Paper presented to the 2002 Automotive News Asia-Pacific Congress, 23 May.

Vatikiotis, Michael. 1984. "Ethnic Pluralism in the Northern Thai City of Chiang Mai." Ph.D. diss., University of Oxford.

Veloso, Francisco, Jorge Soto Romero, and Alice Amsden. 1998. "A Comparative Assessment of the Development of the Auto Parts Industry in Taiwan and Mexico: Policy Implications for Thailand." Massachusetts Institute of Technology, Cambridge, Mass, at http://ipc-lis.mit.edu/globalization/globalization%2000-009.pdf.

Viengrat Nethipo. 2000. "Itthipon nai kan mueang thongthin khong thai: Sueksa korani mueang Chiang Mai" [Political Influence in Thai Local Politics: Case Study of Chaing Mai]. *Warasan sangkhomsat* [Social Science Journal] 31 (2).

Warr, Peter, ed. 2005. *Thailand Beyond the Crisis*. London and New York: RoutledgeCurzon.

Watchara Sinthuprama. n.d. "Setthakit nakhon Chiang Mai lang songkhram lok khrang thi song patchuban" [Economy of Chiang Mai City since the Second World War]. In *Setthakit nakhon Chiang Mai chak adit su anakhot* [Chiang Mai Economy from Past to Future]. n.p.

Wilai Laohakun. 1996. "Poet phot khon dang thue hun arai" [Share-owning by Prominent People]. *Who's Who*, 23 September.

Wingfield, Tom. 2002. "Democratization and Economic Crisis in Thailand." In *Political Business in East Asia*, edited by E. T. Gomez, 250–300. London: Routledge.

Wirat Saengthongkham, Pandop Tangsiwong, and Somsak Damrongsunthonchai. 2003. *70 pi Chirathiwat Central ying su ying to* [70 Years of Chirathivat: The More Central Fights, the More it Grows]. Bangkok: Manager Classic.

Wirat Saengthongkham. 2000. *Yutthasat khwam yai khruea simen thai* [Strategies for Expansion of the Siam Cement Group]. Bangkok: P. Press Publishing.

Wrigley, N., N. M. Coe, and A. D. Currah. 2005. "Globalizing Retail: Conceptualizing the Distribution-based TNC." *Human Geography* 29 (4): 437–457.

Yipphan. 2002. *Che sua yesterday sokkanatakam naithun thai phak kamsuan nai baeng* [Tycoons of Yesterday: The Tragedy of Thai Capitalism: Bankers' Tears]. Bangkok: Multimedia Group.

———. 2004. *Kot thurakit* [Business Clans]. Bangkok: Fresh Publishing.

Yutthasak Khanasawat. 2001. "Tamnan thurakit kha plik thai" [A History of the Thai Retailing Business]. *Warasan songsoem kan longthun* [Investment Promotion Journal] 12 (2), February, 18–23.

———. 2004. "Kan prap khrongsang nai utsahakam pun simen lok" [Adjustment in the world cement industry]. *Warasan songsoem kan longthun* [Investment Promotion Journal] 15 (4), April, 51–57.

Zhang, Y. 2003. *China's Emerging Global Businesses: Political Economy and Institutional Investigations*. Basingstoke and New York: Palgrave Macmillan.

CONTRIBUTORS

CHAIYON PRADITSIL is assistant professor in the Department of Political Science, Burapha University, Chonburi. He obtained his doctorate in political science from Chulalongkorn University. His research interests include the political economy of public policy and community development, especially in the eastern region of Thailand.

CHRIS BAKER is a writer, editor, and translator. He has a doctorate in history from Cambridge University and has published widely on Thailand's history, political economy, and current affairs.

NATENAPHA WAILERDSAK has a doctorate in economics from the University of Tokyo, where she was an Assistant Professor in the Institute of Oriental Culture until 2006. Currently, she is a Visiting Research Fellow in the Faculty of Economics at the University of the Philippines. She has published in English, Japanese, and Thai on business groups and corporate management and governance, including *Managerial Careers in Thailand and Japan* (Silkworm Books, 2005), *Business Groups and Family Business in Thailand Before and After the 1997 Crisis* (BrandAge Books, 2006, in Thai).

NUALNOI TREERAT is associate professor of economics and former director of Political Economy Centre, Faculty of Economics, Chulalongkorn University. Her research interests and publications are in the fields of corruption and good governance, and public policy.

OLARN THINBANGTIEO is lecturer in the Department of Political Science, Burapha University, Chonburi. He is a doctoral candidate in political science at Ramkhamhaeng University. His research interests are local politics and political history.

PASUK PHONGPAICHIT is distinguished professor and chair of the Political Economy Centre at the Faculty of Economics, Chulalongkorn University. She has a doctorate in economics from Cambridge University, and has published widely on the Thai political economy, corruption, illegal economies, social movements, and regional issues. She has been a visiting professor at Kyoto University, Tokyo University, Johns Hopkins SAIS, University of Washington, and Griffith University.

PAVIDA PANANOND is associate professor of international business at Thammasat Business School, Thammasat University. Her research interests cover foreign direct investment and emerging multinationals from developing countries. Her latest publications include "The Changing Dynamics of Thai Multinationals after the Asian Economic Crisis," *Journal of International Management,* November 2007, and "Explaining the Emergence of Thai Multinationals," in Henry Wai-chung Yeung (ed.), *Handbook of Research on Asian Business* (Edward Elgar, 2006).

PORPHANT OUYYANONT is associate professor of economics at Sukhothai Thammathirat Open University. He obtained his doctorate in economic history from the University of New England, Australia, and has been a visiting scholar at Kyoto University. His publication and research interests include the economic history of Bangkok and Thailand, village economy and rural communities, current international economic issues, and economic development.

SAKKARIN NIYOMSILPA is senior analyst at Kasikorn Research Center, and lecturer at Rangsit University. He obtained his doctorate degree from the Research School of Pacific and Asian Studies, the Australian National University. He served as Thai diplomat for a number of years before joining academia. His interests include the Thai macroeconomy and the political economy of industrialization in ASEAN, China, East Asia, and Russia. He has written *The Political Economy of Telecommunications Reforms in Thailand* (Pinter, 2000).

THANEE CHAIWAT is a lecturer in the Faculty of Economics, Chulalongkorn University. He obtained his M.A. in economics from Chulalongkorn University. His research interests include political economy, international economics, and applied econometrics. He has just been awarded a scholarship to study for a Ph.D in economics.

UKRIST PATHMANAND is a senior researcher at the Institute of Asian Studies and a lecturer in the Graduate School, Chulalongkorn University. His research focuses on political development in Thailand and regionalism in the Greater Mekong Sub-region Countries. He is coauthor of *The Thaksinization of Thailand* (Nordic Institute of Asian Studies, 2005), and a regular commentator in the local press.

VEERAYOOTH KANCHOOCHAT is currently reading an M.Phil in Development Studies at the University of Cambridge, focusing on institutional economics. He holds a B.A. in Electrical Engineering and M.A. in Economics from Chulalongkorn University, and has worked on research projects concerning industrial development, free trade agreements, foreign direct investment, infrastructure, and media reform.

VIENGRAT NETHIPO is lecturer at the Department of Government, Faculty of Political Science, Chulalongkorn University. Her research and teaching interests are in local politics, state-society relations, and informal power in Thailand. She has published a number of articles about godfathers and politics.

INDEX